Finding Jacob Wetterling

The 27-Year Investigation from Kidnapping to Confession

Robert M. Dudley

Exposit

Jefferson, North Carolina

LIBRARY OF CONGRESS CATALOGUING-IN-PUBLICATION DATA

Names: Dudley, Robert M., 1966– author.
Title: Finding Jacob Wetterling : the 27-year investigation from kidnapping to confession / Robert M. Dudley.
Description: Jefferson, North Carolina : McFarland & Company, Inc., Publishers, 2016 | Includes bibliographical references and index.
Identifiers: LCCN 2016048430 | ISBN 9781476668925 (softcover : acid free paper) ∞
Subjects: LCSH: Wetterling, Jacob, 1978—Kidnapping, 1989. | Kidnapping—Minnesota—Saint Joseph—Case studies. | Kidnapping—Investigation—Minnesota—Saint Joseph—Case studies. | Missing children—Minnesota—Saint Joseph—Case studies. | Criminal investigation—Minnesota—Case studies.
Classification: LCC HV6602.S254 D83 2017 | DDC 364.15/4092—dc23
LC record available at https://lccn.loc.gov/2016048430

BRITISH LIBRARY CATALOGUING DATA ARE AVAILABLE

ISBN (print) 978-1-4766-6892-5
ISBN (ebook) 978-1-4766-2836-3

Front cover photograph © 2016 iStock

Printed in the United States of America

Exposit is an imprint of McFarland & Company, Inc., Publishers, Jefferson, North Carolina

Exposit

Box 611, Jefferson, North Carolina 28640
www.expositbooks.com

For Jacob,
all the missing,
and all who search.

Acknowledgments

The author wishes to express his sincere thanks to the following for their contributions to this book:

My family, for their patience, support, and understanding throughout the process.

Dianne Rassmussen, Trish VanPilsum, and Patrick Marker for pushing me at all the right times.

Liz Collin, Ellarry Prentice, and Madeleine Baran for their objective and original reporting of the Jacob Wetterling kidnapping case. They are truly credits to their profession.

The staff at the Stearns County Museum, *St. Cloud Times*, *St. Joseph Newsleader*, and St. Cloud Public Library.

Everyone who assisted with the book in any way, whether it was with research, suggestions, inspiration, ideas, information, encouragement, or constructive criticism. A special thanks goes out to Sheryl, Pat, Jim, Aubrey, Natalie, Kyle, Paula, and Natalie.

A very special thank you to Liz Collin at WCCO Television in Minneapolis. She was the first journalist to listen to what I had to say, and one of the few with the resolve to break away from the pack, reporting on the Wetterling case from original and important perspectives.

Other recommended reading:

Three Boys Missing by James A. Jack
Mind Hunter by John Douglas
Striving To Be The Best by Allen Garber

Table of Contents

Author's Note

This book is a comprehensive record of the investigation into the October 22, 1989, abduction of Jacob Wetterling from St. Joseph, Minnesota—second only to the collection of boxes held in the basement of the Stearns County Law Enforcement Center.

Anyone who was living in the Midwest in the fall of 1989 was familiar with the Wetterling kidnapping. It was all over the news. There were newspaper articles, television news stories, posters, billboards, buttons. The story quickly spread across the entire country, even to other parts of the world. Jacob was everywhere—but he couldn't be found.

Although I lived a few hours away from the St. Joseph area, there were many reminders of Jacob's kidnapping over the years. Some came from news reports about new information or leads in his case. Sometimes his face flashed across a screen, such as the scoreboard the Metrodome Stadium in Minneapolis.

But one reminder affected me more than any of the others. A news story I heard on the radio in 2010 piqued my curiosity because, until that moment, I had never given a great deal of thought to the details of the abduction—the location where it had occurred, or the circumstances. My assumption had always been that the kidnapping took place in some suburb of the Twin Cities area, and that Jacob had probably become separated from his parents for a moment somehow, and then grabbed by an opportunistic stranger.

After doing a little research, I was surprised to learn that Jacob's kidnapping occurred in the small town of St. Joseph, Minnesota, on a dead-end road near his home. And that he was taken by a masked gunman in front of two witnesses.

What began with curiosity later evolved into more serious research. That research ultimately led to the name of the man who was a suspect from the very beginning of the case, but who had apparently been lost in the shuffle through the changes of investigative teams during the nearly three decades that had passed since Jacob's kidnapping.

This chronicle of the investigation looks at the case from several perspectives. The account begins with the day of the abduction and the massive media attention that followed. It details the show of support from the local community, then moves on to the investigative effort to find Jacob and his kidnapper, concluding with the story of how an early suspect in the case resurfaced after more than a quarter century.

It should be noted that this book was written without input from the Wetterling family or the Jacob Wetterling Resource Center. As a researcher, my goal has been to make this an objective, dispassionate work. Quotes attributed to Wetterling family members or acquaintances, and persons associated directly with the investigation are credited to their respective media sources. In cases where individuals are mentioned who were involved or questioned during the investigation, but were never publicly named by the media, their names have been changed.

The story of Jacob Wetterling's abduction and the 27-year search for him and his kidnapper is compelling—as mysterious as any such crime could be. Every question that was answered during the course of the investigation seemed only to raise more questions. For millions in the Midwest and across the nation, what happened to Jacob changed the world. No longer would small-town America consider itself safe from the exploitation of children.

1

The Ride Home

*I flashed the flashlight at him. He told me to turn it off. I thought
it was a joke. I kept thinking somebody else was going to jump out
at us.*[1]—Trevor Wetterling

The weather forecast for Sunday, October 22, 1989, promised a
beautiful, unseasonably warm day. Jerry Wetterling had spent a little
time on Saturday evening planning a Sunday of family events. He
talked to his boys about heading to the lake in the morning to do
some fishing. It would probably be the last good opportunity of the
fall season.

Jacob, 11, was the oldest son and was the fisherman of the family.
He agreed to the plan from the start. Younger brother Trevor, 10, opted
to sleep in instead.[2] Patty Wetterling, mother of the four children,
planned to stay home with eight-year-old Carmen, the youngest. Amy,
13, was away at a friend's house.

As predicted, the weather was glorious. The early morning sun
peeked through the autumn-leaved trees that surrounded the Wetterling home. The temperature was already well into the forties and
was climbing quickly.

Jerry was the first one awake that morning. He ventured out on
a four-mile jog while the rest of the family slept. He was a chiropractor in St. Joseph, a budding small town just west of St. Cloud. An
avid sports fan, Jerry was active and athletic.

He returned from his run to find Jacob eagerly waiting in the
kitchen, already dressed for fishing with his equipment sitting by the
garage door. They ate a light breakfast, loaded up their gear in the
family boat and made the ride to nearby Big Fish Lake.[3] It was a 25

minute drive to the lake, which was located a couple miles north of the communities of Cold Spring and Richmond.

The fish weren't biting on that otherwise perfect day on the lake. The quiet October morning was filled with all the spoilings of summer. As noon approached they decided it was not their lucky day and packed up to leave. Jerry and Jacob were avid Minnesota Vikings fans—kickoff for the game against the Detroit Lions was at 12 P.M. so they hustled home to watch it.[4]

Jacob was especially excited about the Vikings' prospects that season. The team had just acquired running back Herchel Walker via trade from the Dallas Cowboys. The Vikings had been playing well lately after a poor start to the season and were hoping to extend their winning streak to four games that afternoon.

Once home, Jerry and Jacob joined Trevor in the living room to watch the game. Walker played well once again and soon the team had a very comfortable lead. Jacob and Trevor—both hockey players—decided to forgo part of the second half and put in some extra practice time at the ice rink. Jacob had recently switched from his familiar goalie position to one using regular hockey skates and he was struggling with the transition. Jerry loaded the hockey gear into the car and drove the boys to the Municipal Ice Arena in St. Cloud.[5]

Hockey was extremely popular in Minnesota. There was hockey, and then there were "other" sports. Although the season was already underway in St. Joseph and the surrounding communities, there were few skaters at the rink that day—most people were outside enjoying the weather. The Wetterlings took advantage of the light crowd and skated hard. Jacob, still uncomfortable with the switch from goalie skates to regular, struggled somewhat.[6]

After they returned home, Jerry told the boys there was still some daylight remaining for a quick game of "OD," or "Offense-Defense." Jerry was the all-time quarterback in the made-up game. Jacob and Trevor took turns playing wide receiver and defensive back, essentially making two one-man teams. The boys adopted special rules to help even things out between Trevor and the older, more physical Jacob. Jacob had three downs to score a touchdown while

Trevor was allowed five downs. Jacob, ever the compassionate big brother, would sometimes "throw" the game in Trevor's favor.[7]

As evening approached Jacob called his best friend, Aaron Larson, and asked him to come over. The pair had been inseparable since shortly after Larson moved to St. Joseph. They had played together on the same football, baseball, soccer, and hockey teams for as long as they could remember. But their sixth-grade schedules had them in different classes and practice times and they rarely saw each other at school. The next day, Monday, was an in-service day for teachers—no school for the boys meant Aaron could stay overnight. Aaron's parents agreed make the short trip to drop him off.

There wasn't much of interest on television that night. One of the networks featured a movie titled *Do You Know the Muffin Man?* The plot involved a man who molested a young boy.

Jerry and Patty had been invited to a party near Clearwater that Sunday evening.[8] They had debated whether or not to attend, and at the last minute decided they would go. Clearwater was a fifteen-mile, twenty-minute drive southeast of St. Joseph. The party was to celebrate the Millstream Arts Festival that had been a recent successful event in St. Joseph— Patty was the chairperson.[9] The party doubled as a housewarming for the hosts, who had recently moved to Clearwater.

Since Amy was away at a friend's house, Jacob was left in charge of minding Trevor and his younger sister, Carmen. Patty ordered pizzas delivery for the kids and then left for the party with Jerry. She phoned home when they arrived at their friend's house and gave Jacob the phone number for the party's host. He was to call if any problems came up.

After sharing the pizza the boys soon became bored. They decided to bike into town to rent a movie at the Tom Thumb convenience store, but Jacob knew they would need to get permission from his parents first. Knowing that his mother would be a hard sell, he devised a plan to gain her approval. He phoned their next-door neighbor, Rochelle Jerzak, and asked her if she would watch Carmen while the boys biked into town. Rochelle agreed. Next, Jacob tracked down a flashlight. He checked the batteries to make sure they were good for the trip to town and back. The boys sorted out their transportation options. Jacob would ride his mother's ten-speed, Aaron would push the scooter while Trevor ride his own bike.[10]

Jacob had put together a sound plan. The boys elected Trevor to make the call to their parents. After a brief discussion with Trevor, Patty denied their request. Although the boys had biked the route many times,[11] they had never made the trip at night.[12] She suggested they might have better luck asking their father, but offered no guarantee of success.[13]

A short time later Jacob decided to make a second call, this time asking for his father. After hearing Jacob's plan, Jerry gave his approval. He understood that Jacob had been going through a tough time lately, and thought that allowing him to pursue a bit of adventure might give him an emotional boost. Jerry did, however, insist that the boys wear reflective clothing. Jacob understood and agreed.[14]

Rochelle came over to the Wetterlings to watch Carmen and the boys headed out shortly after 8:30 p.m. Trevor held the flashlight and led the way, Aaron and Jacob trailed just behind him. All three boys loved sports and silly comedies. The had already decided on the film they would rent, the baseball comedy *Major League*, before they rounded the turn northward onto 91st Avenue.

The Wetterling home was one of a handful situated on one of two quiet cul-de-sacs at the end of 91st—the one-mile stretch was a dead-end rural road. There was only one way into town. There was only one way to anywhere.

It was especially dark outside that fall evening. There was no moon and not a star in sight. There were no streetlights. The boys rode in a tight group so all could benefit from the single flashlight. They had reflective vests on so any passing cars could see them, but they anticipated little traffic on the long dead-end road.

Desolate but smoothly paved, 91st Avenue (today 16th Avenue SE) ran straight northward into town. The route started with a long, gentle climb to the top of a hill, marking roughly the halfway point to town, then an easy downhill ride, then a few more blocks to Tom Thumb.

There were just two houses on the stretch of the road leading up to the crest of the hill, one on either side of the road. The first house was on the right, east side. It was the home of Robert and Rita Rassier. The property was a large farmstead with a long gravel driveway that led a few hundred yards perpendicular from 91st Avenue, then bent northward around a pile of firewood and down a gentle hill on the other side of a large patch of thick woods and underbrush. The farmstead included a large home nestled along the east side of the wooded area, as well as several agricultural outbuildings surrounding the end of the driveway. In daylight, the house and all but two of the buildings were shielded from street view by the hill and the thick wooded area. At night, none of the property's buildings were visible from the road.

The other house was a couple hundred yards further up the hill, on the left. Urban Schreifel's modest home sat just a hundred feet or so back from the road. The area in front of the residence was wide open to the road, with a well-maintained garden alongside the house. A small patch of woods lay from a point just south of the garden a hundred yards or so to the west. Past the garden the woods stretched to the north, arcing around the west side of the home.

The only other homes on 91st Avenue were over the hill. There, the quiet countryside met the southern edge of St. Joseph. The homes in town were close to one another, forming traditional city blocks.

As the boys rode up the hill and neared the first driveway, Aaron thought he heard a noise in the field on their left hand side, opposite of the driveway. He briefly glanced in that direction but was unable to see anything at all in the blackness. Aaron wasn't able to identify the source of the noise and it sounded to him like a something that shouldn't be there.[15] He was curious about the noise but shrugged it off and kept it to himself. He didn't want to frighten young Trevor. They continued over the hill toward town. On their way, one car passed them northbound and they met a couple of cars that were heading south on 91st. As they came into town, they made a right turn on East Baker Street, followed it for a couple of blocks, then turned left toward their destination.

They parked their bikes just outside the Tom Thumb entrance and went inside. They made their way to the video racks and were dismayed to see the vacant video slot where *Major League* should have been. The boys settled on the slapstick comedy *Naked Gun* instead, even though Trevor had seen it several times before.[16] They grabbed the videotape and then darted over to the candy aisle. The female store clerk, a local college student familiar to the boys, asked Jacob to sign out the videotape. When the boys left the store it was a few minutes after 9:00 p.m. They got back on their bikes and started for home.

The hill was steeper southbound on 91st but after a few minutes they reached the crest. It was an easy ride the rest of the way home.

They were just starting down the hill when a man suddenly jumped out from a driveway in front of them.

"Stop!" the man shouted in a deep, commanding voice. "I have a gun!"

The boys skidded to a sudden stop. Trevor instinctively pointed his flashlight at the man, catching a brief glimpse of him. He saw the flash of a silver gun in the man's hand. Trevor could see the man was wearing gloves and a dark mask, like a woman's stocking, with a little ball on the back of his head. He was dressed in dark clothing and a big, dark, puffy coat.[17] Everything about the man was dark.

The first thought that crossed Trevor's mind was that it was just a joke being played by someone from the neighborhood. He almost started to laugh out loud.[18] The same thought crossed Aaron's mind.[19]

"Shut off that light!" the man barked in a deep, raspy voice. Trevor switched off the flashlight.[20]

The man ordered the boys to throw their bikes down in the ditch. The boys offered the man the videotape, but he angrily struck it to the ground. The boys then did as they were told, dropping their candy on the grass around the area of the bikes. Next, the man ordered them to lie in the grass on their bellies. Again, they did as they were told.

The man asked the boys their ages. They blurted out their answers in unison.[21]

"One at a time!" he roared, clearly agitated.[22]

Trevor stated that he was ten. The man then ordered him to get up and run to the woods to the west.

"Don't look back or I'll shoot!" he threatened. Trevor did as he was told.

Next, Aaron said he was eleven, then Jacob also said he was eleven. The man looked at their faces. He then groped Aaron in the genital area with his hands, over his clothing. The masked man then gave Aaron the same instructions he had given Trevor, to run to the woods.

"Don't look back or I'll shoot!" the masked man warned once again.

The man grabbed Jacob from the ditch by the arm, and pulled him toward the gravel driveway that led to the east. As Aaron ran into the woods to the west he quickly caught up with Trevor. They stopped briefly to look back, but saw nothing—Jacob and the man were gone.

The boys ran all the way back to the Wetterling home. Aaron was faster than Trevor but he matched Trevor's pace so he wouldn't leave him behind. After a half-mile run through a field they finally reached the house. Panicked and gasping for breath, they told Rochelle what had just happened. She called home and asked her father, Merle, to come over right away.

Merle Jerzak rushed from next door and instantly noted the horror on the boys' faces—they were white as ghosts and sweating. He saw that Jacob was not there. The boys told him what had happened and he called 911 to report Jacob's kidnapping. It was 9:32. He was still on the phone with the dispatcher when the first Sheriff's deputy arrived at the Wetterling home at 9:40 p.m.

When the masked man stopped the boys on their ride home that night, they could have had no idea that what happened next would change their lives forever. It would change their families' lives and their friends' lives. What happened that night brought the tiny town of St. Joseph, Minnesota, to its knees in shock. No one believed something like this could happen here. No one knew that what would follow would become the largest search and investigation in the history of the state of Minnesota. It became a mystery that gripped the community, the state, and the nation. The kidnapping of Jacob Wetterling brought to the forefront of public mind the realization that what happened that night in St. Joseph could happen anywhere.

2

The Call

The boys went to the store for a video. Jacob didn't come home. He was taken by a masked gunman.[1]—Merle Jerzak, Wetterling neighbor

The following is taken from a transcript of the eight-minute 911 call made by Merle Jezak from the Wetterling home:

911 DISPATCH: 911 emergency.

MERLIN JERZAK: This is Merlin Jerzak from (gives street address) in St Joe, right in the Township. I am right now next door to my neighbor's, at my neighbor's, the Jerry Wetterling family. Some of their boys went down to *Tom Thumb* to pick up a movie and on their way back, someone stopped them and we believe that they have one of the boys because one of the boys did not come back with them. His name is Jacob Wetterling.

DISPATCH: Ok, were they picked up in a vehicle?

JERZAK: Just a second, I will ask (asks the boys). They didn't see a vehicle. This person appeared on the road when they were bicycling back home.

DISPATCH: OK, and they don't know where their brother and friend is at?

JERZAK: They don't know where their brother and friend is at.

DISPATCH: OK, so we are missing two people?

JERZAK: Just missing one.

DISPATCH: One? OK. Did they see the individuals at all?

JERZAK: Yes they did. He had a mask on.

DISPATCH: He had a mask on?

JERZAK: Right.

DISPATCH: The other dispatch right now is dispatching a squad to where you are at right now, OK? In the meantime, I just want to get as much information as I can…. How old is the individual that has not returned?

JERZAK: Eleven.

DISPATCH: Ok, Jacob. It's Jacob, right?

JERZAK: Yes, Jacob. Jacob Wetterling.

DISPATCH: OK, what was Jacob last seen wearing?

JERZAK: He was wearing a red hockey jacket that had Police Department on it. And it has his name on it.

DISPATCH: Police Department written on back?

JERZAK: In white letters.

DISPATCH: Where was the last time they seen Jacob? Where were they at, about?

JERZAK: It was, ah, right at the, ah Urban Schreifel's house.

DISPATCH: OK, give me an idea where that is. Do you know where Dr. Cotton's office is?

JERZAK: Yes, it's about approximately a quarter of a mile up, ah, south from the clinic.

DISPATCH: Hang on a second, OK? (dispatcher relays info to dispatch party)

DISPATCH: Was Jacob riding a bike?

JERZAK: Yeah, he was riding his ten-speed bike.

DISPATCH: Where are the boys at this time?

JERZAK: (gives address and directions to Wetterling residence)

DISPATCH: Can you … give me information on this guy with the mask? I want color, anything those kids can remember.

JERZAK: Um, I think that my best bet is to let Trevor get on the phone here and he can describe to you what he saw…. We have him pretty well calmed down here.

DISPATCH: OK. Hello? Trevor?

TREVOR WETTERLING: Yeah.

DISPATCH: You are talking to the sheriff's office, OK?

TREVOR: Mmhmm.

DISPATCH: I want you to give me anything you can recall about this male party that approached you guys, OK?

TREVOR: Well, he was, he was like, kind of, he was like a man. He was kind of like…

DISPATCH: He was large?

TREVOR: Sort of. OK. He had like, ah, kind of like looks like these nylon things, as a mask.

DISPATCH: Do you know what color it was?

TREVOR: Black.

DISPATCH: A black mask? Do you know what color jacket he had on?

TREVOR: I think it was black too.

DISPATCH: Ok. Did you notice any jeans or anything?

TREVOR: Yeah, just a second. (asks Aaron something inaudible)

DISPATCH: Trevor, do you know what happened to your friend's bicycle?

TREVOR: Um, no, we don't know.

DISPATCH: Nobody knows what happened to that?

TREVOR: Cause we had to just like run off into the woods.

DISPATCH: OK, you guys ran off into the woods but nobody knows what happened to Jacob, right?

TREVOR: Yeah.

DISPATCH: OK. Can you think of anything else? Did the guy have...

TREVOR: What?

DISPATCH: Did the guy have like a deep voice or anything like that you could remember?'

TREVOR: (talks to Aaron) It sounded like he had a cold.

DISPATCH: OK, can you tell me, how big, compared to your dad or somebody how big would you say this guy was?

TREVOR: He was about the size of Merle, the guy you were just talking to.

DISPATCH: OK, same height, same weight?

TREVOR: Yeah.

DISPATCH: OK. Do you remember, and he had on a black mask and a black jacket. Do you know if the jacket was leather or nylon, did it have anything written on it?

TREVOR: We couldn't tell because it was so dark.

DISPATCH: OK. Can I talk to Merlin again real quick? Thank you.

JERZAK: Yes?

DISPATCH: Merlin, how big are you?

JERZAK: (laughs) OK, ah, I am about 195 pounds and 5' 10".

DISPATCH: Where are the woods at that the kids ran into?

JERZAK: (asks the boys: Did the guy tell you guys to run into the woods?) OK, it is a little bit to the south of Urban Schreifel's, um, house. And, um, ah, it runs for about a quarter of a mile west.

DISPATCH: OK, I am hoping if Jacob would have run into the woods or something, if he would have gotten lost or something. Do they know if he actually had contact with Jacob or anything like that?

JERZAK: Yes, they just told me that the guy had a hold of Jacob and told them to run into the woods.

DISPATCH: Told the other two boys to run into the woods. Did they see any weapons at all or anything like that? Guns? Knives?

JERZAK: He had a pistol.

DISPATCH: (relays info to police). Can I talk to Trevor again?

TREVOR: Hello?

DISPATCH: Trevor, did you see the gun the individual had?

TREVOR: Um, we couldn't really see it, but we just, we sort of…

DISPATCH: OK, did he threaten you? OK, do you guys see squad cars outside the residence?

TREVOR: Um, what?

DISPATCH: There should be a squad … can I talk to Merlin again?

JERZAK: Yeah, I think the squad is at my house.

DISPATCH: Is it far? OK, can you guys open up the door and yell out to them.

JERZAK: Yeah.

DISPATCH: OK I will tell them to go … are you north or which direction are you from where the spot is?

JERZAK: Um, South.

DISPATCH: Hold on. Merlin? (relays info to police). I got officer Bechtold in the house.

JERZAK: OK.

DISPATCH: He is going to finish off the call from that end now, OK? More than likely we will be coming out with some dogs and stuff, OK?

JERZAK: OK, good. Thank you very much.

Officer Bechtold entered the Wetterling home and started talking to Trevor and Aaron. Merle Jerzak then called the home where the Wetterlings were attending the party and asked to speak to Jerry.

"Jerry!" Merle said in an excited voice. "The boys went to the store for a video. Jacob didn't come home. He was taken by a masked gunman. I want you to get Patty and come home!"

Jerry hung up the phone and hurried back to Patty. "We gotta go!" Jerry told Patty.

"What's the matter? Are the boys not home yet?" Patty asked, confused by Jerry's tone.

"Jake's not," Jerry answered.

"What?" Patty asked as Jerry hustled her outside.[2]

They left the party without saying goodbye to their hosts. Patty was bewildered and scared. On their way to the car, Jerry told Patty what Merle had told him about what happened to Jacob. The drive home only lasted about twenty minutes by the hands of a clock, but probably seemed like an eternity to the Wetterlings. Patty prodded

Jerry to drive faster, but Jerry objected, saying he didn't want to risk being pulled over for speeding. Patty reasoned that being pulled over would get them a police escort home.[3]

As the Wetterlings turned onto 91st Avenue, they came across a St. Joseph police officer waiting in his squad car by Dr. Cotton's office. He escorted the Wetterlings home from there.[4] A sheriff's deputy was parked in their driveway when they arrived. Once inside, they saw Trevor and Aaron, who looked as though they were in shock.

Stearns County Sheriff Charlie Grafft had been sitting at home watching television when he heard the squad cars screaming by his house, heading west toward St. Joseph, sirens blaring loudly through the crisp night. He called the office a few minutes later to find out what was happening. The dispatcher informed him that a masked gunman had abducted an 11-year-old St. Joseph boy. Grafft hurried to his car and drove the three miles to St. Joseph, stopping briefly at the abduction scene before proceeding to the Wetterling home at the end of the road. He arrived at the house just minutes after Jerry and Patty.[5]

"When I looked at the bikes laying in the ditch and the scooter, the way they were laying there kind of struck a chord in me," Grafft later said.[6]

Grafft's initial instinct had been that the boys, or someone, had played a prank. However, once inside the Wetterling home he saw Aaron Larson and Trevor Wetterling and knew he had a serious situation on his hands.[7]

Grafft had difficulty finding the right words when he addressed Jerry and Patty. Jacob had just been abducted, and although at this point Grafft knew very few of the details involved, he knew enough to realize the task before him and his deputies was going to be a challenge. He felt very uncomfortable with the situation at hand, and just wanted to get out of the house.[8]

Sheriff Grafft knew this was going to be a big case. He also knew this would be seen as something that couldn't happen in a small town like St. Joseph, a peaceful community strongly rooted in family and religion. Above all, knew he would need help.

So began life after October 22, 1989, for the Wetterling family, and for the small central Minnesota town of St. Joseph.

3

Covering the Story

I heard you before I saw you. I heard the thump, thump, thump, and then the chopper came at me right out of the sun. I saw that and I felt hope. I started to cry. I thought, "Now, we're going to find him."—Vernon Iverson, greeting WCCO reporter Darryl Savage

Vern Iverson paced nervously back and forth along the driveway where he had parked his car, just a short distance from where Highway 2 crossed under Interstate 94. His mind wrestled with many ideas about what he could do next to help his friends, the Wetterlings, in their time of great need. Their oldest son had been kidnapped the night before and there had been no sign of him since. Wetterling family members and friends living in the St. Joseph area had already been enlisted to help find Jacob, but there remained considerable work that Vern could help with. There were newspapers to call, radio and TV stations to court, and influential contacts to lean on for favors.[1]

After waiting for what seemed an eternity, Iverson finally heard what he had been waiting for—the faint rumble of a helicopter in the distance. The rumble grew steadily into a heavy thumping sound. Moments later he could see the helicopter coming toward him. Once the chopper was within a couple hundred yards he waved his arms back and forth over his head. The pilot waved back. Iverson hopped back into his car and headed back to St. Joseph, leading the WCCO television station helicopter and crew to the Wetterling residence.

Behind the controls of the chopper as it weaved above the streets of St. Joseph was pilot Dale Dobesh. Also on board were reporter Darryl Savage and photographer Bob Manary. This news team from WCCO in Minneapolis had been airborne early that morning, heading toward Hill City, Minnesota, to cover a story about a small school district being operated by a coalition of teachers due to the lack of a principal. On their way they received an in-flight call from the station redirecting them to St. Joseph. They were informed that an 11-year-old child had been abducted the night before and they were being dispatched to cover the story.[2]

Savage was frustrated with the change in assignment. In recent weeks, he had twice been suddenly pried away from stories he was working on to cover breaking news. Children went missing all the time. The vast majority turned out to be domestic-related and brief in duration. Station policy, much like standard police policy, was to not report on such cases until twenty-four hours had passed. "Why was there such a fuss over this one child?" he asked himself. "What was the big deal?"[3]

He soon came to understand that the abduction of Jacob Wetterling was far from an ordinary missing child case. The days ahead would challenge his perspective on his chosen career and test his objectivity as a journalist—this story would be a life-changing event for Darryl Savage.

For volunteer Vern Iverson, securing WCCO's coverage of Jacob's abduction was just one of the many efforts that ultimately brought massive media attention to the story. He was a friend of the Wetterling family through their mutual Bahai faith. Iverson lived about an hour away in Elk River. Late the night before, he had been on the receiving end of one of a network of phone calls that Jerry Wetterling had started. Jerry had reached out for help from among the Bahai community. Shortly after getting the call from another member, Iverson called Jerry, promising him that he would enlist prayer support from his friends in the Twin Cities area.[4]

Iverson began calling others, but it didn't take long for him to realize he needed to do more than make phone calls. He gathered a change of clothes, hopped into his car and sped west on I-94 toward St. Joseph. On the way he thought about what could be done to help get the word out about Jacob. He recalled a television show he had seen recently about a teenage girl who had disappeared, and how a massive media blitz had helped bring her back home.[5]

That television program was the inspiration for Iverson's personal mission to gain local and national media attention to Jacob's case. His efforts to bring to public attention the story of Jacob's abduction were so zealous that at one point during the investigation the FBI focused on Iverson as a prime suspect.[6]

Iverson set up a makeshift office in Jerry's chiropractic clinic, making phone calls to every newspaper, television station, and radio station he could think of. He was persuasive. He projected a sense of urgency that commanded attention from the other end of every phone call he placed.

The media responded en masse. A flurry of television and newspaper reporters descended upon St. Joseph. Iverson knew the Wetterlings would need to be prepared for the difficult attention the family was about to face. They were oblivious to what was coming, their thoughts centered only on their missing son. Being in the spotlight was the last thing they anticipated.[7]

Vern was right. There soon came a tidal wave of personal questions from the press—often *very* personal, with no respect for boundaries. They asked about their marital status, about Jerry's sexuality, and about the possibility of an extra-marital affair. Nothing was off limits. Iverson warned the Wetterlings the media would be relentless in pursuit of an angle. But the family would have to stand tall in the face of that adversity. The media would provide the attention needed to bring Jacob to the forefront of the public awareness but it would come at the cost of the Wetterlings' privacy, he cautioned them.

There was little hesitation by the Wetterlings. "Whatever it takes to get Jacob back," Patty declared, and Jerry agreed.[8]

Media coverage of Jacob's abduction became a daily staple of local, regional, and state news. National media followed the story in St. Joseph as well. The FBI had very little physical evidence in the case, and they understood the need to rely on media attention to generate interest and leads from the public. Public interest was their best ally in the search for Jacob and his abductor. The Wetterlings, law enforcement, and Iverson worked together to maintain media coverage by keeping the story "fresh" with near-choreographed releases of information.

The search for Jacob Wetterling dominated the *St. Cloud Times* daily newspaper for weeks. Often times, there were multiple stories within a single edition of the paper. There was a steady balance of coverage of the search efforts, human-interest stories and shows of community support. It was the biggest story in the region and commanded everyone's attention. It ultimately took a monumental historical event—the fall of the Berlin Wall on November 9—to eclipse Jacob from the front page of the *St. Cloud Times*.

Iverson's Twin Cities employer, Medtronic, was fully supportive of his efforts to help Jacob's cause. He was allowed to drop his research work at any time, without question or notice, and to take phone calls that pertained to Jacob or the Wetterling family. His office staff was instructed to assist in any way possible. Medtronic even installed a second phone line in his office specifically for Vern to use for the search for Jacob.[9]

Iverson was questioned as a suspect by law enforcement on at least two occasions. His connections in Central America, where the Iversons had lived during the mid 1980s while Vern worked for the Dole food company, were of particular concern to the FBI. They felt there was no way anyone could "work" the media as he had with such precision, without having first-hand knowledge of the abduction. He was questioned at length about his work and personal activities. He agreed to take a polygraph test but the test was never actually administered. Iverson did not object to the FBI's suspicion, for he knew it was a signal that investigators were being thorough with their investigation. Investigators were ultimately satisfied that Iverson was not connected to the abduction. They determined he was simply an enthusiastic, dedicated, and resourceful volunteer.[10]

After 6 months of dedicated service to the Wetterling family, Vern Iverson's health deteriorated to the point he had to withdraw from the search effort. He had spent a week in the hospital for stress-induced symptoms. He was suffering chest pains, and was having difficulty breathing and sleeping normally. He had done all he could for the Wetterlings.[11] It was his determination that helped focus public attention to Jacob's abduction.

Darryl Savage was 29 years old when he became part of the developing story. Up to that point, he felt like his working life had been defined by opportunities "just missed" by a small fraction. He had left his job at KOSA-TV in Midland, Texas, in 1987 to join the staff at WCCO in Minneapolis. Within a month of his departure, Jessica McClure—dubbed "Baby Jessica"—had fallen into an abandoned well in Midland. The story captured the nation's attention for days. Of course, Savage was happy the girl was rescued—but it could have been him covering the story. Lately he felt he had been missing critical reporting opportunities and had no control over his choice of assignments. This was on his mind as he rode in the chopper to St. Joseph.[12]

As pilot Dale Dobesh set the helicopter down on a grassy field near the Wetterling home, Savage noted the grin on Vern Iverson's face. They greeted each other. Then Iverson recounted the feeling that came over him when the helicopter arrived at the rendezvous point on Highway 2.

"I heard you before I saw you. I heard the thump, thump, thump, and then the chopper came at me right out of the sun," he said. "I saw that and I felt hope. I started to cry. I thought, 'Now, we're going to find him.'"[13]

Iverson led Savage and the rest of the WCCO crew to the Wetterling home. Savage was prepared to receive the sort of "unwelcome" that a reporter would typically get from a family in the middle of a crisis. What he got instead was unexpected.

"I went in and my first impression was these people are tired and have been doing a lot of thinking. It was like walking into a room and people stop talking, or when they're deep in conversation and suddenly stop because you're there," he said.[14]

After a brief time in the house, Savage got up to leave for the Del-Win Ballroom command center to get up to speed with law enforcement press release information and to prepare for a noon update of the story. On his way out of the house he noticed a plateful of breakfast food sitting on the kitchen table alongside a set of silverware. Savage sensed that that was Jacob's seat at the table. He paused for a moment, reflecting on that scene, then continued outside. He later realized that when he stepped into the Wetterling home, he had stepped into a "gray zone," where the lines between covering a story objectively from the outside and becoming a part of it were blurred.[15]

Savage led off the WCCO noon broadcast on Monday, October 23, with the first of his many television reports from St. Joseph. He had the Wetterling family on camera. Patty talked about Jacob and pleaded with his abductor to return him to his family. Trevor Wetterling and Aaron Larson talked about what happened the night before.

But it was Jerry's calm demeanor that the viewing public noticed most. He spoke matter-of-factly about Jacob's abduction. There was no bereaved, angry father ready to exact revenge on whoever had taken his son. Jerry Wetterling's seeming nonchalance, coupled with the well-established likelihood of parental involvement in child abductions, led to a public perception that Jerry was somehow involved in Jacob's disappearance.[16]

WCCO consistently began their multiple daily news broadcasts with updates from St. Joseph. Knowing they had little physical evidence to work with, law enforcement officials were cooperative with media requests for information and updates. They knew the media was their biggest ally and best hope to generate leads in the case. Likewise, the media—Darryl Savage in particular—understood the need to keep Jacob's story "fresh" in the public's eyes. Information was dispensed in bits and pieces rather than all at once. The objective was to keep the story in the papers and on the television news daily. Savage had to walk that fine line between objectively performing the job he had come to do and playing along with the situation with a measure of leniency. He and others in the media knew that investigators were often holding back information one day, so they could come back to complete the "picture" on another day.[17]

"We knew we were going to be part of the story, not just covering the story," he said. "It was an uncomfortable thing. The family knew it; the FBI knew it. We were being used in a good way."[18]

Toward the end of the week following the abduction, Patty delivered an emotional radio appeal for Jacob's return. She was barely able to get through the statement before she collapsed into someone's arms. It was a difficult and emotional scene for Savage to experience. His co-worker Bob Manary was reduced to tears. The display of emotion continued the following day at a rally held at Municipal Ice Arena in St. Cloud. Jacob's classmates and other school children, along with parents and townspeople, swayed back and forth and cried as they sang the song "Listen," by Red Grammar. Savage broke down crying himself. He hugged Jerry for the first time.[19]

Savage's bond with the Wetterlings tightened by the day and soon the relationship compromised his professional obligation to the story. At one point the WCCO team was on their way to Cold Spring to report on law enforcement's pursuit of a suspect who had been under surveillance by the FBI for several days. The man was a known sex offender and the news team had been tipped off that an arrest was imminent.[20]

Patty overheard Savage talking to his team over the radio. "Don't go up there," she pleaded. "You'll blow it!"[21]

She felt that the presence of the media vehicles would tip off the suspect and he would run. Savage was torn between doing his job and yielding to Patty's wishes.

As difficult as the story became for Savage, the hard part was leaving St. Joseph.[22] It was difficult for the Wetterlings, too. Patty had confided much to Savage, even telling him about the crazy questions she would field from other reporters. After 12 whirlwind days and nights in St. Joseph, where he felt as though he had been "adopted" by the family and the community alike, Darryl Savage returned to Minneapolis on Friday, November 3.[23]

Jacob Wetterling's abduction continued to garner attention from the national media. A CBS *Evening News* crew came to town to film a story. *Inside Edition*, a popular tabloid television program, ran one earlier in the week. *A Current Affair* ran a story and followed up with regular updates. CNN covered the kidnapping. Appearing on ABC's *Good Morning America* program, Patty and Jerry Wetterling told their story and pleaded with America to help bring Jacob home. Sheriff Charlie Grafft accompanied them to the interview.

People magazine featured Jacob's story in a large spread, including photos of Jacob and a composite sketch of the suspect. Other magazines, including *Time* and *Ladies' Home Journal* also ran stories. The Lost Child Network, based in Virginia, sponsored a national television advertisement that featured a picture of Jacob. Jacob's story reached other continents as well, as updates about the kidnapping appeared in the *Pacific Stars And Stripes* newspaper in Tokyo, Japan.

Professional athletes, sports teams, musical acts, and other celebrities joined in support of Jacob's Hope, a rallying cry for the search that would eventually come to symbolize the plight of missing children everywhere. The Minnesota Vikings came up with the idea of wearing Jacob's name on the back of their helmets. The National Football League would not allow it for technical reasons, but the team showed their support in other ways. Banners with the words "Jacob's Hope" hung from the corners of the Metrodome's end zones. The stadium's scoreboards would sometimes light up with that endearing picture of Jacob wearing his gold-colored sweater.

The Oakland A's standout baseball player, Minnesota native Terry Steinbach, wore a "J" on the back of his batting helmet during the final game of the World Series. The Minnesota North Stars professional hockey team wore the initials "JW" on their helmets in a symbolic display of hope for Jacob. A photo in the November 6, 1989, *St. Cloud Times* showed Vikings quarterback Tommy Kramer on the sidelines during a game sporting a baseball cap that read, "Jacob's Hope–Listen." After the game, Vikings coach Jerry Burns handed out four games balls to players on the team. He held back a fifth game ball, telling the players it was meant for Jacob upon his return home.

The Minnesota Timberwolves basketball team used their home opener of their inaugural 1989 season for Jacob's Hope. The 35,000 fans that attended the game at the Metrodome delivered a standing ovation for Jacob and the Wetterling family just before game tipoff. The Wetterlings stood at center court while Jacob's picture flashed up on the scoreboards. Proceeds from tickets sold during the week were donated to the Jacob Wetterling Fund.

The vast majority of media coverage was positive and supportive. There were some exceptions. When Geraldo Rivera came to St.

Joseph to cover the story, he gave the Wetterlings the impression he would be celebrating the outpouring of support from the community. However, and in keeping with Rivera's reputation as a tabloid journalist, the program focused instead on negative statistical information about child abductions. Patty was outraged and hurt. She didn't understand how that kind of talk could help Jacob and she pleaded with network officials to consider changing the focus of their report.[24]

Rivera made amends in another way, though. He participated in a radio telethon program to raise funds. Rock star Don Henley, of The Eagles, and Minnesota Twins player, Gary Gaetti, also joined in that effort. The 27-hour marathon raised $70,000. The money was split between the Jacob Wetterling Fund, the Kevin Collins Foundation, and Missing Children Minnesota.

Exactly two months after Jacob's abduction, on December 22, 1989, a rumor quickly spread throughout the region that Jacob had been found safe in a Texas hospital. The general mood in the St. Cloud area, and even in the Twin Cities, was ecstatic. Calls flooded the phone lines of newspapers and television and radio stations across the state. Shopping malls and other businesses announced the news across their public address systems.

But it turned out the news was not about Jacob at all. The reports were of an injured soldier named Jason from Fergus Falls, Minnesota, who had been returned to the United States from Panama and was recovering safely in a Texas hospital. People thought they heard the name "Jacob," and the rumor mill started rolling.[25]

The Wetterlings heard about the rumor almost immediately, as friends and relatives called them asking them if Jacob had been found. They had experienced their share of rumors and misinformation over the past few weeks, so they knew not to get too hopeful. When local officials determined there was no validity to the story, rather than react with disappointment the Wetterlings were encouraged by the giddy reaction from the public. Jerry commented that it demonstrated the way people would react when Jacob came home for real.[26]

By October 1990, nearly a year after Jacob's abduction, media attention to the case had waned significantly. Despite an intensive search of the area and an all-out media blitz that reached national proportions, there was no sign of Jacob or his abductor.

In January 1991, CBS sent a free-lance filming crew to St. Joseph to record a segment about Jacob's abduction. Network officials hoped to create a regular series from the program. The Wetterlings were interviewed, as were Rochelle and Merle Jerzak, and several law enforcement officials who had worked the case. The abduction itself was re-enacted for the program, which aired in May 1991, generating several new tips from viewers.

News organizations published an age-enhanced photo of Jacob in October 1991, created by the National Center for Missing and Exploited Children in Arlington, Virginia. The image represented what Jacob might look like at 15, though he would have been 13 at the time.[27]

WCCO aired a two-part report in May 1992 titled "Dimension: A Look Inside the Wetterling File," which leaked information about some early suspects in Jacob's abduction. Though the information released had for the most part already been investigated, and was therefore likely harmless, investigators were concerned the report would cause the public to become apprehensive about confidentiality in reporting potential leads. Furthermore, the program suggested that investigators did not follow up on some leads.[28]

Trish Van Pilsum, a broadcaster at WCCO, said the station's coverage was intended to showcase "some of the highs and the lows in the most intensive search ever conducted in Minnesota."[29] Patty Wetterling called out WCCO for using the story for ratings. "This is not about leaks. This is not about sweeps. This is about Jacob. We've got to stay focused," she said.[30]

Details revealed in the WCCO series included information about Jacob's footprints in the dirt driveway near the crime scene, tire tracks, and a man in black with a gun. The tracks were right at the edge of Jacob's footprints, and were presumed to be those of the kidnapper's vehicle. The presence of the fresh tracks next to Jacob's footprints was an important clue investigators quietly keyed on.

For the next few years the media coverage of Jacob's abduction was relatively quiet. With few new leads there was not much to tell.

But occasionally there would be a splash to rekindle attention on the case. In 1993, the rock band Soul Asylum, who hailed from the Twin Cities, produced multiple music videos for their hit song, *Runaway Train*. Several versions of the music video were broadcast on MTV, featuring pictures of missing children, including Jacob.

BRTN, a Belgian public television and radio station, came to St. Joseph in early 1997 to film a documentary based on the experiences of four American families whose children had been abducted. The film featured Jacob's case, along with those of Jessyca Mullenberg from Eau Claire, Wisconsin, Ernest Choice from Tyler, Texas, and Morgan Nick from Alma, Arkansas. Belgium had experienced a rash of abductions and sexual assaults and was scrambling to implement reforms and the film was intended to show the Belgian public the support and investigative systems that had been developed in the United States.[31]

In June 1999, as the 10th anniversary of Jacob's abduction neared, ABC featured Jacob in their television show *Vanished*. The segment was entitled *A Mother's Search*. By the summer of 1999, all four major television networks had contacted the Wetterlings about producing an update on Jacob's story.

Local media interest of the case was again rekindled in 2004, when investigators revealed that the long sought-after driver of a car that had been witnessed at the scene of the abduction had come forward to tell his story. The incredible story of that driver and the subsequent shift of the investigation's focus are covered later in this book.

The case garnered renewed national attention in July of 2010, when investigators stormed the farm of Robert and Rita Rassier, which was connected to the driveway where Jacob had been taken 21 years earlier. They executed a two-day search involving multiple search warrants and the public naming of Dan Rassier as a person of interest. Dan was the adult son of Robert and Rita Rassier.

In October 2014, regional media coverage of the 25th anniversary of Jacob's kidnapping focused on the Wetterling family's long search. Investigators held a press conference to announce a new effort in the search for Jacob, centering on a handful of billboards that had been put up around the cities of St. Cloud and St. Joseph. The billboards were donated by a local advertising agency and featured a photograph of Jacob as an 11-year-old boy as well as an age-enhanced image. A message on the billboard asked the public to call with any information about the case.

The focus of the billboard campaign in St. Joseph and St. Cloud appeared to be an indication that authorities remained confident that Jacob's abductor was from the area. A billboard was also put up in the town of Paynesville.

The media coverage surrounding the search for Jacob Wetterling and his kidnapper was nothing short of spectacular. The blitz immediately following his abduction captured the public's attention from all possible angles. Over the years, interest was perennially renewed with news updates and other timely reminders from the media. The common thread of all coverage of the case was the hope of bringing him home.

As impressive as that coverage was, it paled in comparison to the outpouring of support from the community. The media may have gotten the message out, but the message itself was the people of St. Joseph.

4

Welcome to
St. Joseph, Minnesota

I couldn't be more proud of the city of St. Joseph. You people are just absolutely giving, and giving, and giving. And Jacob is hearing. We are not going to allow what I call the disease of missing children, abducted children, we are just not going to allow this to continue.—Jerry Wetterling, at a volunteer assembly held at Kennedy Elementary school gymnasium

Stories of out of town visitors like Vern Iverson and Darryl Savage were common around the town of St. Joseph in the days following Jacob's abduction, but most volunteers came from within the city and township of St. Joseph itself. The big-hearted show of support from this small community astonished the droves of law enforcement officials, members of media, and volunteers that descended upon the small town.

With a population of about 2,500 in 1989, St. Joseph was nestled within Stearns County in central Minnesota, along the north side of Interstate Highway 94, scarcely more than an hour's drive from Minneapolis. The town's major landmarks included the St. Joseph Catholic Church, St. Benedict's Monastery, and the all-women's College of St. Benedict. About six miles to the northwest was Collegeville, home to the prestigious St. John's University.

The surrounding area was predominantly rural and was considered a safe place to live and raise a family. Prior to Jacob Wetterling's abduction, the most high profile unsolved cases in Stearns County were the 1944 disappearance of six-year-old Jackie Theel, the murders of the Reker sisters in 1974, and the 1976 bombing of the Kimball Post Office.

The citizens were predominantly Catholic, and many were of German descent. The history of St. Joseph Catholic Church dates back to 1854, although at the time the town was known as Clinton. Several German families settled on the prairie land of central Minnesota and Father Francis Xavier Pierz convinced the townspeople to construct a church building in 1855. Benedictine monks and sisters settled in the area over the next several years. The sisters' convent and school became the centerpiece of town, and it grew into what became the College of St. Benedict. Today it is considered one of the leading liberal arts colleges in the country. The town was renamed St. Joseph in 1870, after the church upon which it was founded.

The hometown residents who gathered at Kay's Kitchen in downtown St. Joseph were the same faithful folks—the community that united in support of the Wetterling family. The locals were the essence of Midwestern friendliness and hospitality. This was a place where few ever gave a second thought to locking their cars when they went into town for groceries or the doors of their homes at bedtime.

Word of Jacob Wetterling's abduction spread like wildfire throughout the town of St. Joseph. By early morning on Monday, October 23, 1989, the news was everywhere, having moved from household to household, and businesses, by word of mouth. The Monday afternoon edition of the *St. Cloud Times* carried a brief article covering the story and there were countless daily updates in the weeks ahead. The *St. Joseph's Newsleader*, a bi-weekly paper, first reported on the kidnapping in its October 27, 1989, edition and continued to feature the story in headlines for months.

From the very first day after Jacob's abduction there was no shortage of volunteers to assist in the distribution of flyers, to help search the woods, or support the search effort in some other way. More than 300 students and staff from nearby St. John's University and the College of St. Benedict gathered to march and pray for Jacob on Monday, October 23. That same night, more than 75 students marched the mile and a half from the College of St. Benedict to the Del-Win Ballroom search headquarters. They sang and recited prayers together. Other students drove to nearby communities and distributed flyers.

A group of concerned community members quickly went into action, organizing the Jacob Wetterling Fund. They put out milk bottles to collect donations around town. Within a few days, others joined the group and set up a board.[1]

Volunteer Ken Twit picked up on an idea he learned about on the radio: he called the Wetterling's home phone number using every area code in North America. His theory was that Jacob might have known his home phone number, but may not have known his area code. Twit dialed about 130 different area codes. Anytime someone answered the phone call, Twit informed them about Jacob's abduction and would ask them to notify investigators if Jacob contacted them.[2]

The primary goal of the Jacob Wetterling Fund was, of course, to bring Jacob home. However, from its formation, the board understood the need to fill any gaps outside the direct investigative efforts. They formed a policy and structure within the organization. One goals was to help others that might find themselves in similar situations.

The children of St. Joseph were in a state of disbelief over what had happened to one of their friends. "The guy who did that probably came from somewhere else," said Jason Eickhoff, an 11-year-old boy. "Nobody around here would do something like that."[3] Like many kids in town, Eickhoff was afraid to go outside at night for some time following Jacob's abduction.

For one classmate of Jacob's, Daniel Ferraro, the abduction hit close to home. His Boy Scout troop had been camping in the area on Saturday, October 21, 1989. He realized that what happened to Jacob the next night could have just as easily happened to him or one of his friends.[4]

Two days after the abduction, a meeting was held at St. Cloud North Community School, where Jacob was in the sixth grade. School staff, counselors, parents, and more than 200 students attended the meeting. The purpose of the meeting was to help everyone cope with the abduction. Principal Ray Pontinen laid out the school's plans to help students who might have difficulty adjusting to their fears. A

Stearns County Sheriff's deputy and several psychologists and social workers joined the meeting. They counseled many students on the first day of school after the abduction.

Many attendees, parents in particular, were frustrated by the lack of definite answers to questions about how to help their children. School psychologist Ruth Kelly advised parents to keep their children on a "tighter leash," but not to the point of scaring them away from their routine activities. "Kids are processing this at a TV level, that this will be happily solved," Kelly said. She cautioned that while parents should not go to the extent of bursting that bubble of optimism, their children "have to know this is real, that it can happen right here in St. Cloud, in St. Joseph, that it's not some TV program."[5]

St. Joseph Police Chief Bill Lorentz held a community meeting at St. Joseph Laboratory School. He answered questions from students and tried to ease their fears. One sharp-minded student asked if the police helicopter used to search the area that night used an infrared camera to search the homes around the abduction scene. Lorenz said the cameras had not been used. Another student asked if the abductor had a car. Lorentz said investigators thought that he did have a car. Children wondered how the kidnapper knew Jacob and the boys would be there at the time of the abduction.[6]

On Wednesday, October 25, St. Joseph Church hosted a gathering of 600 people in prayer for Jacob. Patty, Jerry, Amy, Trevor, and Carmen sat in the front pew, the entire congregation behind them praying for Jacob's safe return. "We came together this morning to ask God's help and mercy. We are here, Jerry and Patty, to do whatever you ask or need until Jacob is found," said Father Tom Gillespie.[7]

Donations large and small came from a wide variety of businesses, individuals, and organizations. The funds were used to offer reward money, distribute posters and mailings, and to help cover private investigative expenses, should they become necessary. Many community events were organized, ranging from cash collection boxes to benefit dances, raffles, and dinners. By week's end, a fund at the First State Bank in St. Joseph had swelled to more than $25,000. The Tri-County Crimestoppers offered a reward of its own for $2,000.

Workers from U.S. West, through their volunteer organization known as the Telephone Pioneers of America, coined the phrase Jacob's Hope. They purchased hundreds of white ribbons and wrote the phrase on each one of them. Soon, Jacob's Hope became a trademark symbolic of the search and of the plight of missing children everywhere. The Pioneers encouraged people to tie white ribbons onto their cars or front doors until Jacob was found.

Reward money continued to accumulate. A group of businessmen from Minneapolis anonymously pledged $125,000 in cash for the safe return of Jacob by 11:00 p.m. Sunday, October 29. The Crime Stoppers reward grew to $25,000.

By Sunday, a week after Jacob had been taken, there was no word of his fate and no sign of his abductor. Mass at St. Joseph Church—seating capacity 700—was overflowing. People filled the aisles, and many more stood outside on the lawn. The mood was somber. The faces of the congregation showed the strain of a long week of fear, shock, and anger.

As Halloween approached, there was an unspoken reluctance by parents and children alike to go out trick-or-treating. Instead, many families hosted or attended private Halloween parties. Downtown businesses donated candy, soda pop and other treats to a school sponsored party.

An editorial in the Friday, November 3, 1989, *St. Cloud Times* highlighted the enormous community support for the Wetterling family. The column, entitled *Our Midwestern Roots are Showing*, noted that it was Midwestern values that were the driving force behind the support for Jacob and his family. It explained that "the nation perceives the small towns of the Midwest as the last bastions of safety—the last place anyone would imagine a crime of such magnitude happening."[8]

With the surrounding area now saturated with fliers, Vern Iverson convinced Patty and Jerry to bring in some outside help to take flier distribution to the next level. That help arrived in the form of San Francisco's David Collins. Collins was uniquely qualified for the task, having coordinated several such mailings over the past five years. More relevant, however, was Collins' personal experience. His son, Kevin, had been kidnapped from a bus stop in San Francisco in

1984. Collins, an unemployed truck driver, had since taken on the role as president of the Kevin Collins Foundation.

The Foundation specialized in mass distribution of information about missing children. At the time, the organization had taken on about 40 cases of child abduction, some which had been solved. However, the majority of the cases handled by the Foundation were not stranger abductions like Jacob's. Most were committed by family members. Those kinds of cases were generally easier to solve. Nearly two weeks had passed since the night of Jacob's abduction. Collins' experience had taught him that public awareness was more critical than police investigation by that point. "In the beginning in these kind of cases, the most important thing is the police department," Collins said. "As time goes on, that reverses and public awareness becomes much more important."[9]

Collins helped volunteers set up the Friends of Jacob Wetterling office, which evolved from the Jacob Wetterling Fund group. Located in downtown St. Joseph, its mission was to coordinate the mailing of fliers and fundraising efforts.

With Collins' help, an organizational meeting for a volunteer mailing effort was held in the gymnasium at Kennedy Elementary School. He had put together a plan to utilize up to 300 volunteers, but as he approached the podium, he saw that a crowd of more than 1,000 assembled.[10] Collins told them they had more help than was needed, that if anyone wanted to leave they could. No one left.

A printing company in St. Cloud donated 330,000 fliers. They were mailed out by the tens of thousands. Volunteers stuffed and addressed envelopes. Posters were shipped to truck stops, police stations, hospitals, clinics, military bases, and national agencies such as the American Medical Association.

The community support from the town of St. Joseph far exceeded Collins' expectations, resulting in an unparalleled distribution of information. Awareness of Jacob's abduction saturated the Midwest. He stayed in St. Joseph for about a week until he was called away to work on another case.

Local businesses continued to demonstrate a high level of support, holding multiple fundraisers and events. The Del-Win Ballroom sponsored a benefit dance and auction. Mark Kurtz, a local artist, donated a golden eagle sculpture. Professional sports teams chipped in to provide prizes. The Minnesota Twins, North Stars, and Vikings donated items including game tickets, jerseys, and other equipment. In the end, more than $20,000 was raised during the event.

Atonement Lutheran Church handed out envelopes to about 400 parishioners. Each envelope contained five fliers for Jacob. Families were asked to mail the fliers to friends and relatives outside the local area. Some businesses donated postage stamps to assist the mailing effort. Others donated envelopes or printing services for reward fliers.

Members of the Minnesota State Outdoor Advertising Association donated advertising space on 75 billboards across the state. Billboards displayed Jacob's picture, the Crimestoppers telephone number, and pleas for information about the case. The photo of Jacob wearing a bright yellow sweater became fixed in the minds of people across the country.

The Lions Club in nearby Richmond launched a $100,000 reward campaign to anyone who returned Jacob safely, or provided information that led to his safe return by November 15, 1989. The reward was offered following the expiration of the $125,000 reward previously offered by the businessmen in Minneapolis.

St. Cloud area McDonald's restaurants donated 25 cents for every order of french-fries sold. Some locations handed out fliers to drive-through customers. The owner of the local Super 8 motel arranged for fliers to be mailed to each of the chain's 660 locations. The *St. Paul Pioneer Press* utilized their 5,000 newspaper stands across the state to showcase posters of Jacob.

A local printing company donated bumper stickers that read "Remember Jacob." Some people admonished the choice of words, however, because is suggested a pessimistic view of Jacob's fate.

St. Cloud-based Anderson Trucking Service put Jacob's picture on semi-trailers, to be seen at hundreds of terminals across the country. Other local trucking companies put posters on their trucks as well. Two hundred large posters of Jacob were displayed at the Metrodome, the Met Center entertainment complex, and other Twin Cities locations.

Volunteers opened an office in St. Joseph with the help of donated filing cabinets, desks, chairs, office supplies, phone lines, and other items. Hotline phones were staffed seven days a week. Apple Inc. donated an assortment of computers and peripheral support equipment.

One of the most memorable events was Hands for Jacob, held on Saturday, November 4. Two students from Cathedral High School in St. Cloud conceived the idea. Radio station KXSS-FM sponsored the event, during which more than 5,000 people joined hands to form a human chain that stretched for nearly four miles along Stearns County Road 75. Minnesota Twins Dan Gladden and Al Newman, along with team president, Jerry Bell, attended the event.[11]

Yet the unified community spirit was accompanied by a collective fear. It wasn't spoken of much outside the home, but it lingered in the air. Kids who would ordinarily be sent on errands into town were accompanied by an adult or simply stayed home. Children who once pedaled their bicycles to school rode the bus instead. Prior to the abduction it was not unusual to see 60 bikes in the racks outside Kennedy Elementary School. In the days after, they could be counted on one hand.

People now locked their doors at night, and many began locking them during the day. Children were asking their parents difficult questions. Will the man try to take me too?

But it was the outward display of community support the public would identify with across the state and the nation. *St. Cloud Times* editor John Bodette summed up the tight-knit effort with his October 28 editorial, written as a message to Jacob: "Each day creative ideas expand the search. Some of the most determined efforts have come from youngsters your age…. You should be very proud of your hometown of St. Joseph. Your friends and neighbors have led the effort to get your plight out to the state and nation."[12]

The 1989 holiday season was approaching, and with it the Minnesota winter. Outdoor gatherings diminished, but displays of lights and messages in support of Jacob took their place. With fewer leads coming in for investigators to follow, media attention began to wane.

Yet the case continued to gain recognition in high places. An

Anoka resident succeeded in getting word of Jacob's abduction to the Vatican through the local Catholic diocese. Pope John Paul penned a letter in support of the Wetterling family. Patty read the letter aloud, her voice cracking emotion: "His Holiness asks you kindly to assure Jacob's parents in his name that he is deeply united with them in this period of trial and joins them in their heartfelt prayers for the safe return of their son."[13]

On December 23, a group of 10 Vietnam War veterans began a 65-mile walk from Anoka to the Wetterling home to raise money and to raise public awareness. They marched into St. Joseph on Christmas Day. Although winter brought an end to the public rallies and events, the community came together one more time. Friends and family gathered at the Lake George shelter to celebrate Jacob's twelfth birthday on February 17, 1990.

The support for Jacob Wetterling and his family from the people of St. Joseph and the surrounding area was overwhelming. By all measures, the energy and commitment demonstrated was unprecedented, and hope for his safe return endured in the hearts and minds of the community.

Jacob's twelfth birthday would become a special day for all other children as well—it was the day the Jacob Wetterling Foundation was born. The organization known as the Jacob Wetterling Fund had been established within days of his abduction, it's primary function to support efforts to find him. The new organization expanded its focus to all missing children and to the prevention of child abduction and abuse by establishing three principal objectives. The first was to educate children and parents to prevent child abductions. Second was to assist law enforcement and families in the development of procedures to implement when the threat of abduction becomes reality. Third was to engage with the political arena in the development of legislation designed to protect children from predators.

The Jacob Wetterling Foundation was immensely successful in achieving those objectives. Among its most significant accomplishments was the enactment of legislation requiring registration of sex offenders with local law enforcement agencies. In 1994, Congress passed the Jacob Wetterling Crimes Against Children and Sex

Offender Registration Act, providing law enforcement with the ability to publicly notify community residents of the presence of known sex offenders, and the requirement that offenders be listed on a national registry.

On the surface, the Jacob Wetterling Foundation appeared to be focused substantially on the issue of child abduction. However, the Foundation recognized that the growing problem of child abductions had in its roots a continuous cycle of sexual abuse. Therefore, much of the energy and resources utilized by the organization were aimed at those roots, by addressing all forms of child abuse and exploitation. The key to successfully suppressing the cycle of abuse, according to the Foundation, was to raise public awareness to a level where witnesses and families would take steps to report suspicious activities by suspected pedophiles and abusers.

5

The Search Begins

*It doesn't pay for us to get way out in the middle of places if you
can't get out there with a vehicle. This guy was in a vehicle, no
doubt about that, so we're concentrating on roads and ditches.*
—Dave Rodahl, Minnesota Department of Natural Resources

Al Garber, FBI supervisor of the St. Paul office Violent Crimes
Unit, was relaxing at home in front of his television on Sunday night,
October 22, 1989. The telephone rang shortly before 10:00 p.m. On
the other end was St. Cloud–based FBI agent Al Catallo.

Catallo informed Garber of Jacob Wetterling's abduction and
the general circumstances surrounding the crime. He immediately
phoned his boss, Jeff Jamar, and suggested that he, Garber, drive over
to St. Joseph the first thing Monday morning if Jacob had not been
found before then. Jamar gave his approval.[1]

When Garber checked in with the local FBI office in St. Cloud
early Monday morning, he learned there had been no sign of Jacob
or his abductor. He left home and headed northwest for the 90-
minute drive to St. Joseph.

Garber was somewhat surprised by Jamar's willingness to agree
to his plan. Throughout Jamar's tenure as his boss, he had been insis-
tent about relegating him to office duty. Garber preferred a hands-
on approach, having worked his way up to supervisor through several
investigative assignments over his FBI career. He preferred to be right
there in the field, working alongside his agents.[2]

Garber arrived in St. Joseph at 9:00 a.m. on Monday, October
23. He went directly to the command post that had been set up at
the Del-Win Ballroom, just a few blocks from where Jacob had been

37

abducted. There, he met with Agent Catallo, Stearns County Sheriff Charlie Grafft, and St. Joseph Police Chief Bill Lorentz. They briefed Garber on the known details of the abduction and summarized the search operation that had been initiated immediately following the abduction the night before.

Grafft recounted the efforts of his deputy staff. He had called in a State Patrol helicopter to search the area. He had personally boarded the chopper for the air search that began at about 10:30 p.m.[3] (The actual time of the helicopter search is an issue of debate. Given that the nearest State Patrol helicopter was stationed 60 miles away in Brainerd, it's probable the search would not have begun until later that night, most likely after about 11:00 p.m.) By midnight, the helicopter was searching a residential area up to a half-mile north of the abduction site.

The chopper's searchlight scanned back and forth several times across the area surrounding the crime scene, scouring the woods and open fields for any sign of Jacob. At one point the chopper was observing the ground so closely, it almost came into contact with utility wires near the scene. A total of 35 deputies and police officers searched well into that first night, ultimately suspending the search at 3:00 a.m.

By Monday there were four helicopters, at least six all-terrain vehicles, and a bloodhound involved in the search. Sheriff's deputies canvassed the neighborhood, interviewing everyone in the area in a door-to-door search for information that could help locate Jacob. Minnesota Department of Natural Resources officers used ATVs to search the area as well. Teams of law enforcement officials and volunteers covered a 25 square mile area around the abduction site. Despite their efforts, no signs of Jacob or his abductor were discovered.

Jeff Jamar, chief of the FBI office in St. Paul, arrived in St. Joseph later in the day and drove over to the Wetterling home to meet Jerry and Patty Wetterling. They discussed the steps investigators had taken at that point and what they were planning to do next.

Investigators scrutinized the Wetterlings as potential suspects. They were taken to the Comfort Inn hotel and interviewed for five hours, sometimes together, sometimes in separate rooms.[4] Questioning covered a wide range of personal and business related areas, including their days of dating at Mankato State University and student teaching in Mexico. Jerry, in particular, was thoroughly vetted. He submitted to a lie detector test but the results showed no indication of deception. The Wetterlings were quickly ruled out as suspects. They were transparent and cooperative, and clearly had nothing to hide.[5]

Jerry was president of the local chapter of the National Association for the Advancement of Colored People. He acknowledged it was possible that his involvement with the organization could be a factor in his son's abduction, but said he had no reason to believe that was the case. He had no enemies or quarrels of any kind with anyone he could think of. No one had ever threatened him or his family in any way. He was at a loss to explain how or why anyone would have ill will toward him or his family. "I don't think it was anyone targeting our family," Jerry said. "He didn't ask the kids' names, only ages.[6]

The air and ground searches were halted on Monday night, about 24 hours after the abduction. Authorities had searched in vain for any sign of Jacob or his abductor. "We've gone over that area fifteen times," Grafft told reporters.[7]

Despite the massive search, few tangible clues were found. Leads came in from the public, but after a full day had passed, there had been no communication of any kind from the kidnapper. Investigators concluded that the abductor had probably left the area with Jacob. Grafft speculated that the kidnapper might have stalked Jacob for several days before abducting him and that the publicity surrounding the case may have driven the kidnapper out of the area. He noted that no ransom demands had been made and said authorities believed the kidnapper was a local sex offender.[8]

"It was someone who knew the area very well," Grafft said. "A person had to have stalked them quite a while to do this. We think it's a sex offender, no doubt about it."[9]

"I'm not an expert on pedophiles," FBI agent Jeff Jamar offered. "But that's one indication to me that this person is a pedophile. There is no question—the child was abducted for a specific purpose."[10]

Jamar and Grafft chose their words carefully. They were referring to the kidnapper's actions—he had groped the genitals of Aaron Larson and Jacob Wetterling as part of his selection process.

Stearns County Deputy Sheriff Jim Kostreba reinforced Grafft's assessment. "It's difficult to say that someone just happened to be in that area at the time," Kostreba said. "It's a fairly remote area and it's not traveled by everybody. You'd have to say the person followed the three boys from somewhere."[11]

Grafft announced that several recently released inmates from the St. Cloud Reformatory had been investigated, but no evidence was found connecting any of them to the kidnapping. One former inmate, a convicted sex offender, was surveilled by investigators, but an inspection of his car revealed that his tires could not have left the tracks in the Rassier driveway.[12] The disclosure about the tire treads was the first hint that investigators had been able to secure physical evidence from the crime scene.

Investigators received more than 300 telephone tips in the first couple of days, and developed more than 100 potential suspects from tips, interviews, and parole records. Several potential suspects were convicted sex offenders.

Rassier driveway. Jacob's footprint was found near the first pole.

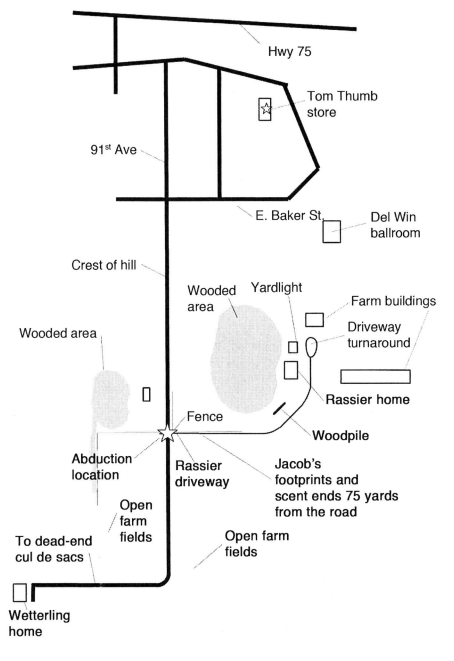

Map of area of Jacob's abduction.

Jacob Wetterling was kidnapped near a mailbox at the end of the driveway to the farm owned by Robert and Rita Rassier. The Rassier's was the residence on the right hand side of the road as the boys were biking north to Tom Thumb.

Dan Rassier, 34, lived in the house at the other end of that long gravel driveway. He lived there with his parents, but they were on vacation in Europe at the time of the abduction. Rassier was home alone the night of October 22. He told investigators and the media he had seen a vehicle quickly turn around in his driveway around the time of the abduction. He also told them about an unusual car he had seen in his driveway earlier that day.

Sometime in the middle of the afternoon, Rassier heard something going on outside as he was in his second-floor bedroom, organizing his record collection. He got up from his desk to investigate and saw a tan-colored car speeding down the driveway. In a cloud of dust, the car made a fast, 180-degree left hand turn-around near the farm buildings, then sped back out the driveway toward 91st Avenue. He described the car as similar to a 1970's Chevrolet Monte Carlo. Rassier said he had never seen anything like that on his family farm before. The man behind the wheel of the car was driving "like his life depended it." After the car left, Rassier returned to his record collection.[13]

In the late afternoon, he took a break from the records and went for a short run. It was unseasonably warm that Sunday. He ran across a field on the farm, along a path that led to the Del-Win Ballroom, where a polka festival was going on. From there he headed west to 91st, then back south toward home. It was early evening by the time he returned from his run. He remembered that he picked up the Sunday newspaper by the mailbox and then continued up the long driveway. He showered, made himself some dinner, and went back to his desk.[14]

Rassier said his dog, Smokey, started barking at some point after dark. Hearing a car coming up the driveway, Rassier got up from his desk, turned off the light, and went over to his second floor bedroom window to look outside. He wondered if it was the same car he had seen earlier. As it came closer, he realized it was a different car. It was moving pretty quickly, but not as fast as the car that had come through in the afternoon. This car made the same left hand, 180-degree turn. From the vantage point of the window, Rassier said he thought he could see a woman or a boy in the passenger seat—he or she appeared to have their hands covering their eyes. After turning around, the car sped back down the driveway, just like the other car.[15] Rassier described the vehicle as a small dark car, probably blue, with headlights close together.

Shortly after seeing the car, Rassier said he finished with his record collection and went to bed and fell asleep. He was awakened some time later by the sound of Smokey barking again. Rassier went to the window and saw people with flashlights by the firewood pile, just up the driveway from the house. Thinking they might be stealing firewood, he went to investigate. He turned off the lights inside the house so he would not be seen and went outside. He saw there were several men with flashlights by the woodpile.[16]

Rassier went back into the house and called 911. The time of the call was 11:23 p.m.[17] The 911 operator informed him that a child had been abducted, and that the people with flashlights were police officers searching for the boy.[18]

After completing the call, Rassier grabbed a flashlight and went outside to see if he could help. He spoke with Stearns County Sheriff's Deputy Bruce Bechtold. Rassier offered to search the farm's outbuildings, and proceeded to check each of the buildings. Afterward, he said, he figured there wasn't much more he could do, and since he had to work the next day, he went back to bed.[19]

The next morning, Rassier left for work and started to drive his car down the driveway, but was unable to cross the crime scene tape investigators had hung across the driveway. Rassier said he got out of the car, crossed the tape and jogged down the driveway to ask the officers how he could get out. He said they became upset with him and directed him to drive through the shallow grassy swale alongside the driveway.[20]

Despite having this second contact with officers in his driveway that morning, Rassier said no one questioned him until Monday morning, at his teaching job at Rocori School in Cold Spring. A pair of investigators pulled him out of his classroom for a search of his car and an interview that lasted about 45 minutes. They did not search Rassier's office or band room.

According to Rassier, he first told investigators about the two cars he witnessed when they interviewed him at school. He said the interview was when he first learned Jacob Wetterling had been abducted at the end of his driveway, and that he had no idea the kidnapping had taken place so near his family's property. Rassier said it occurred to him then, for the first time, that the car he witnessed Sunday evening was probably related to the kidnapping.[21]

On Monday, a bloodhound tracked Jacob's scent from the road, up the Rassier's unpaved driveway for about 75 yards, to the place where Jacob's last footprints were found in the dirt, with a fresh set of car tire tracks alongside. Detectives interpreted the footprints as evidence of resistance by Jacob. A Nike shoe, similar in style and size to the shoes he was wearing, was used to help identify the prints as Jacob's. The bloodhound did not indicate Jacob's scent beyond that point. Detective Steve Mund of the Stearns County Sheriff's Office made plaster casts of several footprints and tire tracks found in the driveway.[22]

Don Banham, a K-9 officer from the Minneapolis Police Department, worked his dog, Amos, tracking Jacob's last footsteps. Banham noted that the dog's strong reaction to Jacob's scent was a critical part of the early investigation. A personal belonging of Jacob's was used to train Amos to the scent. "It was a real strong track and then all of a sudden the track ended," Banham said. "I believe that the dog was indicating correctly, it told me that Jacob was at that point and turned around and went the other way, either in a vehicle or back on foot."[23]

Investigators took casts of tire tracks near the scene but did not communicate a high level of certainty that the tracks were those of the kidnapper. Minnesota Bureau of Criminal Apprehension Director Mark Shields said he was "not confident" that the kidnapper made the tracks, noting they were considered as possible evidence at that point.[24]

Within days, the number of law enforcement officers involved in Jacob's search had grown to more than 50. It quickly became clear that the Del-Win Ballroom could no longer house the growing base of operations. The office was relocated to the basement of the Law Enforcement Center in downtown St. Cloud. Investigators sent photographs of Jacob to law enforcement agencies within a five-state area.

Captain Jack Kritzek of the SCSO created a computerized file for logging information that came in from tips and investigators. As leads were generated, they were sorted into "A" and "B" groups. "A" leads were critical information to be investigated immediately; the "B" leads to be investigated soon. Steve Mund and Lou Leland of the SCSO, and Frank Whippler from the Benton County Sheriff's Office, sorted the leads.[25]

Leland was the lead detective for Stearns County and was considered an expert in the psychological evaluation of suspects. He had been on a hunting vacation out west when Jacob was kidnapped, but flew back when he was informed of the abduction. According to a fellow investigator, Leland was upset about being relegated to sorting leads in the basement and would have been more useful in the field, utilizing his skills for interrogating suspects.

As tips poured in from concerned citizens, investigators zeroed in on a small red car that had been seen in St. Joseph over the course of the past three weeks. The car was reportedly seen on 91st Avenue on the night of the abduction. A similar car was also reportedly seen multiple times parked at the Del-Win Ballroom, just a couple blocks away from the Tom Thumb where the boys had rented the video. The driver was described as a Caucasian male, 25 to 30 years old and weighing 185 to 190 pounds. Authorities identified as many as two-dozen red cars to investigate in possible connection to the promising lead.[26]

An abandoned red car was reportedly seen parked near the south end of Lake Owasso in Ramsey County. A tip about the 1987 Mercury car came into a Twin Cities television station from a caller that said they thought that a body had been removed from the car and tossed into the lake. According to BCA director Mark Shields, investigators searched the area around the lake on Wednesday October 25, 1989, on foot and by helicopter. The car was located but quickly ruled out because its tire tracks did not match those at the abduction scene. Investigators decided not to drag the lake.[27]

Investigators ultimately ruled out the suspicious red car that had been seen in St. Joseph. An art student from St. Cloud State heard that authorities were looking for a small red car, and came forward to explain that he owned a red car and had been in the area multiple times in recent weeks looking for scenes to sketch. Investigators did not consider him a suspect.[28]

Police in La Crosse, Wisconsin, investigated a report that a man fitting the description of Jacob's kidnapper was seen by an employee of the Quillin's IGA store. He said the man acted nervous and asked for change for calls he made from a pay phone. The man was driving a tan-colored Chevrolet Citation. The license plates were checked and found to belong to a man from Mackinaw, Illinois.[29]

Authorities said they identified four suspects within a couple of days of Jacob's abduction, but were able to clear them by confirming their alibis. Three of the men had criminal records for sex offenses and had been released from correctional facilities or treatment programs in recent months.[30]

By Wednesday, October 25, authorities were investigating the likelihood that Jacob's abduction was related to a January 13, 1989, abduction and sexual assault of a twelve-year-old Cold Spring boy named Jared.

Jared was walking home alone from downtown Cold Spring at about 9:45 p.m. on a Friday night, when a man in a car approached him and asked for directions to a local residence. As Jared started giving directions, the man got out of the car and grabbed him by the shoulders, forcing him into the car.[31] The man then drove a few miles to a rural area just north of Richmond, where he sexually assaulted Jared, then released him on the way back to Cold Spring, near County Road 158, on Highway 23, at about 11:00 p.m.[32]

Jared described the car used by his abductor as dark blue in color—a late-model, mid-sized four-door with blue interior and a luggage rack on the trunk. The abductor was described as a white male in his mid-thirties to early forties in age, approximately 5'8" tall, 170 lbs., with a small gut, broad shoulders, rough dark skin, large ears, large nose and dark hair. The man was wearing black boots, a gray vest, a brown baseball cap and a camouflage shirt and pants similar to military-issue type clothing.[33] He seemed to know the area around Cold Spring and Richmond quite well.

Although the information was not disclosed publicly at the time, the key to investigators linking Jacob's and Jared's cases was that the abductor had groped the boys over their clothing. As Wetterling Task Force investigators would later learn, it was a common element in other unsolved sexual assaults that had occurred in the neighboring community of Paynesville a few years earlier.

The SCSO conducted the investigation into Jared's abduction and assault, with detectives Lou Leland and Doug Pearce leading the way. Within three days of Jared's abduction, Stearns County Sheriff's Deputy Robert Zieglmeier received information about a possible suspect in the kidnapping: Danny James Heinrich, of nearby Paynesville. Heinrich drove a 1987 dark blue, four-door Mercury Topaz. Other descriptive details of the car were remarkably consistent with the vehicle Jared had described.[34]

Zieglmeier learned that Heinrich was in the military, either the National Guard or Army Reserves, and that he was known to frequently wear military fatigues. Heinrich's physical description at the time was that he was 5'5" tall, weighed 160 pounds, and had brown eyes and brown-colored hair.

On January 17, 1989, Pearce gathered six photographs of various men whose physical characteristics were similar to what Jared had described—including a current photo of Heinrich. Jared viewed the photos and identified Heinrich and one other man as resembling his abductor.[35]

Danny Heinrich was employed at Master Mark Industries at the time of Jared's abduction and assault. On January 18, 1989, five days after the incident, detectives Pearce and Leland drove to Master Mark to look at Heinrich's vehicle, a 1987 Mercury Topaz. They matched the license plate number with motor vehicle records to confirm that it belonged to Heinrich. They noted that the interior was gray-colored and there was no luggage rack—the only details that differed significantly from Jared's description.[36]

There is no record to indicate that Pearce or Leland interviewed Danny Heinrich about Jared's January 1989 abduction as part of their investigation in his case.

In February 1989, the Tri-County Crimestoppers offered a

$1,000 reward for information leading to the arrest of Jared's abductor. The reward was published in the *Cold Spring Record*, the *Paynesville Press*, and the *St. Cloud Times*, with a police artist's sketch of the assailant and detailed descriptions of him and the car.

Near the end of October 1989, within a week of Jacob's kidnapping, authorities released information about a kidnapping attempt that had occurred in the Township of St. Joseph in July, along with a the sketch of the assailant. Nine-year-old "Andrew" had narrowly escaped being abducted when a man in a van pulled up alongside him and asked him his age. When the man tried to get him inside the van, Andrew was able to run away. The would-be kidnapper was described as a white male in his late twenties,

Original police sketch of Jared's abductor, February 1989 (Stearns County Sheriff's Office).

with dark brown hair, dark eyes, a slender build and fair complexion, with a mole on his forehead. He was driving an older, light tan van with white trim and rust along the bottom edges.

Andrew's mother said that at the time no one would believe them when they told of the incident. The SCSO didn't even inform the St. Joseph Police Department about the report until after Jacob was abducted three months later.[37] Andrew's mother indicated that after Jacob was taken, there was speculation locally that the kidnapping was for ransom. Andrew's father was a doctor and Jacob's father was a chiropractor—many people theorized that the abductor was selecting children whose parents would have money.

Investigators explored the connections between the two cases. They felt the use of the gun in Jacob's abduction might have resulted from a prior failed attempt. "Because the man used a gun, which is a very high-risk thing to do, we've concluded that he may have tried and failed before," FBI Agent Jeff Jamar explained.[38] "The key aspect of this guy is, he did ask the boy his age," FBI spokesman Byron Gigler said, adding that Andrew's assailant was a "strong potential suspect" in the Wetterling case.[39]

In an unusual coincidence, the day of Jacob's abduction, October 22, happened to be Andrew's tenth birthday.

Following Jacob's abduction, the FBI questioned Andrew's neighbors and found several witnesses who had seen the suspicious van in the neighborhood prior to the kidnapping attempt. The sketch of the assailant, as well as information about him, promptly generated more than 1,500 phone calls to search headquarters. Despite a considerable number of leads and witness statements, the man's identity was never determined.[40]

Additional details about Andrew's near-abduction and the man driving the van came to light a few weeks after Jacob was taken. Three different families in the St. Joseph Township area—including two that lived near Andrew's home—came forward to relate incidents they had witnessed.

One 11-year-old boy said that a man in a similar van took his picture and then drove off. It happened about two weeks after Andrew's abduction attempt. The boy said he had been fishing from a dock on a lake when he saw a van stop close by. The driver leaned out the window and took his picture. "I turned around and looked at him and he backed up, turned and got the heck out of there," the boy said.[41]

He described the man as having black hair and said he was holding eyeglasses in his hand while he took the picture. The boy said he had been scared to tell anyone about the incident because he was afraid something might happen to him if word got out. The FBI obtained this information while questioning boys in the school district.[42]

Another young boy from Andrew's neighborhood told his parents he saw a van matching the description on the same day of the abduction attempt, although he noted nothing unusual about the sighting.

The mother of another St. Joseph family reported seeing a similar van almost every day for three months—June through August of 1989—in an area about seven miles from Andrew's neighborhood. Her family was building a new home and the van had been parked across the street whenever she arrived there at about 6:00 p.m., and would remain there until about 9:00. She never got a good look at the driver. She thought it was unusual, but had not felt compelled to call the police until authorities released a sketch of the van in November.

"He wasn't on our land, and he didn't do anything," she said. "But I would always say 'oh, there's that van again. I would watch him and he would just sit there. He wouldn't move. I used to think he was hunting, because that's how long he sat."[43]

It occurred to her after hearing news of Andrew's attempted abduction that the man may have been watching the group of kids that were always playing outside with her own four children. After the house was completed and the children were no longer playing outside, the van wasn't seen there again.

John Douglas, the FBI's legendary profiler, was brought into the investigation from the headquarters in Quantico, Virginia, to create a psychological and physical profile of Jacob's abductor. Such profiles had proven to be accurate in about 90 percent of cases. In Jacob's case, Douglas concluded that the perpetrator was a white male, probably 25 to 35 years old, employed in a low-skilled job, and had little contact with the public. He thought the man might have acne, facial scars or some other physical deformity.[44]

Several aspects of Jacob Wetterling's kidnapping were unusual. The assailant wore a mask and used a gun. He had been particularly brazen in committing the crime in front of witnesses and then letting them leave. Douglas suggested he had a recent high-stress event in his life that triggered high-risk behavior. The use of the gun indicated he may have attempted a similar crime but failed. His acquaintances would probably have noticed a heightened level of anxiety in him in the days after the kidnapping.

John Douglas wrote several books about the cases he worked during his storied FBI career. He advised investigators to keep tabs on main suspects, especially near the first anniversary of the crime. A violent criminal, he wrote, almost always visits the victim's grave near anniversary dates, especially around the first anniversary. He explained that violent criminals who commit murder often bury their victims' bodies in a location that is familiar to the criminal, somewhere he feels comfortable.

The FBI profile was released in hopes that someone would recognize the suspect. Chief Jeff Jamar acknowledged, however, that investigators had not yet developed a strong theory of what had happened to Jacob.

Wetterling Task Force investigators actively sought tips from the general public. They wanted to know if anyone saw anything out of the ordinary or any unusual people prior to Jacob's kidnapping. St. Joseph resident Cindy Lovold remembered seeing a man in Cash Wise Food Mart several times. She called the task force with a description of the man dressed in military fatigues. She said he stood out to her as being unusual because he looked creepy.[45]

On Thursday October 26, a group of 30 volunteers from several surrounding counties came to St. Joseph with horses to search the area around the abduction site once again. The horseback search began about a mile east of St. Joseph, then crossed through the Sauk River and headed west toward St. Joseph and beyond. The search party was looking for any sign of Jacob or an article of his clothing that may have been left behind or snagged on a branch. No evidence was found.

The use of horses offered several advantages over searching on foot. Sitting at a higher elevation, a searcher can cover more ground on horseback and get into areas of rough terrain that could be difficult to traverse on foot. Riders are able to pick up on cues from horses, which have a keen sense of sight and smell. "You learn to read your horse," said Capt. Bryan Hagen, a member of Dakota County Sheriff's Mounted Patrol. "You watch his ears, and if they come up and the horse starts looking around, you follow where they're looking."[46]

By the end of October there were 70 law enforcement officers, including 20 FBI agents, working full-time on Jacob's case. That number of agents was typical for investigating a child kidnapping—but Jacob's case proved to be anything but typical. Investigators worked 14 to 16 hours daily, most receiving no days off during the first few weeks of the search. Tips poured in from the public and officers were kept busy following up on all of them.

The headquarters at the Law Enforcement Center held several tables filled with phone books, telephones, notebooks, and office supplies. Despite the fact that additional phone lines were installed, there were times when all phone lines were busy fielding calls and tips from the public. This was particularly true following any national media coverage of the story.

Within a few days of the kidnapping, the Minnesota State Attorney General announced he had contacted the attorneys general of Wisconsin, Iowa, Illinois, North Dakota, and South Dakota. Officials from those states agreed to upgrade their investigations from "high alert" to "extremely high alert."[47] It seemed the entire Midwest was on the lookout for Jacob Wetterling.

According to Dan Rassier, investigators first searched his family's farm six days after the abduction, on Saturday, October 28, 1989. Rassier was present in the morning when investigators arrived. He said they asked him then, for the first time, about the cars he had reported seeing in his driveway the Sunday before. By then, Rassier said, an assortment of all terrain vehicles, cars, and horses had trampled over the tire tracks. He said he was frustrated that investigators had failed to investigate the tracks earlier. Investigators inspected several pairs of Rassier's shoes and determined that none of them were consistent with the shoe impressions they had discovered in the driveway. This was the first indication by investigators that they had recovered what were believed to be the kidnapper's shoeprints.[48]

Rassier left the property to play music for a wedding that Saturday, so he was not at home during the actual search of the property. However, family members told him that investigators spent considerable time searching his bedroom that day. Detectives administered a polygraph test to Rassier that Saturday night but, he said, law enforcement did not reveal the results to him. He also agreed to travel to Minneapolis to be questioned under hypnosis by Dr. John Rhetts, but he said he was not told if that questioning revealed any information relevant to the case.[49]

On Saturday, October 28, the search for Jacob got another infusion of help, this time from the Minnesota National Guard. More than 100 troops from the St. Cloud-based Guard unit were brought in to perform another thorough search of the area under orders from Minnesota Governor Rudy Perpich. The team of troops utilized a pair of helicopters to search by air, while others in the unit searched the terrain on foot. Another helicopter from the Department of Natural Resources also joined the search. Areas along the Sauk River were searched, as were the nearby granite quarries in the Township of St. Joseph. Searchers walked in a tight group, no more than arm's length apart from one another, as they plodded through densely vegetated areas, junkyards, barbed wire fences, buildings and other obstacles.

The only significant find of the day was a white sock that was discovered about 100 yards south of the abduction site. Investigators brought in a bloodhound dog to track a scent from the sock but the dog was unable to track the scent further than the nearby road. Days later, laboratory testing revealed that the sock was not related to the investigation. Investigators were back to where they started. They had no physical evidence other than Jacob's footprints in the driveway where he had been taken, and the tire tracks nearby.

The Guard search continued all weekend and into Monday. By the end of the three-day search, more than 300 troops, Department of Natural Resources officers, and volunteers had covered thousands of acres of land and numerous buildings in the area. More than 36 square miles had been thoroughly searched in the Townships of St. Joseph, Rockville, and Collegeville.

Dave Rodahl of the Minnesota Department of Natural Resources led one of the search groups. His unit focused on the area encompassed by 287th Street, Stearns County Road 160, and Island Lake Road, concentrating on areas easily accessible by vehicles, including an abandoned farm site on 287th Street.[50]

"It doesn't pay for us to get way out in the middle of places if you can't get out there with a vehicle," he said. "This guy was in a vehicle, no doubt about that, so we're concentrating on roads and ditches. If you can't get there with a car, you can't get there. We hope that's the angle (the abductor) has been using."[51]

Law enforcement authorities set up roadblocks in St. Joseph on Sunday, October 29, one week after the kidnapping. Passing motorists were questioned during traffic stops that began at 7:30 p.m. and continued through 10:00. Authorities hoped to find any delivery drivers, hunters, or others who might normally drive through that area on Sunday nights. More than 2,000 vehicles were stopped and about 40 people were questioned at length but no meaningful clues were produced.[52]

One of investigators' best leads to date developed on Monday October 30, after a witness reported seeing a man and a boy matching Jacob's description stopped along a road near the city of Hector. The man was driving a white, late model General Motors vehicle. The man appeared to be in his late twenties and stood about 6'1". According to the witness, he may have had a gun. He had a dark complexion and was wearing gold or silver glasses, a brown or tan cap, and a light gray jacket with white lettering on the sleeves.[53]

The witness agreed to be hypnotized to glean as many details as possible from him. He told investigators that the boy he saw with the man appeared to be urinating alongside the road. He described the boy as having brown hair, wearing a red jacket with blue letters, and a pair of blue sweatpants—clothing generally matching the description of what Jacob was wearing when last seen. The witness said the boy got back in the car with the man and they sped off as he approached them. The driver ran a stop sign and headed eastward on Highway 212.

About an hour later, a Sheriff's deputy spotted a similar car eastbound near Victoria. He followed it to Eden Prairie and stopped the driver. The 34-year-old man was arrested for possession of two loaded handguns without a permit. He was driving a 1978 white Chevrolet Malibu and was alone in the car. Investigators assembled a lineup but the Hector witness was unable to identify the driver as the man he had seen earlier that day. Investigators lost confidence in the lead a few days later, after the witness became less certain of what he had seen[54]

Within ten days of Jacob's abduction, investigators had compiled a list of hundreds of possible suspects. More than 100 had already been eliminated. Most were local men with histories of child sexual abuse.

"We feel based on crime scene analysis that the abductor was from this area," said FBI spokesman Byron Gigler. "Interviews, the profile, research by our behavioral science unit all lead us to the strong opinion that the individual was familiar with this area, that he lived or worked here at one time and still has friends and associates here. He knew his way around."[55]

In an unusual development, an inmate at the state prison in Stillwater, Minnesota, told a fellow prisoner that he had kidnapped Jacob. The prisoner shared the information with the FBI and Carmen Piccarillo, an agent from Garber's unit, promptly went into the prison undercover. The suspect told Piccarillo that he wanted to pay to have his car destroyed. The car was located and torn apart by FBI lab technicians, but no evidence was found. The suspect's rural farmhouse was searched, but again, nothing. Garber and Minnesota BCA agent, Dennis Sigafoos, attempted to interview the suspect but he was uncooperative.[56]

Ground searches of the area were called off about two weeks after Jacob's abduction. In all, more than 300 square miles of fields, rivers, woods, farms, and homes had been searched. Much of the area had been searched multiple times but no real clues had been discovered from the efforts.

With tips from the public beginning to slow somewhat, authorities released the sketch of the van used in the attempted abduction of Andrew that summer. Additional details about the van were released: it was a 1970's model, with a white bumper and a cracked blue-colored bug deflector in front. It was a utility-type vehicle with black-wall truck tires, two rear windows and handles on the back doors. Sheriff Charlie Grafft noted that investigators quickly became busy with up to 200 callers, many giving similar descriptions of what they had seen.

The investigation soon became focused on finding a man who was seen acting suspiciously at the Tom Thumb store just before Jacob was abducted. He was seen standing outside the convenience store at about 8:45 to 9:00 p.m., just minutes before the abduction. A father and his four-year-old daughter went into the store and noted a man standing by the door staring at them.

The store clerk reported seeing the man standing by the store's ice machines when she emptied the trash bins at 9:00 p.m.[57] She later told investigators that Jacob, Trevor, and Aaron came into the store minutes later, and gave no indication that they had seen the strange man.[58]

On November 6, 1989, the FBI released a sketch of the man, described as a white male in his 50's, about six feet tall, having a large build and weighing about 200 lbs. Witnesses described him as having white hair and a receding hairline. FBI spokesman Byron Gigler told the media that this man was not a main suspect, but they had a sense of urgency in identifying him. "We have been working diligently from day one to locate him," Gigler said. "We're appealing to the public to contact us if they feel they know this man."[59]

It was believed the same man had been seen that same day at about 3:45 p.m., outside a Quik Mart convenience store in nearby Avon. A married couple and their two daughters reported seeing a man with a piercing stare as he leered at customers.[60] He did not speak or make any purchases. His odd behavior was noticed by other customers—one family was so upset by his presence that they left the Avon store without making a purchase.[61]

On Sunday November 5, exactly two weeks after Jacob's abduction, a woman working at the Tom Thumb reported that a man came into the store about 9:00 p.m. and started talking and laughing about Jacob's abduction. "They'll never find that boy," he reportedly said.

A police sketch of the man was similar to one made of the man with the piercing stare seen at the store the night of Jacob's abduction. He was described as being six feet tall, weighing 200 lbs., balding with gray hair. He drove away in a dark-colored car.

On November 6, 1989, a young girl in Minot, North Dakota, reported she had seen a young boy matching Jacob's description with a suspicious looking man. She told authorities she was looking at a poster of Jacob at a local shopping center when the boy walked up and asked her for help. He was wearing a red hockey jacket with patches on the front and a hockey logo on the back. The man then yelled for the boy to come back. He was wearing a long coat, and she indicated that he gave the impression that he had a weapon hidden underneath. The girl's mother reported seeing a tan van matching the description of the van involved in Andrew's kidnapping attempt. The FBI interviewed the girl and her mother, according to Minot Police Lt. Armin Lennick.[62] However, the girl quickly changed details of her statement and other people at the mall were unable to corroborate her original story. The lead was dismissed.[63]

By the end of the first week of November, investigators had received more than 12,000 tips from the public. What was missing, though, was the one call that would lead authorities to Jacob and his kidnapper. Patty Wetterling made a public plea for people to come forward with information, stating her belief that someone in the area knew something and that they should come forward.

While tips generated from media coverage and sketches of the suspect had so far failed to produce any arrests, the publicity did help solve a pair of cases in Shreveport, Louisiana. A 10-year-old Bossier City boy had been assaulted, and an 11-year-old girl from Shreveport had been raped. Later, when 10-year-old Amy Mihaljevic of Bay Village, Ohio, vanished from a local shopping mall, callers who had seen the sketch of the suspect in the Wetterling case pointed to a James Edward Vachuska. Vachuska was arrested and charged in the assaults of the Bossier City boy and Shreveport girl, but apparently was not involved in the Mihaljevic kidnapping. He had been released from prison in June 1989, after serving nine years for assaulting two children in the late 1970s.[64] Investigators determined that Vachuska was not involved in Jacob's abduction.

The attention to other abductions across the country highlighted the fact that authorities were stretched thin in covering a tremendous array of leads and information. From Texas to Nevada, and places in between, reported sightings of Jacob kept investigators scrambling. A sighting in Joplin, Missouri, and a pair in Rapid River and Marquette in Michigan's Upper Peninsula turned up nothing.[65]

On Wednesday, November 8, 1989, the attempted abduction of a nine-year-old in New Brighton, Minnesota, sparked a new surge of leads. The boy had been delivering newspapers with his cousin, and was riding his bicycle home by himself when a man drove up and ordered, "Get in the car, your parents want me to take you home."[66]

The boy sped off on his bike toward home. The man followed him briefly but drove off when the boy reached his house. A sketch of the driver resembled the sketch of the man seen at the Tom Thumb in St. Joseph. The boy described him as in his mid-fifties, balding and gray-haired, with a rough-sounding voice. The boy's cousin said he noticed a gray car following them as they finished delivering their papers, but it wasn't until the two separated at the end of their route that the driver tried to entice the boy into his car.[67]

Agent Jeff Jamar noted that investigators had identified six Minnesotans with criminal sex offense records against boys, and whose physical descriptions closely resembled the man described by the New Brighton boy. However, all six had alibis for the night of Jacob's kidnapping and the kidnapping attempt in New Brighton.[68]

With little to no physical evidence to go on, investigators were heavily reliant on leads from the public. False leads consumed valuable resources. In mid–November, someone called the Missing Children's Network, reporting that Jacob was still in St. Joseph. Other leads came from people who thought they had seen Jacob, some reporting that he was at a specific location. In all such cases, the FBI had to investigate to the fullest extent possible.

Yet another attempted abduction occurred on Friday, November 17, 1989, in Roberts, Wisconsin, just east of the Twin Cities. A 13-year-old boy was on his way home from basketball practice when a man in a car approached him. The driver rolled down his window and yelled to the boy in a deep voice, "Get in the car."[69]

Aware of Jacob's kidnapping, the boy ran home as fast as he could. The driver was a white middle-aged man wearing a black ski mask. The car was believed to be a tan 1984 or 1985 Lincoln Town Car.[70] "He saw a car parked on a driveway leading to the schoolyard," said Agent Byron Gigler. "He saw it for some time as he was walking up to it. He heard the window go down. A dome light came on. He yelled at him in a commanding voice."[71]

Investigators noted similarities between Jacob's abduction and this attempt in Roberts. Both men wore masks; both spoke in commanding voices. Both incidents occurred at night and involved boys about the same age. And both occurred within two miles of Interstate 94.

In November, Governor Rudy Perpich enlisted the help of Minnesota's 2,000 deer hunters in the search for Jacob. He directed the state Department of Natural Resources to contact license holders and ask them to report any suspicious activity or people.[72]

Investigators remained positive. Stearns County Deputy Jim Kostreba noted that each day officers expressed confidence that they would find Jacob. Most investigators had breakfast at home with their families each morning, but ate their other meals at the Law Enforcement Center in St. Cloud.

By the week of Thanksgiving 1989, leads in Jacob's case were dwindling to the point where reductions of investigative staff became necessary. The Minnesota BCA removed six of eight officers working the case. "We're at the point here that we are so busy with so many major cases throughout the state. It was one of those tough decisions I didn't want to make, but I had no choice," said BCA Superintendent Mark Shields.[73] The FBI cut agents from 20 to 15 by Thanksgiving.

Meanwhile, a 10-year-old Red Wing, Minnesota, girl saw a man wearing a ski mask and driving a car erratically on a rural road. A young boy was inside the car, pounding his hand against a window. She jotted down the license plate number and gave the information to her bus driver.[74] The girl said the boy resembled the pictures of Jacob she had seen. The story gained credibility when a 16-year-old girl gave a similar account that took place in the area about fifteen minutes earlier. The incident was later discounted, however, after the driver of the car was located. The man and the boy had been hunting in the area and had swerved to avoid hitting children they had seen by the road.[75]

In the latter half of November, authorities released another sketch of the suspect—a composite of the three previously distributed sketches, created on the assumption the earlier witnesses may have been describing the same person: the man with the piercing stare at

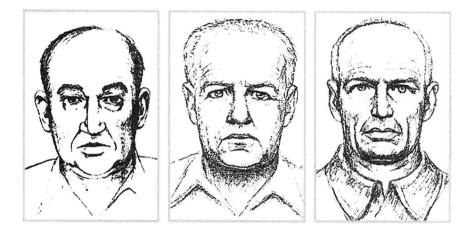

Left: Sketch of man seen at the Tom Thumb store on the afternoon of October 22, 1989. *Center:* Sketch of man seen at the Tom Thumb store November 5, 1989. *Right:* Sketch of man in attempted kidnapping in New Brighton (Stearns County Sheriff's Office).

the Tom Thumb the night of the abuction; the man who laughed about the abduction in the Tom Thumb two weeks later; and the man who had attempted the kidnapping in New Brighton on November 8.[76]

Meanwhile, another man who was once a suspect in Jacob's abduction, but had been previously cleared, told investigators that Jacob had been killed and his body taken to an abandoned meat packing plant in a city with the word "Falls" in it. The FBI followed up with a bulletin to all law enforcement agencies in Minnesota on November 18, requesting that they check any former meat packing facilities plants in their areas. Chippewa Falls, Wisconsin, police investigated the defunct Packerland plant, but found nothing.[77]

Composite of three sketches (Stearns County Sheriff's Office).

Within four weeks of Jacob's abduction, investigators had interviewed 1,200 people who had reported suspicious activity, had fielded tips from more than 100 psychics, and had investigated and cleared 525 potential suspects. They anticipated questioning hundreds more in the coming weeks.[78]

By Thanksgiving, the FBI issued a plea for more information on three cars and drivers that were seen in Jacob's neighborhood prior to his kidnapping. "After intensive investigation in that neighborhood, these vehicles are ones that were pointed out as not fitting in," said Byron Gigler. "We're very anxious to identify the drivers of the vehicles."[79] Sketches of two of the drivers were released. Witnesses were unable to provide a good description of the third man, so no sketch was done.

The first sketch was of a man with a full, dark-colored beard, wearing a cap. Numerous witnesses saw him on 90th Avenue about six weeks prior to the kidnapping. His car was described as older and maroon in color. It had rectangular taillights, similar to a 1976 Pontiac Catalina. The back end the car was jacked up. Two witnesses reported seeing the vehicle parked on the street at night; both times the vehicle left when someone approached it. The car was also seen in the area once during the daytime.[80]

The second car was seen one week before the abduction on 95th Avenue, near Seventh Avenue SE, in a neighborhood across a field and west of the scene of the abduction. It was a small, red car with white trim, believed to be an older model, about the size of an American Motors Pacer or Gremlin, and its rear tires were either oversized or the back end was elevated. The car had dealer logo plates on the back license plate holder and the logos had red and blue lettering on a white background. The driver had medium length hair and wore glasses and a cap.[81]

The third car was a red-orange colored station wagon that was also possibly jacked-up in the rear. It was seen either October 21 or 22 near the Wetterling home on Kiwi Court. A similar car had been seen on 91st Avenue on October 22 at about the time of the abduction. It may have been one of several vehicles that passed the boys on their way to Tom Thumb that night. (As of late November 1989, authorities had been able to locate only one of those cars.) The boys reportedly saw no cars on their way back home from the store.[82]

Trevor and Aaron were interviewed three times, and each time their story was consistent. They did not see or hear a car. However, a neighbor did tell investigators that he heard tires squealing at about 9:00 p.m. that night.[83]

After Thanksgiving, the number of law enforcement officers working Jacob's case had been reduced from 50 to 30. Investigators had pursued more than 13,000 leads, but they still had not publicly identified a prime suspect. The sketches of the men and descriptions of the cars seen in the neighborhood of the abduction site generated only about 50 calls.

Occasionally, people claiming to be psychics made calls to Crimestoppers. All such leads were checked out: investigators reasoned that people who were reluctant to come forward might use psychic claims as a ruse to give legitimate tips without being identified. They produced no credible information. One psychic lead had the FBI searching a four county area around Mason City, Iowa, but nothing was found there.[84]

At the end of November, a person of interest who had been previously questioned in connection to Jacob's abduction was involved in a standoff with Sheriff's deputies at his home. A man in his fifties, he had initially come to the attention of investigators because he resembled the sketch of the man seen at the Tom Thumb store around the time of the kidnapping. He also resembled the man seen at the store two weeks later, and had been questioned in mid–November. He had not been ruled out but was also not considered a prime suspect.[85]

He barricaded himself in his home on Crestview Drive in the Pleasant Acres development of St. Joseph and threatened to shoot himself or anyone trying to enter his home. Sheriff Charlie Grafft reported that the man was taken into custody at 9:00 a.m. Wednesday, November 29. He was taken to St. Cloud Hospital for 72 hours of observation for mental instability.[86]

Authorities did not publicly state that the Pleasant Acres resident was the same man wanted for questioning after being seen at Tom Thumb store on October 22. But it is interesting to note that, beginning with the November 30, 1989, edition of the *St. Cloud Times*, the two original sketches of the man at the store were no longer included in articles related to the abduction.

Investigators followed up on another kidnapping attempt in Monticello, Minnesota, on Thursday, November 30. A 15-year-old boy was walking home from basketball practice at about 7:30 p.m. As he passed a parked car outside of the Pizza Factory restaurant, near the corner of Broadway Street and Highway 25, a man rolled the window down and asked the boy if he needed a lift. When the boy said no, the man ordered him to "just get in the car!"[87] When the man gave the order a second time, the boy ran into the Monticello Sewing Center, where his parents were shopping.

The boy described the man as white, approximately 30 to 40 years old, with long sideburns.[88] Restaurant employees were able to give a partial license plate number of a suspicious car. Investigators immediately tracked it to a Fridley man, who was questioned that night but cleared. Police made a public appeal to customers who were in the restaurant between 7:00 and 8:00 p.m., to come forward with any additional information.

A Fridley boy reported another kidnapping attempt the following day, December 1. The 10-year-old was reportedly followed by a brown van twice that Friday—once in late morning and again in midafternoon. This marked the fourth attempted kidnapping in the area in the six weeks since Jacob's abduction, although the Fridley incident was determined to be unrelated.[89]

One factor that hampered efforts was that the investigative agencies had little experience in handling such cases. The attempted abduction of Andrew earlier that summer showed how the lack of an inter-departmental communication failed in terms of awareness and preparedness for future incidents in the area. In mid–December, authorities reiterated that Jacob's kidnapping was likely connected to the January abduction of Jared in Cold Spring. "We feel there's a very definite connection," Sheriff Charlie Grafft said.[90]

The FBI interviewed Jared three times in December 1989. The similarities to his assault and Jacob's abduction were striking. Investigators noted that the abductor in both cases exhibited a commanding presence. "This guy was very aggressive, very commanding, almost like a military man," said Byron Gigler.[91] In both cases, the victims' genitals were groped.

Authorities released a ninth and final sketch of the man believed to be involved in Jared's assault. This one was particularly significant because the suspect was not wearing a mask. An experienced FBI artist from Washington, D.C., created the sketch after a lengthy meeting with Jared and his parents.

The FBI took several weeks to be certain that Jared's description of his attacker was accurate and that circumstances of both cases pointed to a single suspect. That information was developed after three interviews with Jared. "We didn't want to put out an artist conception like this one unless we were certain," said Jeff Jamar.[92]

Sheriff Charlie Grafft pointed out the differences between this sketch and the one of Jared's perpetrator that had been released in February 1989. He explained that the original sketch had been created immediately after the assault, and that this new sketch was after Jared was better able to recall details of the man's face. "He's a sharp, very intelligent young man," Grafft said of Jared. "He was able to give a lot of details."[93]

The sketch generated another burst of new tips in Jacob's case. Hundreds of calls came pouring in within a couple days of its release. "The phone has been ringing off the hook," said Grafft. "We've got a lot of local calls and some from outstate. Everyone seems to know the man. Now if we can just find him."[94]

FBI sketch of Jared's abductor, December 1989 (Stearns County Sheriff's Office).

WE *MUST FIND* THESE MEN...

SO **JACOB** CAN BE FOUND.

Age: 40 to 50 years old;
Height: 5'8" tall; Husky shoulders;
Low, raspy voice;
Bold, authoritative manner

JACOB WETTERLING:
Age: 11 years; Height: 5'0";
Weight: 75 pounds; Hair: Brown;
Eyes: Blue; Mole on left cheek

CALL: (612) 259-3981

1-800-255-1301

Jacob,
we love you and we'll
never stop looking for you
— Mom + Dad

JACOB WETTERLING FOUNDATION
Phone 612-363-0470
You can help. Please read the other side.

STRANGER ABDUCTION

Poster featuring sketch of Jacob's abductor (Stearns County Sheriff's Office).

"We're pretty confident that this is one and the same person," stated Byron Gigler. And they were fairly certain they were looking for someone who lived in central Minnesota. "He's either from the area or dog-gone familiar with it," said Grafft.[95]

On Tuesday, December 19, a Redwood Falls, Minnesota, boy reported yet another abduction attempt. It happened at about 4:30 p.m. as the he was biking home from an eye doctor appointment. A man pulled alongside him, rolled down his window and said, "Get in the car, kid."[96] The man was wearing a ski mask and spoke in a rough voice.

The boy fled on his bike but the man did not follow. The boy described the vehicle as a two-door, medium-sized red car with black door guards and masking tape on the driver's window. He described the man's voice as raspy and low, like he was a smoker or had a cold. Over the course of the investigation, there had been many reported attempted abductions—many of them false. But in this case adults who knew the boy vouched for his reliability.[97]

Meanwhile, investigators searched for yet another suspicious vehicle that was reportedly seen in St. Joseph about a week before Jacob's kidnapping. Witnesses described the car as a four-door, dark brown station wagon, believed to be about a 1970 model. It had a luggage rack and rust on the doors and fenders. The car bore an orange and black sticker on the back bumper that read "Catch Me If You Can"—the title of locally produced 1988 film.[98]

On New Year's Eve 1989, the FBI announced they were cutting more agents from Jacob's case. Four agents had been sent home two days earlier and the remaining eight agents were expected to wrap up the investigation of all remaining leads within a few weeks. From that point forward, the investigation would be led by the SCSO. More FBI agents would be brought back into the case as dictated by new information or developments.

Once all open leads had been reviewed, investigators acknowledged that they were now focused on a small group of potential suspects, although none were specifically named. In the two-and-a-half months since Jacob's abduction, investigators had received more than 18,000 leads, developed more than 20 sketches, interviewed thousands of people, checked out dozens of false sightings, and investigated two fake confessions from Minnesota men. Despite extensive search efforts, virtually no physical evidence was discovered, with the exception of Jacob's shoe print, the adjacent tire tracks and the shoe prints believed to belong to the abductor. "We've practically vacuum-cleaned the entire township," said Sheriff Grafft.[99]

Of the short list of suspects, one had been under suspicion for about a month. Another resembled the man seen at the Tom Thumb store just prior to the kidnapping.

To be sure, investigators had thoroughly vetted all suspects. Dwayne Hood, a journalism graduate from Nashville, Tennessee, found himself a potential suspect after he showed interest in obtaining copies of *St. Cloud Times* newspaper articles printed in the days following Jacob's kidnapping. The next day, an FBI agent paid him a visit. Hood was impressed with the amount of information the agency had already collected on him. The FBI agent photographed his car and removed its rear tires to take detailed photos of them. They took front and side mug shots of Hood. (The focus on the rear tires indicated investigators believed it was likely that the abductor had driven forward out of the Rassier driveway, rather than backed out of it.[100])

Although the Wetterling Task Force had not solved his disappearance by January 1990, the work they did yielded much information about other crimes in the area. Several men were investigated and arrested for a variety of sex-related crimes.

Among them was 42-year-old Duane Allen Hart, who was arrested for sexual misconduct involving multiple boys in northeastern Kandiyohi County. He was charged with incidents that occurred from 1987 through the fall of 1989 in the Paynesville and Belgrade areas. He worked as laborer and truck driver on a potato farm and typically lured boys by offering them drugs, alcohol, or money.

Investigators followed leads of the reported assaults of several young boys in the Paynesville area in 1986 and 1987, abduction attempts committed by a man believed to be on foot. There were also reports of attempted abductions by perpetrators using vehicles. Witnesses in those assaults reported a man who wore black clothing and sometimes wore a ski mask.[101]

On March 9, 1986, a 12-year-old boy was walking near the G&T Foods store when a man driving an older blue, four-door car approached him. The man asked the boy if he wanted to go for a ride. The boy declined.[102]

In August a 13-year-old boy was attacked from behind and threatened by his assailant but was able to escape.

In November, another 13-year-old Paynesville boy was attacked but was unable to get away. Like the boy in the August attack, he was approached from behind before being sexually assaulted. The incidents were detailed in the *Paynesville Press*, prompting police to issue a warning to parents to keep their children indoors after dark.[103]

By May 1987, there had been a series of five reports involving boys ranging in age from 12 to 16, with no prime suspect identified. Another assault occurred in mid–May. Sgt. Bill Drager told the *Paynesville Press* that police needed all the help they could get from the public. "After this guy grabs the boys he tells them, 'Don't turn around or I'll blow your head off,'" he said. "And in at least one instance he used a knife."[104]

In all cases the boys had been in the downtown area prior to being assaulted. Drager indicated that he thought the assailant was either following them home from downtown or was heading them off and waiting to ambush them.[105]

The man in the Paynesville cases was described as 5'11", not fat, but chunky. He wore a mask on several occasions. One victim described the mask as looking like it was made out of candy-striped carpet. He always wore black or dark clothing and was seen with a blackened face in the May 1986 incident. Some of the boys said the man could run very fast. He was careful about not leaving evidence, but in one instance a cap had fallen off of his head as he ran away from the scene. Paynesville police believed one man committed all the assaults.[106]

Duane Hart had been an early suspect in the Wetterling kidnapping, but investigators discounted him in favor of suspects who more accurately fit the profile. There were substantial dissimilarities between the charges filed against Hart and the circumstances surrounding the abductions of Jared and Jacob. Despite these differences, Kandoyohi County Judge Arthur J. Boylan banned the media from publishing Hart's photograph for fear it would jeopardize the ongoing investigation.[107]

Hart grew up in Paynesville, but lived south of Belgrade at the time of his arrest. He had no prior record for sex-related offenses but did have several drunk driving convictions. Forrest McKinley of Paynesville, Hart's one-time foster father, said he suspected Hart had been abusing boys but never had proof.[108]

According to a former neighbor of McKinley's who was familiar with the investigation, the FBI had monitored the McKinley home near Lake Koronis. He thought they were waiting for Hart to possibly visit his former foster parents' vacant property. However, the FBI may have actually been monitoring another home—Danny Heinrich's father lived close to Lake Koronis.

Hart's mother, Mary Hart, of Paynesville, said she was "shocked" by the allegations against her son. "They're just looking for a patsy," she said, after learning that Hart's arrest had been a result of the investigation into the Wetterling case.[109]

In late January 1990, investigators were interested in putting Hart in a lineup before Jared, although Hart did not closely resemble the sketch of the man Jared had described. Jared participated in line-ups with Hart but did not identify him as a possible assailant.[110] Still, FBI spokesperson Jeff Jamar said Hart was "absolutely not out of the picture. We have to explore whether he's a suspect or not."[111]

Hart's attorney, public defender John Holbrook, later said Hart had been all but cleared in Jacob's abduction. This was supported by comments made by Kandiyohi County District Attorney Mike Lynch.[112]

Hart told a private investigator the FBI had suspected him for the 1976 bombing of a post office in Kimball, Minnesota.[113] Assistant Postmaster Ivend Holen was killed in the blast. The FBI concluded that the bomb was mailed inside a package containing a metal fishing tackle box. Holen had apparently tossed the package in a pile intended for delivery somewhere north of Kimball.[114] Hart said the FBI came to his building and took away tools they suspected could have been used to make bombs.

Hart remained living in the Paynesville area until he moved in with a family near Sibley Park, between Belgrade and New London, in the latter half of the 1980s. He was living there at the time of his arrest in January 1990. Hart told an investigator that he had sexual relationships with a pair of teenage brothers in the household where he lived. Their mother learned of the abuse only after Hart was arrested and charged with six counts of sex crimes, which had been committed against her sons and two other juvenile boys. She said the FBI investigators had spoken to her while they were investigating Hart for a possible connection to Jacob Wetterling's abduction, as well as Jared's assault. Investigators asked her if Hart had access to a fairly new blue car, and if she thought Hart was capable of committing a kidnapping. She told them she didn't know about a blue car, and didn't think he was capable of kidnapping a child.

Hart gave the private investigator an alibi for the night Jacob was kidnapped: he had been 45 miles from St. Joseph at Mud Lake, west of New London, with one of his victims. The FBI interviewed the boy in 1990 and corroborated the story.

Hart was apparently quite candid in his discussions with the investigator, detailing the methods he used to entice his victims. More revealing was Hart's apparent willingness to help identify who was responsible for Jacob's kidnapping. There was one man in particular he pointed to in February 1990—Danny Heinrich.

According to Hart, Heinrich matched many of the descriptive points of Jared's abductor. He drove a fairly new, dark blue, four-door. He spoke with a raspy voice when excited. He frequently wore camouflage clothing and black boots, and had a fascination with police scanners.[115]

Meanwhile, Paynesville Police Chief Robert Schmiginsky came to Wetterling investigators in January 1990 to remind them about the cluster of assault cases in Paynesville in 1986 and 1987. He advised them that Danny Heinrich was a suspect in those cases and should be considered a suspect in Jared's case. And, because the Wetterling team had already established a link between Jared's and Jacob's abductions, Heinrich should be considered a suspect in all the cases. Furthermore, the car that Heinrich had owned at the time of Jared's abduction, a 1987 Mercury Topaz, was strikingly similar to the car Jared had described.

The FBI conducted surveillance on Heinrich for weeks, and detectives located the Mercury Topaz. The FBI forensics lab determined that fibers from the back seat of the car were similar to fibers found on Jared's snowmobile pants.

Heinrich was arrested and brought in for questioning. FBI profilers were consulted and suggested a specific interrogation strategy. Special lights and a flag were brought in, and the furniture was arranged in a particular way. Agent Steve Gilkerson was selected to perform the interview and was given a script of specific questions. Upon questioning, Heinrich immediately denied all involvement, refused to talk and requested an attorney.

Had Heinrich's questioning occurred under other circumstances, things might have gone differently. The FBI had arrested him just as they were withdrawing from the case due to a lack of leads. In what seems to have been a case of territorial friction between departments, Stearns County officials were against the arrest since they hadn't been involved in investigating him. When Heinrich lawyered-up, the Stearns County District Attorney dropped the charges. The SCSO and the BCA were upset with how the FBI handled the suspect. Heinrich would eventually fall off investigators' radar as they developed other suspects.[116]

The SCSO was actively involved in the Wetterling case from the start, but ultimately was not properly trained nor prepared to carry out an effective long-term investigation into the abduction of a child. As an investigative agency, the FBI's experience in such cases meant that they naturally led the initial phases of the investigation. As the SCSO took over the investigation in full, it committed sizeable resources to the case for the next several years. The case was never closed or shelved and has always been treated as an active investigation, never as a cold case.

6

Bare Trees

Because we have some top suspects ... we are confident we can get this case solved. It's hard to say. The right information could come in this afternoon and we could make the arrest tomorrow or today.—Stearns County Sheriff Jim Kostreba

On February 13, 1990, the mutilated body of a young boy was found near the Ford Dam in the Mississippi River in St. Paul. He appeared to be roughly Jacob's size and age. His hands, feet, and head had been severed from his body. Authorities initially feared it was Jacob.

However, one of the boy's feet was found after a search of the river. Comparing it to Jacob's baby footprints, authorities concluded it most likely was not him. The Ramsey County medical examiner later determined that the body contained embalming fluid.[1] Exploring a connection with local cult activity, authorities soon discovered the body had been stolen from a crypt at the Lakewood Cemetery in Minneapolis.[2]

Just as a sense of normalcy had begun to return to St. Joseph, the fear that had ruled the community for months was reignited. On Friday, March 16, 1990, 12-year-old Jason was riding his all-terrain vehicle, delivering newspapers near his home in the Pleasant Acres subdivision in St. Joseph. At about 4:30 p.m., a man driving an older green van pulled up and, beckoning Jason toward the vehicle, asked for directions to someone's home. Jason, declining to go near the van, told the man he didn't recognize the name. The man then told Jason he had another address he was looking for and again asked him to approach the van. Finally, he offered the boy money to come over to the van. Frightened, Jason sped off on his ATV. After riding a couple of blocks away, he turned around and saw that the van had left.[3]

Jason drove home and told his mother what happened. She immediately called 911 to report the incident. Later that afternoon, a Stearns County deputy drove through the neighborhood, but he did not come to her house. After an hour passed, she again called 911 to express concern that the deputy had not stopped to talk to her son. Still, no officer came.

She was further upset when she learned that a neighbor had seen a similar suspicious-looking van in the neighborhood several times while jogging. When asked by the media to explain the response to the call, SCSO Deputy Jim Kostreba acknowledged that the deputy could have stopped; he pointed out, however, that his office had fielded a lot of similar calls in the last few months.

"Since the Jacob abduction, we've gotten probably hundreds and hundreds of these types of calls," he said. "We do get a car to the area and check it out."[4]

There were several quarry pits in the St. Cloud area and investigators were aware they could be a likely place to hide a body. The quarries supplied stone to the Cold Spring Granite Company in Cold Spring and were inactive over the winter months. In mid–April 1990, a helicopter scanned the half-dozen pits for three hours as deputies performed a ground search, but found nothing related to the case.[5]

Authorities questioned 57-year-old Ronald K. Howard, a Wisconsin man, in late April 1990, in possible connection to Jacob's kidnapping. Howard, a convicted sex offender, was arrested in New Lisbon on a probation violation after being questioned about the reported enticement of two young girls. The attempts to lure the girls reportedly occurred in Waupaca and Shawano counties in northeastern Wisconsin. Howard's car matched the general description of the car reported in the enticement attempts.[6] FBI spokesman Byron Gigler explained that Howard was being looked at in the Wetterling case as a matter of routine investigation.

"He has come to our attention based on a couple of things," Gigler said. "Individuals who are familiar or have observed this individual say he resembles one of the artist's conceptions in the Wetterling case, especially the drawing of the individual in a baseball cap."[7]

Two Stearns County deputies and an agent from the Minnesota BCA interviewed Howard. He appeared to be living out of his car and had been witnessed pulling down posters of Jacob in Michigan and other states. He explained to detectives that he had done this because he wanted to be the only one to find Jacob and collect the reward money.

Investigators learned that Howard traveled about 8,000 miles a month and kept detailed records of his travels. A search of his car revealed a cup of candy, pictures of children taped to the windshield and dash, vent holes in the trunk, and placemats from many of the restaurants where he had eaten. Hair samples and clothing fibers were examined for possible links to Jacob's case but no evidence was found and he was cleared of involvement.[8]

In May 1990, a $50,000 reward offer was suddenly quadrupled to $200,000. Sheriff Charlie Grafft explained that half of the money was for Jacob's safe return, the other half was for information leading to the arrest of a suspect. The new reward structure was an attempt to reach out to a woman who had previously called with credible information, but had not left her name or called back.[9]

"The caller had specific information involving a suspect in Jacob's abduction and it was indicated that the call was being made within a couple of miles of the abduction site," Grafft said. "We want to draw her out."[10] Authorities were unable to identify the caller or the possible suspect after considerable effort.

Investigators focused on events that were going on the day and night of Jacob's abduction. There was the polka festival at the Del-Win Ballroom, just a few blocks from the Tom Thumb convenience store. The live music event started at 2:00 p.m. and went until 10:00 p.m. It was possible someone may have witnessed something, or perhaps the perpetrator had actually been at the festival and saw the boys go to the store.[11]

Up to 1,000 people attended and investigators wanted to speak to as many as possible. Radio announcements asked festivalgoers to come forward. It took months of interviews—authorities even tracked down a man living in Japan who had attended, and had stayed at the Super 8 in St. Joseph that night.[12]

Despite having found no sign of Jacob in nine months, investigators expressed confidence he could still be alive. News reports in July 1990 suggested that investigators had a "seclusion" theory: that he was still alive and with the person who had kidnapped him. Statistics showed that long-term abductions were likely to result in the death of the victim. Investigators reasoned, however, that if Jacob had been murdered they probably would have found his body soon after the abduction.[13]

Sheriff Grafft announced in July that he planned to retire the following January. Speaking at a campaign fundraiser event for State Senator Joe Bertram, he told attendees 47,000 tips had been investigated. He expressed frustration with a case that continued to baffle investigators but said he was optimistic it would be solved soon.

In the months following the abduction, there were several prank calls from people claiming to be Jacob Wetterling. One of them had investigators scrambling for days. Crimestoppers received the call at 5:00 p.m. Friday, August 3, 1990, from a phone booth in the small farming community of Forrest, Illinois. The caller, a boy, asked for help and said he was with a man but didn't know the man's name. The call lasted less than one minute, and the boy repeatedly said he had to go.[14]

Authorities quickly published Jacob's picture and an article in the local newspaper, the *Fairbury Blade*. They asked for the public's help in identifying the boy who had placed the call. They speculated that the call came from a booth near the intersection of Illinois State Highways 24 and 47. An employee from a local convenience store called and was interviewed by the Livingston County Sheriff's Department.[15] She said that on Friday, August 3, she had served a man and a boy matching Jacob's description and saw the boy making a call from the payphone across the street a few minutes after leaving the store. They then got into a red station wagon.[16] The Forrest lead went cold after no one else came forward with information.

Another possible sighting in Illinois developed on August 10. A pair of girls reported meeting a boy named Jacob at a swimming pool the day before. They were at the police station complaining about a group of boys that had been harassing them, when they noticed a poster of Jacob hanging on a wall. They told police that the Jacob they met looked just like Wetterling. They saw the boy at the pool again the next day and took pictures of him. The police tracked down the boy at his family's home where he had been living for five years.[17]

On October 3, 1990, in Reno, Nevada, a young boy and two men came into a store at 9:00 a.m. on three consecutive days. On the third day, a clerk asked one of the men if the boy was his son. He laughed and said boy was not his son. The three never returned to the store after that, so the clerk became suspicious and called authorities. Shown a poster of Jacob, the clerk told a detective the boy looked like Jacob.[18]

On October 20, 1990, the eve of the first anniversary of Jacob's abduction, Sheriff Grafft announced that investigators were looking into a promising lead involving an out-of-state man who had been seen in St. Joseph about three weeks before. "He looks pretty promising," Grafft said. "This may be the man we're looking for. I won't get excited until we get the photos and the person that called in the tip says 'Yeah, that's him.' Then we'll turn things upside down."[19] No further information about the suspect was offered and no further details were reported in the media.

After the first anniversary passed, things went relatively quiet for some time. The SCSO had been in charge of the investigation since January 1990. Despite the lack of significant progress, they kept a steady staff of investigators working on the case.

Jacob's thirteenth birthday was on February 17, 1991. Grafft took the opportunity to remind everyone that Jacob's case remained a priority. "There's always something that we're working on," he said. "In fact, we believe right now that we have four or five suspects that we're checking out. Some have just surfaced; some we've gone back to because new information came in on them."[20]

The SCSO continued to receive a few leads. As many as five investigators were still assigned to the case, following up on the handful of tips that came in daily. About half of the tips were from out of state and most were from people who thought they had seen the abductor or believed they had seen someone that looked like Jacob.

One call was of particular interest, but it wasn't a tip. In January 1991, a man called the counseling line of the television show *The 700 Club* and asked if someone would go to hell if he knew where Jacob was. Patty Wetterling appeared on the program to appeal to the man to come forward again, but he did not call back.[21]

Patty made another plea to the general public in May 1991, in the form of a mass mailing of 10,000 copies of a letter asking for help in the investigation. The letter was distributed locally to residents of St. Joseph, Cold Spring, Avon, and western St. Cloud. "A lot of people believe that somebody knows something," she said. "I guess that's the hard thing for me to live with—that someone would know something and not come forward. We don't need 10,000 calls. We need one call."[22]

In July 1991, private investigator Roy Stephens of Omaha, Nebraska, claimed he had information connecting Jacob's abduction to a pedophile ring. Stephens had been involved as an investigator in the 1982 abduction case of Johnny Gosch in Des Moines, Iowa. Gosch disappeared while delivering early morning newspapers in his neighborhood. His mother came forward saying she believed four men were responsible and that Johnny was being used for pornography or sex. Former Nebraska State Senator and attorney, John DeCamp, later attempted to tie the Gosch kidnapping to the Franklin Credit Union scandal centered in Omaha, and a pedophile ring operating out of the same area.

Stephens had gained notoriety in 1990 when he provided information that led to the conviction of a man involved in the 1987 kidnapping of Jill Cutshall in Norfolk, Nebraska. Wetterling investigators looked into Stephens' claims but were unable to find any evidence to corroborate them.[23]

Some leads were quite bizarre. Hunting expert William Urseth told of one in his 2010 book, *The Line*. Urseth and his hunting companion traveled to Bottineau, North Dakota, in the fall of 1991 for a goose hunt. Dave Clark, a local farmer, cooked breakfast for the pair each morning. Urseth soon learned that Clark, known locally as the "Water Witch," was a local legend for his ability to locate underground sources of water and oil using unconventional methods. One night he knocked on their cabin door and asked the hunters if they had ever heard of Jacob Wetterling. Urseth, a Minnesota native, said that he knew of Jacob's story. Clark asked him if he wanted to know where Jacob's body was buried. Without waiting for a reply, Clark pulled out a map and pointed out roads that lead from St. Joseph to a park in Sioux Falls, South Dakota. Urseth asked Clark if he had given that information to the FBI. Clark said he had but that they thought he was crazy.[24]

Meanwhile, Stearns County investigative staff continued working diligently on the case and maintained daily contact with the FBI office in Minneapolis. Charlie Grafft had retired as County Sheriff and turned the reins of the investigation over to the new Stearns County Sheriff, Jim Kostreba.

On October 22, 1991, exactly two years after Jacob's abduction, authorities searched for him in a pond in St. Cloud. A person walking in the nearby wooded area the weekend before found a cross bearing the name "Jacob" on it. It measured ten inches by twelve and was found leaning on some rocks adjacent to the pond. An examination of the cross revealed that it had been placed there recently. Nothing was found during the initial search so the pond was drained and search dogs from the Minnesota Search And Rescue Dog Association were brought in. The dogs showed an unusual level of interest in a tree, whose branches had fallen into the pond. The pond, which was up to seven feet deep in places, was very murky with a muddy bottom. Investigators were unable to find anything in the pond or in the wooded area surrounding it.[25]

An age-enhanced photo of Jacob was produced in January 1992, predicting how he might look at roughly age fifteen. A flier including the photo was mass mailed across the nation, prompting about 75 tips, most of which came from outside the state of Minnesota.[26]

Investigators were interested in a St. Cloud man later in 1992. Matthew Feeney, a Catholic youth camp counselor, was charged with molesting several boys at a summer camp. Investigators found that Feeney appeared to be fascinated with the Wetterling kidnapping and investigators soon learned that Feeney was in the Wetterling's neighborhood within minutes of Jacob's abduction, dropping off another child after a weekend camping trip.

Feeney was originally from the St. Paul area. He was a respected actor and talent agent, and a successful member of the entertainment community. After graduating from high school, he spent several years in the St. Joseph area serving as the director of youth ministries at St. Joseph Catholic Church. In the summer months, he was a counselor at a Catholic youth camp near McGregor, Minnesota. The children called him "Matti."[27]

By 1992, Feeney was a convicted sex offender. He admitted that he had molested several boys as they slept in their cabin while at the camp in the late 1980s and early 1990s. He admitted to detectives that he had fondled approximately ten to twelve boys in their sleep. These assaults occurred while Feeney was serving as a Catholic youth counselor. Some of the boys recalled the abuse and were able to describe details to police. Feeney was sentenced to six months in jail, ten years of probation, and mandatory sex offender treatment.[28]

During the course of the investigation into Feeney's alleged assaults, he drew attention from investigators for possible involvement in Jacob Wetterling's abduction. Feeney turned his personal journal over to investigators at one point. In it, he allegedly wrote about his attraction to young boys and identified himself as a child molester and a monster. He also wrote about Jacob. He reportedly wrote that he wanted to visit the Jacob Wetterling Foundation on a weekly basis and that he hoped Jacob's abductor would slip up and reveal Jacob's whereabouts.[29]

According to investigators, Feeney also had a hand-written letter that appeared to be intended for one of his victims. In the letter, he apologized to the victim and seemed to answer a question about Jacob: "About Jacob Wetterling, no. I didn't do a thing, but sometimes I wonder. I have an airtight alibi. I was camping and (victim's name) was with me and witnesses saw us with his dad twenty minutes after the fact. What I'm scared of is: What if I had been asleep that night? Could I do something that terrible and complex in my sleep?"[30]

Soon after Jacob's abduction, Feeney took two young boys for a drive past the Wetterling abduction site. They stopped at the site and he told the boys what had happened there. One of the youths later recounted how Feeney's vehicle looked like a cop car, with a CB radio, a nightstick, and a large flashlight inside. That young man eventually became a camp counselor himself and later acknowledged that, after sex abuse allegations against Feeney surfaced in 1991, he started thinking differently about the visit to the abduction site.[31]

Stearns County investigators cleared Feeney of involvement in Jacob's abduction. A pair of witnesses said Feeney was in the St. Joseph area at the time of the abduction, but that he had been with them when the crime occurred. Investigators also noted that Feeney's methods of luring his victims—gaining their affection with gifts and engaging in conversation with their parents—were not consistent with the circumstances of Jacob's abduction.

A May 1992 two-part television news report on WCCO revealed previously unreleased details of the investigation. *Dimension: A Look Inside The Wetterling File* said that more than 26,000 leads had been received in the nearly three years since Jacob's abduction. Investigative reporter Trish Van Pilsum revealed that a case detective had received a phone call from a woman about a week after the kidnapping. The woman claimed she knew a man who often wore black clothing and carried a gun, and told the detective that the man had changed all the tires on his car the day after Jacob's abduction. Sheriff Kostreba was interviewed for the program and he indicated that his department was actively investigating three or four main suspects in Jacob's case. There were about two dozen more that had been investigated but not yet cleared.[32]

In October 1992, FBI files revealed that a former Catholic priest from Stillwater, Minnesota, had been questioned on December 7, 1989, as a possible suspect in the Wetterling kidnapping. Father James Porter confessed to FBI agents that he had molested 40 to 50 boys in the 1960's while living in Massachusetts. Porter was accused of sexually assaulting boys in three different states but no evidence was found to link him to Jacob's kidnapping.[33]

John W. DeCamp, an attorney and former state senator from Lincoln, Nebraska, came to Minnesota in February 1994 to promote his book, *The Franklin Scandal*. He suggested that members of a pedophile ring that operated out of the Midwest might have taken Jacob. He based his theory on information from children and young adults who had been involved with the group. Although the scandal was publicly derided as being a hoax, De Camp argued that it was real.[34]

DeCamp further claimed to know of three individuals who had seen a person matching Jacob's description in Madison, Wisconsin, and also in Council Bluffs, Iowa. He said that the sex-ring successfully brainwashed children into believing they were not wanted at home.[35]

In October 1995, Sheriff Kostreba said that there were still four top suspects in Jacob's kidnapping. Two were from central Minnesota, though neither was a stereotypical pedophile. The other two were not from the area but were pedophiles. Aside from those top suspects, he added, there were another half-dozen possible suspects investigators had been unable to rule out.

Search warrants released publicly by WCCO-TV in May 1996 revealed information about three suspects in the investigation. Although two of them had been ruled out, the third had not yet been cleared. Authorities moved quickly to get the documents resealed by the courts.[36]

One of the suspects was a 60-year-old man who had confessed to Jacob's kidnapping a month after it had occurred. He told investigators that Jacob's clothing could be found in his basement, but investigators did not find any evidence to corroborate the story. The man suffered from Alzheimer's disease and was dismissed as a suspect.[37] Although authorities did not say so, he may have been the same man who had barricaded himself in his house and had a standoff with Stearns County deputies in November 1989.

Another suspect mentioned in the warrants was a student from St. Cloud State University. Investigators searched his room and found unusual writings about the Wetterling's religion, the Baha'i faith, as well as "missing" posters of Jacob. The student was cleared, and committed suicide a few months later.

The third and final suspect was a Paynesville area man that fit the description of the man that had assaulted 12-year-old Jared in January 1989. Investigators said Danny Heinrich had not yet been cleared in Jacob's case. A search warrant indicated his home was searched in January 1990. One paragraph in the warrant was blacked out without explanation—the reason for this was never revealed.[38]

On February 23, 1996, Father Tom Gillespie was abruptly removed from his post at St. Joseph's Catholic Church, where he had been pastor since 1986.[39] He had been one of the first public figures to come out in support of the Wetterling family. St. Joseph parishioners remained in the dark about the reasons for Gillespie's removal for several years. Eventually, St. John's Abbot John Klassen assembled a parish meeting to inform parishioners that Gillespie was one of ten priests and monks currently living under restrictions at St. John's Abbey due to allegations of sexual abuse of children. Media reports revealed that Gillespie had committed acts of sexual abuse at another parish in the 1970's. An Abbey spokesperson told parishioners in St. Joseph that it had been an oversight that the meeting wasn't held back in 1996, when Gillespie was removed from the parish.[40]

In 1997, St. Paul police served 44-year-old David Paul Weiss with a search warrant after he was arrested August 6 on charges of sexually assaulting a 15-year-old boy. According to the warrant, Weiss had discussed the Wetterling case with at least one of his assault victims. Weiss' roommate told investigators that Weiss had confided to him that he knew of a body that had been hidden in the cemetery at Fort Snelling. The police took Weiss to search the cemetery but no evidence was found.[41]

Police reportedly found child pornography, movies, a digital camera, boys' clothing, and a youth jock strap in Weiss' possession. Media reports also stated that a jar containing testicles was found, but they were later determined to be canine. DNA testing showed no connection between Weiss and Jacob's kidnapping.[42]

Information about the Weiss case was forwarded to the Stearns County Sheriff's Office, and Sheriff Kostreba acknowledged that several people had contacted his office about possible ties between Weiss and the Wetterling case. Some media outlets touted Weiss' arrest as a big break in the case but no link to Jacob's case had been established.[43]

Patty Wetterling issued another public appeal letter in October 1998, addressed to Jacob's abductor. She pleaded with him to come forward to tell her what had happened to Jacob, asked him to contact her directly. "I really want this guy to call," she wrote. "This is an appeal from me. I think we deserve to know some answers, and there's at least one person in the world who knows them."[44] SCSO Detective Dave Nohner said Patty's letter prompted about a half-dozen significant leads.

The ABC television show *Vanished* featured Jacob's story in its June 24, 1999, episode entitled *A Mother's Search*. St. Paul television station KSTP followed the program with a story of its own, featuring an interview with a prison inmate who claimed to have seen two young men and a vehicle near the location of Jacob's kidnapping around the time of the crime. The claim was consistent with the story behind the "Stearns Truth tapes," which had surfaced locally in 1997. In the tapes, two brothers alleged that an acquaintance of theirs had kidnapped Jacob. Sheriff Kostreba told reporters that the lead had been thoroughly investigated, that he knew the source of the lead, and that it was unreliable.[45]

The tapes were a controversial series of audio recordings made by a local bail bondsperson, Ann Forrester, and were said to be recordings of conversations between Ann and three young adult siblings. Two brothers, Edward and Joseph Lawrence, and their sister, Bethany Lawrence, discussed a man named Randy Penney in the recordings.

The Lawrence brothers alleged that one or both of them were at the scene of Jacob's abduction, and that Penney had taken Jacob. The tapes indicated apparent discrepancies as to whether or not both brothers were present at the abduction scene. A private investigator that spoke with Joseph Lawrence on several occasions noted that he changed his story several times regarding his whereabouts on the night of the kidnapping. There were also other inconsistencies in the tapes. Bethany Lawrence said that Jacob was brought to her house soon after the abduction, but her description of his clothing was not consistent with what he was known to be wearing.

Investigators publicly declared that the source of the information in the tapes was unreliable, but stopped short of saying that the entire story was a fabrication. They also would not say whether Randy Penney was considered a suspect. However, a member of Penney's family confirmed that the FBI did investigate him. The individuals involved in the accusations appeared to have had ulterior motives to implicate one another in various crimes. Forrester insists that the "Stearns Truth Tapes" were real, and claims that a former Stearns County investigator fled with the tapes when he left the Sheriff's Office.

During the summer of 1999, 19-year-old Katie Poirier was kidnapped from the Moose Lake, Minnesota, area. She was murdered and her burned body discovered in an ash pit. Surveillance footage from the convenience store where Katie worked led to the arrest of Donald Blom, of Richfield. Blom, 50, admitted that he had kidnapped and killed Poirier. Investigators reviewed the files on Blom for a possible connection to Jacob's case.[46] Blom had a history of rape and kidnapping and had been sentenced to 40 years in prison after a 1976 conviction. He served just three years before being released in 1979. Blom was ultimately convicted of killing Poirier but was never charged with or connected to the other crimes.

A September 1999 report in the *Minneapolis Star Tribune* revealed that the Wetterling Task Force had first investigated Blom under his birth name, Pince, in 1989. He had been imprisoned for six years on a rape conviction, and had been released in March 1989. Investigators questioned him and his wife about the Wetterling kidnapping and established Pince's alibi—we was in Red Wing, 130 miles away.[47]

In January 2001, police detectives on an unrelated investigation arrested 56-year-old Richard Feit of Shakopee, Minnesota, for possession of child pornography. Answering an ad placed in a Detroit-based magazine by a government sting operation, Feit ordered a videotape of a child engaged in a sex act. U.S. Postal Service agents arrested him when the package was delivered to his home.[48] When Feit's arrest was publicized, a Wisconsin woman noted his resemblance to one of the composite sketches in the Wetterling case and phoned authorities.[49] Feit passed a polygraph and gave other verifiable information and was cleared.[50]

St. John's Abbey came under police scrutiny a second time in May 2002, when Stearns County Sheriff Jim Kostreba and Deputy Doug Pearce met with Abbot Klassen to review the Abbey's records on monks. Their review related primarily to the unsolved cases of the abduction of Jacob Wetterling and the 1974 stabbing deaths of the Reker sisters. Although the public had not been aware that the Abbey had been investigated in connection to the Wetterling case, the monks on restriction at St. John's had been investigated from the beginning.

By the fall of 2003, fourteen years had passed since Jacob's abduction. The investigation had suffered a number of ups and downs, but still mainly lacked one thing: evidence. All authorities had to go on were Trevor's and Aaron's eyewitness accounts, and the tire tracks and shoe prints in the Rassier's driveway.

In October, their luck would finally change. One small mystery that had dogged investigators privately for fourteen years was about to be resolved.

7

The Turn

We cannot lose the momentum in this investigation. We're going to systematically process all leads and information that comes in to find a resolution. I strongly feel that we're now looking in the right direction.—Stearns County Sheriff John Sanner, on the 15th anniversary of Jacob's abduction

For the first fourteen years following the abduction of Jacob Wetterling, investigators focused their efforts on locating the car that left the tire tracks alongside Jacob's footprints in the Rassier's driveway. They sought the public's help in finding several vehicles witnesses had reported seeing in the neighborhood in the days and weeks prior.

One witness, Dan Rassier, had reported seeing a car, possibly driven by the kidnapper, speed down the quarter-mile long driveway on his family's farm before making a 180-degree turn near his house and driving off toward 91st Avenue. His account was supported by the presence of fresh tire tracks on the gravel driveway. Bloodhounds had led investigators to what were believed to be Jacob's last footprints, which ended abruptly about 75 yards east of 91st, on the driveway. All of this supported the long-standing theory of abduction by vehicle.

Investigators believed that all other unusual or suspicious cars seen in the area had been accounted for over the years. This one unidentified car, they believed, was the key to solving the case. What was unusual, however, was that they did not publicly disclose their search for the vehicle Dan Rassier described—the small, dark car with lights close together. To date, the only reference made to the car was in Rassier's quote in the October 24, 1989, *St. Cloud Times.*

Longtime Stearns County Deputy John Sanner became the Sheriff in 2003. A change of luck in the Wetterling case coincided with his taking office.

In the fall of 2003, a retired U.S. Marshal had met a man, Kevin Hamilton, through a mutual acquaintance. During their discussion Hamilton admitted that, out of curiosity, he had driven to the crime scene the night Jacob was abducted. He said there were no officers at the scene when he arrived—all he saw were the bicycles in the ditch. The Marshal was shocked by Hamilton's story and assured him that investigators had been looking for him since the day after the kidnapping.[1]

Hamilton came forward on October 21, 2003.[2] The shocking new information he provided reinvigorated the case. The revelation that a curious driver had contaminated the crime scene jolted investigators.

But at the same time, the case seemed to go cold. It was determined that Hamilton was telling the truth and he was cleared of involvement. The tire tracks, for years believed to have been made by the kidnapper's car, may actually have been left by Hamilton minutes after the crime had been committed. In shifting their focus, investigators then overlooked key pieces of information that would not come to light until another ten years had passed.

Kevin Hamilton told investigators he had been at his girlfriend Gina Phipps' house near Kay's Kitchen in downtown St. Joseph the night of the abduction. Several members of Phipps' family were also there playing card games. The family had a police scanner in the kitchen and shortly after 9:30 p.m., as they were wrapping up the games, they heard a report about boys on bikes at the Tom Thumb store. Moments later, they noticed police cars speeding eastbound through town.[3]

Hamilton and Phipps went outside, got into her car, and attempted to follow the route the police had taken. Phipps' car was a late model Pontiac Grand Prix and was silver in color. Hamilton drove near the Del-Win Ballroom but saw no sign of the police cars there. Next, he drove south on 91st Avenue. They drove up over the hill but there was still no sign of any police. They then turned left onto what they thought was a gravel road, but soon realized they were on someone's driveway—the Rassier's driveway.[4]

Seeing that there was nowhere to turn around, Hamilton continued all the way up to the Rassier home and made a sweeping left turn before heading back up the driveway toward 91st. When they reached the end of road, the couple noticed the bikes in the ditch across the street, directly in front of them. Hamilton said he thought about getting out and picking the bikes up, but decided against it. They drove back to town and stopped at the Tom Thumb convenience store.[5]

Hamilton noticed there was a car parked at the store that looked like an unmarked police interceptor. He went inside and saw there were a male store clerk and a male customer in the store. Although the female clerk that served Jacob and the other boys was scheduled to work until midnight, Hamilton said he did not see her. He asked the clerk if someone had called the police about kids on their bikes. The customer told Hamilton he was a "medical cop" and asked if the police should be called. Hamilton was caught off guard by the customer's odd comment and left the store.[6]

As the couple drove back to Phipps' house, Hamilton saw a St. Joseph police car parked by Dr. Cotton's dental office. Hamilton pulled into the driveway, got out, and told the officer his name. He told the officer about the bikes he had seen in the ditch at the end of the driveway. The officer brushed Hamilton off and told him that police already knew about the bikes. Hamilton then backed out of the driveway and drove to Phipps' house.[7]

The officer at Dr. Cotton's office and was likely waiting there to escort the Wetterlings the rest of their way home.[8] Unfortunately, he did not report his encounter with Hamilton to anyone, so the presence of another vehicle at the crime scene remained unknown for the next 14 years.

Hamilton told investigators something else that was interesting: Phipps' Grand Prix had a brand new set of tires installed at a local Goodyear shop one week earlier.[9]

In another unusual twist to Hamilton's tale, he said that about a week after the abduction he drove by the crime scene again, this time during daylight hours. As he was leaving, heading north, he was certain that he saw the "medical cop" and his police interceptor-type vehicle again. Hamilton said he and the man locked eyes as they passed by each other.

Hamilton later said that during his interview investigators told him they wanted him to come back to look at some photographs and possibly identify the "medical cop." He was disappointed they never followed through with the photo lineup, because he felt the man may have been involved in the kidnapping, or may have witnessed something.[10]

Hamilton's story may have explained the fresh tire tracks in the Rassier driveway, but the car he was driving did not match the description of the car seen by Dan Rassier. Still, with the source of the tire tracks now clear in the eyes of investigators, they concluded there was a strong possibility that Jacob's abductor had been on foot. And if he was on foot and on a dead end road, it was therefore likely that the perpetrator lived nearby.

"No doubt this new piece of information has renewed interest in the case," Sheriff Sanner noted. "(It's) blown new investigative life into it. We've got something fresh."[11]

SCSO Captain Pam Jensen and BCA Agent Ken McDonald reviewed a number of pieces of evidence in January 2004. They listened to the original 911 call Merle Jerzak made on the night of Jacob's abduction. They keyed on what Aaron Larson said, that the boys did not see a car at the abduction scene. They reviewed Dan Rassier's November 1989 interview under hypnosis, noting his unusual reactions to questions about the car he said he saw, and about Jacob Wetterling. Rassier broke down crying during some portions of the interview. Lastly, Jensen and McDonald reviewed the information from Kevin Hamilton.[12]

What was missing from the reasoning Jensen and McDonald had followed to the abduction-on-foot theory was a review of the tire tracks found in the driveway at the point where the bloodhound lost Jacob's scent. Over the course of the investigation, several cars had been cleared of involvement based on tire tread pattern or tire size. There was no indication investigators had considered the tire

size or tread pattern of the car Hamilton was driving when they concluded that Jacob had been abducted on foot. It was an oversight that
would not come to light for many years to come.

Jensen and McDonald interviewed Dan Rassier at the SCSO on
February 7, 2004. The interview with Rassier was made from the
standpoint of eliminating the car Rassier claimed he had witnessed.
Rassier was questioned as to why his dog, Smokey, would not have
been barking during the abduction that occurred at the end of his
quarter-mile long driveway. Jensen and McDonald suggested that
Rassier might have caused the noise in the grass that Aaron Larson
heard. They suggested that the 911 operator may have been leading
the boys into saying the abductor had a gun and spoke in a raspy
voice. They repeatedly accused Rassier of kidnapping Jacob; he
insisted each time that the abductor must have been driving the car
he saw that night.[13]

On February 12, 2004, agent McDonald and Stearns County
investigator Troy Jansky visited the Rassier farm. They spoke to
Robert and Rita Rassier, telling them that their son, Dan, was considered a suspect in Jacob's kidnapping. They searched the family
computer, but found nothing of concern.[14] Later that month, Sheriff
Sanner disclosed publicly for the first time that investigators had
interviewed a neighbor and possible suspect in the kidnapping.

"It's a real possibility that our suspect lives within the general
vicinity of the abduction," Sanner said. "We're rethinking the entire
scenario. The abduction could've occurred with the perpetrator on
foot."[15]

Sanner noted that investigators had interviewed hundreds of
potential suspects over the years and cautioned that the questioning
of this particular suspect should not be viewed as significant. Just
prior to going public with the new information, SCSO officials met
with the Wetterlings to discuss the new direction of the investigation.
This new series of events was just one among many the family had
seen over the years. There had been countless leads, false sightings,
new suspects, and promising tips. What was different this time was
that it marked the first time a significant turn in the case had been
made public.[16]

Patty Wetterling was cautiously optimistic. "We've had a lot of significant leads about sightings," she said. "But you just can't throw all your eggs in one basket. I don't get a gut feeling or a sense that we're closer. But there's new energy to it."[17]

The idea that someone local could have abducted Jacob Wetterling sent another shock wave through St. Joseph. The startling realization that the kidnapper could have lived near the crime scene renewed feelings of uncertainty in the community.

"I think people are wondering and thinking back. It's hard to believe that it could be someone local," said St. Joseph resident Bud Reber. "People are wondering who it could be. They're thinking back to people who lived there at the time. You just never know."[18]

With the new focus on the likelihood that a neighbor could be involved, Patty appealed to the public for information from a different perspective. After the abduction, investigators had gone door to door asking if anyone saw anything unusual. "What they're asking now," she said, "and what I'm asking, is for people to talk about the usual. Who was usually around? Who was usually there on a Sunday night?"[19]

"We are more convinced that this occurred by somebody local, somebody on foot," Sheriff Sanner added. "We are more convinced of that now than we ever have been."[20]

Retired Sheriff Jim Kostreba—who had been chief deputy when Jacob was kidnapped and remained involved with the case for the rest of his career—wasn't so sure. "I don't know if you'd call it a gut instinct," he said. "But I always have had a feeling that this one could be cleared."[21]

Kostreba acknowledged that Kevin Hamilton's story offered an innocent explanation for the tire tracks in the Rassier driveway. But he distanced himself from the on-foot theory pushed by Sanner. Kostreba still believed there was a vehicle involved, explaining that it would have been difficult for the abductor to disappear with Jacob so quickly on foot.[22] But the information Hamilton provided had brought the case back to the public, and Kostreba felt they were the ones who could help solve it.

Everett Doolittle had been an investigator with the Minnesota

BCA since the beginning of the case. In 2004, as the fifteenth anniversary of Jacob's abduction neared, Doolittle pointed out that going back to the beginning of the investigation was a common method for solving older cases. He advised current investigators to go back and re-examine all the information, looking for links that hadn't been made earlier, taking a second look at suspects who had been previously cleared, but perhaps should not have been.[23] Doolittle's cold case unit of the BCA had utilized the same methodology to solve two major murder cases, including the 1992 murder of Linda Jensen in Big Lake, and the 1978 slayings of Alice Huling and her three children in Fairhaven Township.

"In almost every case, the person told someone," Doolittle said. "The answer is out there somewhere. The key is to find it. Time becomes your friend for that, not your enemy."[24]

Former BCA Agent Dennis Sigafoos had been assigned to the Wetterling case in 1989. In light of the new developments, Sigafoos revealed his perspective with regards to the investigative effort.

"My deal has always been, start in the neighborhood and stay in the neighborhood … unless something takes you out of the neighborhood," Sigafoos said. "If there was no car, then obviously we would have been in there even harder. Maybe a hell of a lot more could have been done."[25]

Retired Wetterling Task Force detective Neil Neddermeyer, who worked the case for five months, added that Jacob's kidnapping was "a crime of opportunity, probably led on by a fantasy in the back of the abductor's mind."[26]

Although investigators did not state so publicly at the time, the neighbor they were taking a closer look at was Dan Rassier. Patty Wetterling wrote a personal letter to him later in 2004. According to Rassier, the letter appeared to have come through the Stearns County Sheriff's Office. In it, she asked him to please come forward, to admit that he committed the abduction, and to tell investigators what had happened on the night of Jacob's abduction. Rassier did not acknowledge or respond in any way to the letter, and the information in it would not be publicly known until several years later.[27]

Following the 2004 search of the farm, Rassier said the BCA

asked him at one point to confess to the crime, telling him that during his 911 call he sounded much too nervous to simply be concerned about someone stealing his firewood. Rassier said he laughed at the request.[28]

For investigators, the contention that Rassier sounded nervous during his 911 call would later prove to be a thorn in their side. In 2013, it was revealed by an investigative reporter that they had neglected to save the tape of Rassier's call.[29]

A new computer generated age progression image Jacob was released in the fall of 2004. The face looked very familiar to employees of Marvin Windows of Warroad, Minnesota, who called authorities claiming it resembled one of their coworkers . When questioned, he denied he was Jacob Wetterling and refused to submit to DNA testing. But his fingerprints were on file in Arizona and he was eliminated.

While Stearns County investigators were piecing together the new theory of the abduction, Jared came forward to share the story of what happened to him in Cold Spring. He told Twin Cities television station KARE 11 that he believed his abductor and Jacob's were one in the same. A two-part series of news reports highlighted similarities between the cases. KARE 11's coverage of Jared's story produced a flurry of tips from the public.

"Nothing he is saying on TV is anything we didn't already know," Sanner said of Jared. "The only benefit I see in what he's doing is rejuvenating interest in a very old case."[30]

As Jared went public with his story, Sanner was downplaying possible links. While he acknowledged the cases had some similarities, and that these had been considered from the beginning of the Wetterling investigation, he cautioned that the links were weaker than previously believed. "The similarities are there and you cannot get beyond that," he said. "But are they really and truly connected? Until we get resolution, I don't know that we can answer that with any certainty."[31]

Investigators kept their eyes on Dan Rassier, setting up surveillance on him from October 15 through October 19, 2007. On November 7, agent Ken McDonald applied for and was granted a mail cover through the U.S. Postal Service to monitor Rassier's mail. Nothing unusual was intercepted during the four-week review.[32]

The investigation took another unusual twist in December 2008, when police searched the Milwaukee home of Vernon Seitz following his death. Seitz owned Vern's Barbershop in the southwest Milwaukee suburb of St. Francis. He had come to the attention of the Milwaukee Police Department after his psychiatrist said Seitz told her in November 2008, that he wanted to confess to killing a boy in 1959. Seitz died a month later, before police had an opportunity to interview him about the possible killing.

When police searched Seitz's home, they discovered an eerie trove of materials in the basement, related to Jacob Wetterling and to other missing children. Items included child pornography, children's clothing and shoes, posters and videotapes of missing children, tufts of hair, bondage devices, books about cannibalism, and a handgun. Some of the clothing had blood and other biological materials on them.[33]

Items found in the basement that were related to Jacob including printed "missing" posters, videotapes, and a map of the town of St. Joseph. A portion of the floor had newly poured cement, which was jackhammered open, but no additional items of interest were discovered.

Outside, investigators found unexplained piles of dirt in the backyard. The dirt was sifted and tested for evidence of a crime but nothing was discovered.

People who knew Seitz reported that he sometimes talked about his personal reasons for his abiding interest in missing children cases: he claimed he had been abducted himself in 1959.

Police investigated Seitz for a possible connection to the Wetterling case, as well as to another abduction from Victoria, Canada, in 1991. They found that soon after Jacob was kidnapped, Vernon Seitz made two trips to St. Joseph to offer his help to the Wetterling family. After his visits, a wall in his barbershop displayed a laminated poster of Jacob. Patty Wetterling told the *St. Paul Pioneer Press* that Seitz claimed to be a psychic and had given her a painting of Jacob. She said he seemed to care and that he shared with her that he had good personal reasons for offering his assistance.[34]

Seitz's family was asked about his claims of being abducted as a teenager, but they were unable to corroborate his story. At the conclusion of their investigation, police were unable to establish a link between Seitz and any missing children.[35]

Analysis of hair and blood samples from Seitz's home provided no connections to any missing children or crimes. Investigators reasoned that the hair likely came from customers at his barbershop. No explanation was found for the presence of blood in the home.

One of the videos found in Seitz's home was of Jacob Wetterling, taken prior to the kidnapping. It was a startling revelation, seeming to indicate Seitz may have been stalking him. There was a reasonable explanation, however. One week before the abduction, Jacob and his classmates made a video of themselves for a class project. Jacob was recorded reciting his list of personal favorites, such as food, movies, etc.[36] The video was aired on television after Jacob was taken—Seitz most likely recorded the broadcast.

In January 2009, the Milwaukee Police Department released a statement that Vernon Seitz was not involved in Jacob's abduction, or in any other cases of missing children. Sheriff John Sanner, whose office had worked with Milwaukee police, concurred with the determination.[37]

A fire at the Rassier farm on June 4, 2009, destroyed a woodworking shop and a machine shed. Dan Rassier reported the blaze at 2:39 a.m., saying that he had been awakened by a noise outside. Robert Rassier had been staining some pieces of wood the previous afternoon and put the stain rags in a garbage container outside of the woodworking shop.[38] The State Fire Marshal Division of Minnesota's Department of Public Safety could not determine the cause or source of origin.

Although the pace of new leads had slowed to a standstill for several long periods, there remained a sense of urgency about finding out what happened to Jacob Wetterling. "After twenty years, you would think it would lose its traction," Sheriff Sanner said. "Not this case. I'm not about to say we give up."[39] Indeed, the collective investigative effort by the FBI, the Minnesota BCA, and SCSO was impressive. They had followed up on tens of thousands of leads, and interviewed nearly 8,000 people over two decades.

Yet no publicly known, significant arrest had ever been made. An update on the case by the *St. Cloud Times* newspaper in October 2009 offered a glimpse into the efforts that had been made. SCSO Captain Pam Jensen and BCA Special Agent Ken McDonald were the active investigators at the time.

Jensen explained that the investigation continued to take them out of the state of Minnesota, despite the principal theory that the abductor lived near the crime scene. For example, men arrested on charges of child pornography were automatically checked out for possible involvement. Detailed timelines of their activities were created to determine their whereabouts at the time of the kidnapping. The records of every person interviewed over the years were kept in storage, and reviewed again from time to time. Reflecting on the beginning of the investigation, Jensen noted that the scope of the search expanded so quickly that it became difficult to manage. She acknowledged that, in hindsight, investigators should have kept their focus on local suspects.[40]

As of October 2009, the SCSO indicated they were focused on five local suspects. Agent McDonald felt it was likely that the abductor had seen the children on their way to the Tom Thumb store, and knew they would be coming back the opposite way. The area of the abduction was so remote, that it was very unlikely that someone unfamiliar with 91st Avenue was involved.[41]

Dan Rassier and Patty Wetterling ran into each other in October 2009, at a health club in St. Cloud. Patty asked him if they could talk. Rassier agreed to meet with Patty, acknowledging that twenty years was too long to not talk. According to Rassier, he and Patty met for about an hour. She asked if maybe he had tried to pull a prank on the boys the night of the abduction, and perhaps something went wrong. He assured her he hadn't attempted any prank and that he had nothing to do with Jacob's abduction.[42]

During his meeting with Patty, Rassier suggested where a body could be hidden on his family's farm, saying "the person in the area who probably did this could have taken Jacob's body and hidden it in our gravel pit."[43]

But the chance meeting between Rassier and Wetterling was not a chance meeting at all. The SCSO had carefully orchestrated it and Patty was wearing a recording device. During their conversation, he told her about the car he saw turning around in his driveway. It was the same story he had told all along. Patty asked several questions; Rassier responded to some of them speculatively, surmising what the abductor may have done with Jacob's body. He suggested that investigators handled the investigation poorly in the beginning.[44]

The focus on local suspects that began in 2004 reached a stunning climax on June 30, 2010. Authorities stormed the Rassier farm with a search warrant. For two days, Sheriff Sanner evaded media questions about the reasons for investigators' presence on the property. "I do understand that the public is interested in what's going on," he said. "I don't want to do anything at this point to compromise any potential prosecution."[45] The FBI, the BCA, SCSO, and the National Center for Missing and Exploited Children were involved in the search.

Patty Wetterling expressed approval that investigators had gone back to the beginning of the case for answers. She said that both her family and the Rassier family had been "traveling on parallel tracks." Both families wanted answers to what happened more than twenty years ago. She believed they might be on the verge of finding closure from a search of the property.[46] "Jacob's last footsteps are shown on that driveway," she said.[47]

Aerial photos taken on the first day of the search showed that investigators were focusing their attention on the five outbuildings on the property. The operation involved as many as seventeen vehicles and pieces of equipment. A special K9 search dog unit was brought in from Louisiana.[48]

Investigators returned to the Rassier farm with another search warrant on Thursday, July 1, 2010. They also brought in a backhoe and several dump trucks. Six truckloads of dirt were removed from a location about 1,000 feet away from the house. The dirt was moved to the Stearns County public works facility to secure it inside a fenced-in, locked building.[49]

A total of four search warrants were executed at the farm during the two-day search. The warrants were sealed, which meant that investigators were not required to file them in court. This was to prevent the warrants from becoming available to the public.[50]

The *St. Cloud Times* expressed concern about the secretive nature of the search in a July 3, 2010, editorial. Acknowledging the promise of progress in the case, the *Times* blasted the court-ordered silence surrounding the sealed warrants. The editorial went on to criticize the SCSO for being unclear about the reasons for the gag order. The newspaper requested a copy of the judge's orders to seal the warrants but the county attorney's office refused the request.

The *Times* identified three circumstances under which the state of Minnesota allows warrants to be sealed. The first is when making search documents public would render a search unsuccessful. The second was when making the warrant public would create risk of injury to innocent people. The third was when the warrant's disclosure would severely hamper the investigation. None of these applied, the editorial argued.[51]

On Saturday, July 3, 2010, three days after the search of the Rassier farm began, Sheriff John Sanner declared Dan Rassier, age 54, a "person of interest" in Jacob Wetterling's disappearance. Sanner's statement marked the first time in almost 21 years that authorities named a suspect. He announced that a number of items had been taken from the property. Analysis was needed to determine if they were evidence of a crime. The process was expected to take weeks, or even months.[52]

In an interview with a television news reporter, Rassier himself revealed some of the items investigators had taken from the property: a cedar chest, an umbrella stand, a lawn chair, and a box containing newspaper clippings, photographs, and videos related to the kidnapping. Rassier also acknowledged that investigators had previously searched the property in 1989, and again in 2004. During the latter, they searched a family personal computer, but not his own computer. Investigators have never revealed whether or not that search led to the discovery of any information relating to the Wetterling case.[53]

Dan Rassier had been a schoolteacher in the Rocori school district in Cold Spring and Richmond since 1978. He acknowledged that investigators had interviewed him numerous times over the years.

He had submitted to DNA testing, lie detector tests, and hypnosis. Rassier claimed innocence of involvement in Jacob's abduction. He said he supported the search effort and emphasized that he had been cooperative with investigators from the beginning. He was concerned, however, with how the negative attention had affected his elderly parents.

"For over twenty years, we have experienced our own never-ending nightmare," Rassier said. "We realize it's nothing like what the Wetterlings have gone through."[54]

Rassier told the *St. Joseph Newsleader* he had "witnessed many peculiar things" on the day Jacob was abducted—things that had "coalesced in his mind as vital connections pointing the way to solving the crime." He indicated his frustration that nobody had followed through with the information he had so willingly shared with authorities. Rassier declined to specify the "things" he saw, saying that he had trust issues with the media. Upon further questioning he did admit that the "things" he saw were people and/or vehicles. He also declined to specify what he saw because he did not want to tip off anyone guilty of the abduction.[55]

"I am an innocent witness to what happened," Rassier told *Newsleader* reporter Dennis Dalman. "But I definitely saw something. All the investigators know the information I told them."[56]

Asked if he had anything to do with Jacob's abduction, Rassier said "I had absolutely nothing to do with anything with Jacob. I didn't do it. I had nothing to do with it."[57]

As of 2010, Rassier had received no complaints in 32 years of teaching and there were no disciplinary actions in his personnel files. But the school district had been making cuts to the music program in recent years. Rassier stated that while the spotlight was on him, his biggest concern was the pending budget cuts. His classroom was assigned a paraprofessional as a monitor to begin the fall 2010 semester. The school's principal hired the monitor as a result of parental concern.[58]

In September 2010, three months after the search of the Rassier farm, Sheriff Sanner announced that no significant findings had developed. Preliminary lab results were "unable to establish, distinguish, or identify potential evidence," he said. The community's renewed hope for a resolution in the case was deflated. The disappointment was not discouraging to Sanner, however. He reiterated that Dan Rassier remained a person of interest in the case, despite the lack of evidence developed from the July search of his residence.[59]

"If I was the suspect, I wouldn't take this as a signal to relax," Sanner said. "This doesn't change a thing."[60]

Sanner said evidence taken during the search would be retained for future testing. He believed that advances in technology could one day produce the physical evidence needed to make an arrest. The monitor that had been assigned to Dan Rassier's classroom was promptly removed following Sanner's announcement.[61]

After the search of his family farm, Rassier began to engage himself more aggressively with the news media. He granted interviews with several newspapers and television stations. During a September 2010 interview with KSTP in St. Paul, he had been forthcoming about the items taken during the search, which included ash from a burning pit, and some pages from his journal.[62]

According to Rassier, the ash probably contained a number of items, including animal bones the family dog had dragged in from the woods, and remnants of old unwanted clothing. He said the journal entries included his thoughts on the case and he hoped investigators would find information there to help solve it. He pledged to do whatever he could do to help solve the case, but said he was not confident that the case could be solved.[63]

The last comment was met with scrutiny by some—the remark was interpreted as defiant, like something "only a guilty person would say." What Rassier meant, however, was that based on how he saw investigators handling the case, they stood little chance of solving it. He had willingly shown investigators the box of newspaper clippings and other items, and was surprised when they didn't ask if he had more information.

Rassier said investigators asked him if he or the family owned a silver handgun. He told them the family owned no handguns, only a few hunting rifles.[64]

In an October 6, 2010, interview with KARE 11, Rassier said he helped search the farm's outbuildings the night of October 22, 1989, after learning from deputy Bechtold that a child had been abducted that night. Rassier acknowledged that he did not have a good alibi for the time that Jacob was abducted but that he was cooperative with police from the very beginning. He said that he had done everything possible to help investigators solve the case.[65]

In 2012, Rassier made headlines again when he told the Associated Press he had written and mailed a five-page letter to fourteen different investigative and state agencies. In the letter, he complained about how he had been treated by law enforcement for the past two years. He claimed that his civil rights had been violated and that authorities had abused their power in naming him as a person of interest in the Wetterling case.[66]

"Is it considered legal for law enforcement to give the public the perception I am guilty of something when I'm not?" he wrote. "To destroy our family's name the way they did because they had a 'hunch' is, in itself, a serious crime. Nothing can make it right now. The damage has been done. But to leave the whole thing open to speculation and open to the public's imagination is just wrong!"[67]

Rassier claimed in his letter that Sheriff Sanner leaked information about him to the press in 2004, as investigators were changing their theory of about the abduction. He further claimed that during the July 1, 2010, search of his family's property, Sanner twice chided him, saying, "This is what happens when you talk."[68]

Regarding Captain Pam Jensen, Rassier cited examples of why he didn't trust her. He listed several concerning things that happened under Jensen's watch, including the physical assault of his mother.[69]

Rassier's harshest words were for Minnesota BCA Agent Ken McDonald. He said that McDonald twisted his comments out of context and used "select ideas" to solve the crime. He said that McDonald pulled his elderly mother off her chair and dragged her to the floor before finally pushing her out of the house. Rassier claimed that his mother's left arm was severely bruised for a week.[70]

FBI Agent Shane Ball was the lone investigator that Rassier had any kind words for. He said Ball was the only one who gave Rassier a business card and was willing to talk to him.[71] Although it would take several years to come to fruition, Ball's apparent willingness to listen to Rassier may have been an indication of things to come in the future of the investigation.

To the students and parents of Rocori school district in Cold Spring, Dan Rassier has been a well-liked and respected teacher for more than 35 years. For decades, his students have affectionately known him as "Mr. Be-Bop." He has no criminal record. He is considered one of the finest trumpet players in the state of Minnesota and is an avid long distance runner. Among the people who know him personally, he is consistently described as a nice guy, the person least likely to harm another.

But for Stearns County authorities, as of 2015, Dan Rassier was the only man ever publicly named as a person of interest in the abduction of Jacob Wetterling. Although 21 years passed before Rassier was named, it is apparent that investigators considered him a suspect from the beginning. What they lacked was solid physical evidence. In naming Rassier a person of interest, following the 2010 search of his family farm, Stearns County authorities relied almost exclusively on circumstantial evidence, and extraordinary statements from Rassier himself.

Of primary concern to investigators was Rassier's account of the cars he said he witnessed on his driveway on October 22, 1989. He said he told a number of investigators, from the beginning, that he saw two cars—one in the afternoon, one in the evening. He insisted that he told the same story several times during the first few weeks of the investigation.

The car Kevin Hamilton said he was driving on the night of the abduction—mid-sized, light-colored—did not match the description of the vehicle Rassier saw in his driveway—small, dark-colored. Hamilton told detectives how he had turned around by the farm buildings, making a 180-degree turn to the left, just like the cars Rassier described. If Rassier's account of the two cars was truthful, then Hamilton's car was actually the third that day to drive all the way down the long driveway, and make a quick 180-degree left-hand turn.

Another problem investigators had with Rassier's description of the cars was that he didn't report seeing them until the next day, when detectives questioned him at his place of work. It was unclear why he didn't mention them during the two encounters he had with police officers at his home on Sunday night and early Monday morning.

This alleged delay posed a credibility problem in the eyes of investigators. By Rassier's own admission, it was unusual for a car to turn around in his driveway. Yet, he said he witnessed two cars doing just that on the same day. He said the cars were driving fast, especially the car he saw in the afternoon. It was puzzling then, that if the cars were indeed so out of the ordinary, that he didn't make the connection more quickly that one or both may have been involved in the kidnapping.

But if Rassier did inform investigators about the cars, it's unusual that law enforcement officials made no pleas asking the public to help identify those vehicles. Investigators had made a point of publicizing the descriptions of other cars, so if Rassier's story is true, why didn't they make a plea to identify the car he claimed he saw at around the time of the abduction?

Rassier has never retained an attorney through all the years of questioning and scrutiny. He has said that he has been consistent in his story since the beginning and that he had nothing to do with the kidnapping of Jacob Wetterling. Investigators implied that he had changed his story.

Another significant problem for investigators in naming Rassier was that, for nearly fifteen years, they believed that Jacob's case was related to the abduction of Jared in Cold Spring. Investigators have also suggested that Rassier was a suspect from the very beginning of the Wetterling investigation. Yet Rassier has said he was never questioned about Jared's abduction. (He has a solid alibi: on the night of January 13, 1989, Dan Rassier was playing a concert with a friend at the American Legion in Eden Valley, twenty minutes from Cold Spring.)

If Rassier could not have been Jared's assailant, then it seems contradictory that for so many years investigators were certain of a link between the two cases, *and* that they considered Rassier a suspect in the Wetterling case.

Indeed, the investigation into Jacob Wetterling's kidnapping never lacked for a number of possible suspects. What was lacking was physical evidence and information from a witness or someone the abductor may have confided in.

The immediate and massive media coverage of Jacob Wetterling's kidnapping in 1989 rapidly garnered regional and national attention. That attention, in turn, led to many dead-end leads and false sightings across the country. In retrospect, the widespread coverage of the case probably had the unintended consequence of directing the investigation away from a local perspective early on, prolonging it for years.

On multiple occasions, Stearns County officials indicated they had a handful of top suspects, and another group of possible suspects that they hadn't been able to clear in the case. But for all the efforts put forth by dozens upon dozens of investigators, as of October 2015, no one had been charged, and only one person of interest had been publicly named—Dan Rassier. There were still no clues as to Jacob's whereabouts.

But the search would go on, now with the help of ordinary citizens, examining the facts and evidence in their own homes. Online sleuthers were looking for Jacob Wetterling's kidnapper, exchanging ideas and reviewing information old and new.

8

The Sleuths

I get slightly obsessive about working in archives because you don't know what you're going to find. In fact, you don't know what you're looking for until you find it.—Antony Beevor, Military Historian

It was a Saturday morning in the spring of 2013. I was sitting in my car in the parking lot outside the Great River Regional Public Library in St. Cloud, Minnesota. The library doors would be opening in a few minutes. I gathered a few research related materials, a pen, and a few dollars for the second floor copier. That's where I would spend the next several hours poring over reel after reel of microfilm archives of the *St. Cloud Times* newspaper.

I had been researching Jacob's Wetterlings case ever since hearing about the search of the Rassier farm in July 2010. After several months of casual online research, I found myself poring over thousands of posts on the online sleuthing site, Websleuths.com. The members of the online forum frequently speculated about potential suspects in Jacob's case, ranging from early suspect, Duane Allen Hart, to the present-day news revolving around Dan Rassier, among others. Questions raised on *Websleuths* piqued my curiosity further, and it was this thirst for answers that brought me to the media center of the Great River Regional Library.

The library's media center was a fairly expansive space dominated by computers spread across several rows of tables and chairs. On the far side of the library's technology area was a massive wall of steel cabinets that held thousands of reels of regional and national newspaper and magazine archives. I had decided to take a chronological approach for this and subsequent research sessions. My strategy was to gain an understanding of what was going on in the St. Cloud area in the fall of 1989.

After getting a sense of what was going on in St. Cloud at the time of Jacob's abduction, I spent the rest of the day printing page after page of newspaper articles that covered the crime. The articles would be read later from the comfort of my living room in Eau Claire, Wisconsin.

One of my earliest and most significant finds was an October 24, 1989, article in the *St. Cloud Times*, with a direct quote from Dan Rassier, in which he reported seeing a small car in his driveway at the time of the abduction.

"I saw lights kind of close together, like a small car," Rassier said. "It caught my attention because it's unusual for a car to be out here at that time."[1]

Rassier said that when he arrived at home on Monday night, October 23, 1989, he was met near the end of his driveway by Kirsten Haukebo, a reporter for the *St. Cloud Times* newspaper. He said that he told the reporter about the cars he had seen on Sunday.

That quote in the *St. Cloud Times* struck a chord in me immediately, because for the past three years all anyone knew was that Rassier had been named a person of interest in Jacob's case. He was the man who lived with his parents at the other end of the driveway from which Jacob had been kidnapped more than twenty years ago. The revelation was significant because Rassier had recently put himself in the spotlight again, coming forward publicly to proclaim his innocence. Since the search of his family farm in 2010, he had been saying publicly that he saw a car in his driveway at about the time of the abduction. Overtones from investigators and media accounts seemed to suggest that Rassier had changed his story over the years, and many who followed the developments closely, including myself, felt that was the case.

Another good find was a mysterious sketch that had been posted on *Websleuths*. It was featured in a front-page Crimestopppers article about Jared, the 12-year-old boy who had been abducted and assaulted in Cold Spring on January 13, 1989. Local police resources had developed the original sketch of Jared's assailant. It portrayed a young-looking man with dark hair and a hat. The better-known sketch of Jared's assailant wasn't produced until after Jacob's abduction. A highly trained FBI sketch artist developed that sketch in November 1989.

I continued to locate and collect newspaper archives online and in libraries, building a chronological collection that would eventually span more than a thousand pages of documents. I found that by collecting and cross-referencing similar articles from different newspaper sources, I was able to uncover additional details of investigative findings and activities. Reporters from different papers would report the same story in different ways, often reporting different bits of information than the others. It wasn't so much that the reports differed much, or were contradictory; it was more that smaller details were excluded in one report, but included in another. Putting all that information together often helped complete the picture a little more than it had been before. One by one, I would invariably find in nearly every article a bit or two of useful information. Gradually, I was able to build a more complete puzzle.

I shared much of my findings on *Websleuths*. I found a trove of information that seemed to have disappeared from the short list of well-known facts of the case, and I frequently shared copies of articles with blog writer, Joy Baker. Baker had been doing her own sleuthing on the Jacob Wetterling case, focusing on speaking with Dan Rassier and Kevin Hamilton, among others. Baker followed the *Websleuths* forum very closely but was not a registered member, and therefore was unable to access posted attachments of articles, maps, and the like. She would frequently ask me to review and provide copies of documents that were posted by others, or to provide copies of sources of information that I posted there myself.

In July 2013, I learned that Al Garber, the FBI agent who had supervised the early Wetterling investigation, had written a book, *Striving To Be The Best*. The book was a memoir spanning Garber's entire law enforcement and government service career. I promptly ordered the book and read it with great interest, hoping that Garber had included some information about his work in the Wetterling case. What I found intrigued me more than any information I had found to date. Garber detailed his involvement as the FBI supervisor of the Wetterling investigation over several pages of the book.

Of particular interest to me was information that Garber presented concerning a man who had been surveilled for weeks after Jacob's abduction and who was ultimately arrested in Jared's case. Fibers found in the car the man had owned at the time of Jared's abduction were consistent with fibers from Jared's snowmobile pants. The interview room had been set up with special lights, a flag, and the furniture arranged in a certain way. This information led me to believe that the man was probably a military man as suggested by the profile given by the FBI's profiler, John Douglas.

I was very intrigued by the man described in Garber's book. It seemed likely that he would have been the man involved in Jared's abduction and assault. And, with early Wetterling investigators' strong belief that Jacob's case was connected to Jared, I believed this was a man that needed to be tracked down. By this point I had read hundreds and hundreds of pages of newspaper articles, dozens of web pages, and thousands of posts on Websleuths.com—and not one of them had ever mentioned a man being arrested in either Jared's or Jacob's case. Garber's book would turn out to be the second major find of my research effort.

By this time in 2013, Joy Baker had met Jared and had been working with him on his own abduction incident. She was communicating with him regularly and learning a lot of information about his case that hadn't been released publicly until she shared the information in her blog. Baker learned about Duane Allen Hart's 1990 arrest for sexually assaulting several juvenile boys, from a *Websleuths* member in June 2013. Baker pursued Hart quite heavily, and soon her blog entries demonstrated a heavy leaning toward Duane Hart as the likely suspect in Jared's and Jacob's cases.

I scanned copies of the relevant pages of Garber's book and emailed them to Baker. Based on correspondence between Baker and myself, it was clear that she believed that the man described by Garber was Hart. I disagreed, and set out on a campaign to learn more about that man. I contacted Garber via email, and Garber agreed to answer questions about the investigation. However, Garber could not remember the name of the man he had described in his book. When asked specifically about Duane Hart, he told me that he didn't recall Hart's name and expressed doubt that he was the man who had been arrested in Jared's case.

I completed my search of archives of the *St. Cloud Times* in the summer of 2013, and then started researching other local newspapers. I found relevant articles and advertisements in the *Cold Spring Record*, and several other documents at the Stearns County Museum in St. Cloud. I continued to share information with Baker, and suggested to her that the newspaper archives held a trove of key information about Jacob's and Jared's cases.

Then, in August 2013, I subscribed to the online archives of the *Paynesville Press*. I had received a tip from a *Websleuths* member that there were articles about Belgrade resident, Duane Hart, in the archives. Sure enough, there were several articles detailing Hart's January 24, 1990, arrest for assaulting boys in the area. There were also several front-page articles concerning assaults on young boys in Paynesville in 1986 and 1987. The articles detailed the efforts of the Paynesville police to identify the assailant in those cases. There were multiple warnings to parents to keep their kids home after dark. One of the articles mentioned that the Wetterling Task Force had so far been unable to connect Hart to Jacob's kidnapping or to the series of assaults that had occurred in Paynesville in the late 1980s.

Knowing that Baker was primarily interested in Hart as a suspect in Jacob's and Jared's cases, I contacted her about the *Paynesville Press* archives. She read about the unsolved cases of attempted assaults in Paynesville from 1986 to 1987 and publicized them on her blog.

Baker and I sometimes compared notes on information we had found over the course of our research. In one discussion, I mentioned that I had found an article from 1990 where Trevor Wetterling had described Jacob's kidnapper as wearing a dark puffy coat, like a quilted winter coat. I explained that Trevor had gone to a closet to retrieve the coat to demonstrate to a reporter. Baker said that description was similar to the coat that at least one of the victims in the Paynesville assault incidents had described.

I continued to pursue the angle of the man arrested in Jared's case, as described in Garber's book. Frustrated and determined to find out more about the man, I began emailing several current and former newspaper and television reporters, writing to as many as ten reporters beginning in the summer of 2013. I focused my efforts on contacting reporters who had covered the Wetterling case over the years. None of them responded. I followed up several times with Garber as well, but to no avail. I emailed Stearns County investigators about the man in Garber's book, suggesting that the man warranted further attention. I contacted Fox 9 reporter Trish VanPilsum about stories she had done about a Paynesville man while with WCCO, but my pleas went unheeded. It frustrated me that no one responded to my pleas to investigate the information that I knew had never before been publicly reported, but was probably quite significant.

Meanwhile, Baker continued to hone in on Duane Hart. She spoke with many of the Paynesville assault victims, gathering information from them and subsequently focusing on how that information fit into her theory that Hart was responsible for all the attacks and abductions. Zeroing in on a single theory and suspect is not uncommon. It is something that even well-trained investigators are prone to do. Baker continued to push Stearns County investigators in the direction of Duane Hart. Captain Pam Jensen, Stearns County's lead investigator working the Wetterling case, interviewed Duane Hart at the sex offender hospital in Moose Lake, Minnesota, in December 2013. BCA Agent Kent McDonald joined Jensen for the interview.

During the interview, Duane Hart denied involvement in all of the crimes. The Paynesville assaults, Jared's abduction and assault, Jacob's kidnapping—he denied all of it. Hart did allow the investigators to take a DNA sample. Investigators had obtained DNA analysis results for the baseball cap that had been left behind by the man who was responsible for the Paynesville attacks. Jensen and McDonald wanted to compare Hart's DNA to that found on the hat.[2]

On December 31, 2013, I started a project I had been contemplating since Thanksgiving. Frustrated by the apparent lack of interest from investigative journalists, I decided to undertake an effort to put all the relevant details of the Jacob Wetterling case in one place. I decided to write a book, and I hoped that if the book were put into the right hands it could jostle someone's memory or attract the attention of the right person to help solve the case. I titled it *It Can't Happen Here*, conveying the collective sense of shock that overcame the public at the time of Jacob's kidnapping.

Knowing that my research was beginning to delve into discussions with individuals familiar with the Wetterling case, I contacted Patty Wetterling by email in February 2014. In my lengthy email, I informed her that I had been researching Jacob's case for a few years and had come across information that I felt had been forgotten over the years, and was writing a book that I hoped would help solve the case. I offered the Wetterlings an opportunity to review the book prior to publication. After getting no response from Patty, I forwarded the email to Alison Feigh at the Jacob Wetterling Resource Center, and asked her to forward the email to Patty. Patty later responded with a brief email, declining my offer.

For a case that was nearly twenty-five years old and seemed to have gone cold, there was no lack of amateur sleuthers quietly "working" the case. While online sleuthers speculated with each other about a wide range of theories, Baker and I pushed a lot of buttons independently, trying to draw attention to clues that seemed to have been left behind along the way. We both were beating the drum in search of answers, but each of us ultimately forged different paths on how to go about accomplishing that. Baker utilized her blog to focus on finding and speaking with more victims of the Paynesville assaults, and trying to tie them to Duane Hart, while I set out to build a complete history of the Wetterling investigation, to include those assaults as well as other possibilities and potential suspects.[3]

In March 2014, the DNA analysis came back on Duane Hart's sample. It was compared to the baseball cap that had been left behind during one of the attacks in Paynesville. Results indicated that Duane Hart could not be excluded as a contributor to the DNA found on the hat. That information fueled further investigation into the possibility that Duane Hart was involved in all the cases.

As the 25th anniversary of Jacob's abduction neared in the spring of 2014, media attention to Jacob's case bloomed once again. This time, the attention resulted from the efforts of blog writer, Baker, and Jared, the victim of a January 13, 1989, abduction and assault in Cold Spring. Working together with the hope of solving Jared's assault, Baker publicized the reported sexual assaults on teenage boys in the Paynesville area that had occurred between 1986 and 1987. The *Paynesville Press* newspaper had reported on these assaults a number of times when they occurred in the late 1980s, and the Wetterling task force investigated them at the time.

Television station WCCO ran with the story of renewed attention to those older cases in several parts in May 2014. Despite documented information to the contrary, Esme Murphy's coverage suggested that the 1986–1987 assaults had never been investigated following Jacob's abduction in 1989. The reports also alleged that it was several weeks after Jacob's abduction before investigators considered a possible link between the abductions of Jacob and Jared.[4] However, that assertion was inaccurate based on newspaper articles from October 1989. Those articles, particularly those in the *St. Cloud Times*, indicated that investigators went public with the potential link almost immediately after Jacob's abduction, and on multiple occasions afterward.

In May 2014, other media reports suggested that Delbert Huber, of Paynesville might be a suspect in Jacob Wetterling's kidnapping. Baker had blogged about Delbert and his possible involvement in Jacob's case. She had explored Huber and the characters from the Stearns Truth Tapes, among others, in her blog. Delbert Huber and his son, Tim Huber, were already in prison for the 2011 murder of Timothy Larson. According to the reports, investigators received tips from the public that Huber resembled a sketch of a man who was seen lurking at the Tom Thumb store at about the time that Jacob was kidnapped. The 2014 media flurry prompted Stearns County investigators to question Huber again, this time in prison. Huber had been questioned in the Wetterling case several times as far back as 1989, but was never named publicly as a suspect in the case.[5]

The publicity efforts of Esme Murphy and Joy Baker focused on the likelihood that Duane Hart was the man responsible for the Paynesville assaults in the late 1980's and Jared's abduction and assault.

By extension, it also meant that they were pushing the agenda that Hart was also responsible for Jacob's abduction. Baker said that she was frustrated with Stearns County investigators for not listening to her pleas about the Paynesville incidents.[6]

She sent many leads to Stearns County, and although she frequently complained about Stearns County investigators stonewalling her, it appeared that she was successful in shifting their focus away from Dan Rassier and toward Duane Hart instead. Baker may have had unreasonable expectations regarding communications with the Sheriff's Department. Naturally, investigators are gatherers of information, and would not share case information with an amateur sleuth such as Baker. Baker would eventually demand a meeting with Pam Jensen, the lead investigator working the Wetterling case. Jensen advised Baker that she hadn't discovered any new evidence in the case, and hadn't given Stearns County any information they didn't already have.[7]

During the summer of 2014, I informed Baker that I was writing a book that I hoped would help solve the Wetterling case. Other than telling the Wetterlings themselves about the book, Baker was the first person that I had told. Regrettably, our working relationship began to suffer following that disclosure. Baker and Patty Wetterling had become friends by that point, and Baker seemed to have taken on the role of family advocate, which became evident in her blog writings going forward. Despite our differences, I continued to support Baker's efforts by sending her information and tips and defending her work on online forums. Unfortunately, the differences between Baker and I were a microcosm of the apparent division between investigative agencies during the early days of the Wetterling investigation.

Stearns County investigator Pam Jensen and BCA agent Ken McDonald drove to Moose Lake in August 2014 to interview Duane Hart once again. This time they were armed with the DNA evidence that showed that Hart might have been the man who had left the cap behind during one of the Paynesville incidents. Again, Duane Hart denied any involvement in any of the cases that Stearns County and Joy Baker were looking to him for. He denied any knowledge of the baseball cap. Hart acknowledged that recent news media and Baker's blog were pointing the finger at him, and he told the investigators that he felt like he was a suspect in the kidnapping of Jacob Wetterling.[8]

Jensen and McDonald asked Hart where he was storing his personal belongings while he was incarcerated at Moose Lake, where he had been for most of the past twenty-five years. Hart claimed that he had no possessions outside of the treatment facility. McDonald later followed up with another investigator to review the facility's visitor logs and phone logs to determine if Hart had any visitors. The investigator listened to at least one of Hart's phone calls and learned that Hart wanted someone to sell or get rid of items in his storage locker. Previously, Hart had denied having any personal items outside of the Moose Lake facility.

Stearns County and BCA investigators did not believe Hart's denials. On August 22, 2014, BCA agent Ken McDonald secured a search warrant to listen to Hart's phone calls and review all visitor logs and phone call records for Duane Hart, dating back to July 2013, when Baker first began publicizing Hart as a possible suspect in Jacob's kidnapping. The search warrant cited Hart as a viable suspect for Jacob's kidnapping and all the crimes that had been associated with it. The warrant allowed investigators to record and listen to all of Hart's phone calls. Additionally, the warrant provided access to the facility's behavioral reports, investigative reports, and treatment records that may have involved discussions about sexual assaults, kidnappings, and storage of personal items outside of the sex offender treatment facility.[9]

By the late summer of 2014, I had gained a reputation as someone who was digging deep into the Wetterling case. I began to receive contact from individuals who purported to have sleuthed or gathered information about the Wetterling case in the early days of the investigation. In one instance, a former New York City police detective, who was retired and living in central Minnesota, sent me a two-inch thick file of documents. I had spoken with the former detective over the phone several times over the course of my research, and although I found many of the former detective's theories to be rather bizarre,

I was always interested to learn more about different suspects or theories of the case.

Upon reviewing the file, I discovered that it contained a host of interesting documents relating to several subjects I recognized as having been investigated over the course of the Jacob Wetterling kidnapping case. There were copies of lie detector tests, maps of the abduction site, some sketches and photos that I had never seen before, as well as written transcripts of dozens of audiotapes that were known locally as the Stearns Truth Tapes. There was a letter from a behavioral psychologist from Quantico, Virginia, and there were court records and investigative notes concerning convicted child molesters.

There was one interesting set of documents that stood out from the rest. It was a collection of hand-written notes that had been copied, and they appeared to have been written about Duane Allen Hart, the man who had been an early subject of investigation in the Wetterling case. I was surprised by the notes and intrigued by their potential significance. The former detective who had sent this two-inch thick file had spoken several times about many of the documents in the file, but he had never mentioned anything about the notes pertaining to Duane Hart. I wondered if the former detective had even been aware of their presence in the file?

The information contained in the notes was stunning. The notes, which were written by a private investigator in February 1990, were difficult to decipher in places. They were very detailed and quite revealing about Hart's life from childhood to the late 1980s. I was quite familiar with Hart, as his name had come up as a subject of the Wetterling investigation several times in the newspaper archives I had researched. Hart also seemed to be the primary focus for a small number of amateur sleuthers. But for me, and most others, Hart never quite fit the crime. Hart was a groomer, and it seemed he had manipulated access to many young boys—it was unlikely that he would have a need to abduct a boy to satisfy his sexual deviancy.

I reviewed the notes over and over again, each time picking up on something new I hadn't noticed before. It was clear to me that Duane Hart, a convicted sex offender, had been somewhat forthcoming in his discussions with the investigator. He openly admitted to having had sexual relationships with dozens of individuals, and was rather frank about his drug and alcohol use. In fact, the notes seemed to indicate that Hart was attempting to help investigators narrow the search for the man responsible for Jared's assault and Jacob's abduction.

When Hart was shown several sketches of possible suspects in both cases, he identified a handful of men as possible, but suggested one man in particular, Danny Heinrich, who he thought matched the description and sketch of the man in Jared's case in Cold Spring. Hart identified Heinrich in particular because he often wore military type clothing, drove a dark blue car, had a hand held police scanner, and had a rough, raspy voice when excited. He indicated he heard the man had been arrested for Jared's assault because he owned a fairly new blue car. Each of those items was consistent with descriptions from Jared's account of his abduction and assault.

The following weekend was Labor Day weekend, 2014. The long-anticipated episode of John Walsh's *The Hunt*, featuring the Jacob Wetterling case, was to air on Sunday night. The show opened with a disappointing re-enactment of Jacob's abduction. There were street-lights and an eerie crescent moon included for effect. Neither was an accurate depiction of the actual abduction scene. Rather, the dead-end road had been completely dark on the night of October 22, 1989.

The show focused on the possible connection between Jacob Wetterling's abduction and the Paynesville incidents that had occurred between 1986 and 1988, and the January 13, 1989, abduction and assault of Jared in Cold Spring. The episode featured the efforts of Joy Baker and made a compelling argument that all those cases were connected.

For folks who knew the case well, however, the show was recognized as a thinly veiled program about Duane Allen Hart. Hart was not specifically named during the program, but there was little doubt that he was the man that Baker was pointing to in trying to connect the cases together. She reasoned that Hart had been in prison since shortly after Jacob's abduction, and that no abductions were reported after Hart's arrest on January 24, 1990. She further suggested that the Paynesville incidents had occurred during times when Hart was not in jail on alcohol or drug-related charges. When court records indicated that Hart was likely to be in jail, there were no assaults reported in Paynesville.

The logic behind Baker's theory on the dates was hard to ignore. On the surface, it made good sense. And, as she pointed out during the program—how many psychopathic pedophiles could there be in a fifteen to twenty mile radius between St. Joseph and Paynesville? As it turned out, there were a lot more than most people could have imagined.

From my perspective, Hart had never been very high on my list of suspects. Everything I had read and learned about Hart seemed to indicate that he was on Wetterling investigators' radar since immediately after Jacob's abduction. With all the media speculation surrounding Hart and the Paynesville assaults, I briefly entertained the notion that Hart could indeed have been the perpetrator in all those cases. In the end, though, I remained skeptical. I had learned through three years of research precisely how emotionally charged theories and closed-minded multi-media had propelled speculation about other potential suspects in the Wetterling case. Examples included the characters and saga told by the Stearns Truth Tapes, Tim Huber, and Dan Rassier.

I argued that Jacob's abductor was more likely to be someone whom Hart had abused than it was Hart himself. The premise was that the abductor's fixation on young boys might have derived from "learned" behavior. The theory is based on the cycle of abuse that often typifies child molesters, the very cycle of abuse that has been taught by the Wetterling Foundation for decades.

Regardless of whether or not Duane Hart was a suspect in the Paynesville cases or in Jared's case in Cold Spring, I understood that it was highly unlikely that criminal charges would ever be filed against Hart, or anyone else, in those cases. For one thing, even if investigators were to develop strong evidence against Hart or another individual in those cases, potential prosecution would be hindered by statutes of limitations.

Furthermore, there would be other difficulties in prosecutors using connections between Jacob's kidnapping case and the Paynesville cases or Jared's case. Those difficulties would come in the form of unintended consequences of Baker delving into the Paynesville cases and Jared's case. As the Paynesville cluster of cases attracted publicity and the suggestions of Hart's possible involvement became the subject of wide speculation, several of Hart's victims from the 1980s began comparing notes with each other and also with the Paynesville cluster victims. They openly discussed Hart's methods for grooming victims, his control tactics, and even his behavior during sexual encounters. Many of the victims in these cases had become convinced of Duane Hart's guilt.

Such cross-contamination of witness accounts could pose a serious hindrance to potential prosecution, particularly in Jacob's case due to the likelihood that Jared's and Jacob's cases were related. The witness accounts were so badly distorted by the fall of 2014, that they would likely be ineffective against anyone who would ever face charges in Jacob's case. According to multiple sources, these discussions became so widely known that Stearns County Sheriff's deputies were sent out to ask individuals to stop talking to each other about their experiences with Duane Hart or the Paynesville perpetrator. Without a confession by Jacob's abductor, or the discovery of his body or some other key physical evidence, prosecution of a defendant in Jacob's case would be all but impossible.

I pored over the Hart Notes again and again. I forwarded the notes to Joy Baker in early September 2014, knowing that she hadn't seen them before and that she would have an interest in them due to her pursuit of connecting Hart to the abduction and assault cases. In the email to Baker, I accompanied the Hart Notes with comments that the private investigator had said that Duane Hart had suggested one of the Heinrich brothers, either Danny or David, as a likely suspect in the assault of Jared. Baker then forwarded the Hart Notes to Patty Wetterling, and commented back that Patty had never seen them before.[10]

On September 10, 2014, I forwarded a copy of the Hart Notes to St. Cloud-based FBI Agent, Shane Ball and Stearns County. In my emails to Ball and Stearns County, I noted that it was clear from the Hart Notes that Hart had been looked at by Wetterling investigators in connection to the Paynesville cases and for Jared's and Jacob's cases. I offered to speak with investigators about possible suspects that Hart had provided in the notes, and other information and connections that I had uncovered in my research. I received no response.

Then, on Saturday evening, September 13, 2014, FBI Agent Shane Ball emailed me and asked about the source of the Hart Notes. I responded to Ball with a detailed explanation of how I had come across the notes, and who had authored them. I immediately notified Baker and Patty Wetterling of Ball's apparent interest in the notes.

I had sent several tips to Agent Ball in the past, and I knew that there was a level of implied significance to the fact that Ball had inquired about the source of the Hart Notes. Sending tips to the FBI and to Stearns County was typically a one-way communication, with no response expected or received. Ball was relatively new to the St. Cloud office and the Wetterling case, but he had always demonstrated an interest in listening and learning more about several suspects.

Understanding the significance in Ball's inquiry, I called the private investigator once more, reviewing with him again the time he spent with Hart in his jail cell. By that time, he had received a copy of the notes from me, and had a chance to review the notes for himself. The investigator reiterated that it was his professional opinion that Hart was probably not involved in the Paynesville incidents, nor in Jacob's or Jared's cases, because those assaults did not fit Hart's modus operandi. Hart was a groomer. He used drugs, alcohol, and money to secure sexual favors from juvenile boys and adult males. There was no doubt in the private investigator's mind that Duane Hart had suggested Dan Heinrich as the likely abductor in Jared's case, and therefore in Jacob's case as well.[11]

With that, I followed up with an email to FBI Agent Ball on September 14, 2014, suggesting that Duane Hart had pointed to Dan Heinrich as the likely perpetrator in the cases. Heinrich's name was all over the notes, and it was usually marked with an asterisk or other indicator, and it was boldly circled on the front page of the notes.

The notes made reference to Heinrich's fascination with police scanners, the fact that he owned a fairly new, dark blue four-door car, and would often wear camouflage clothing, that he had a raspy voice when he was excited—all of which were details that were consistent with what Jared had described about his abductor. Furthermore, the notes indicated that Hart had heard that Heinrich had been arrested in the cases at some point. I concluded that Heinrich was probably the man that had been detailed in Garber's book. The similarities were too powerful to ignore.

I forwarded to Baker my emailed tip to FBI agent Ball about Dan Heinrich as a likely suspect. Baker and I had previously discussed the Hart Notes over the phone and I shared my insight that it appeared Duane Hart was trying to help investigators identify Jacob's abductor. There was, of course, little doubt that Hart had committed atrocious acts against children, and it was readily apparent that he had left a wide swath of hurt and destruction in his path.

The Hart notes were the climax of my research, and I knew it would be very unlikely that I would come across anything else as significant. Despite that, I continued with my research and worked to touch all points, ask questions, crosscheck information between similar newspaper articles, and so forth. I would occasionally take breaks from my research, but always came back for another round of reviews, looking for those little bits of information or making connections I hadn't picked up on the last few times through my mountain of materials.

I had done some of my research at the Stearns County Museum in St. Cloud. Sarah Warmka, a museum archivist, quickly took an interest. Warmka also happened to be the leader of the Granite City Book Club. Once I shared with Warmka that I was writing a book about the Jacob Wetterling kidnapping, she invited me to present a discussion to the club. They agreed to schedule the discussion prior to publication, as I wanted to get feedback from readers about the material in the manuscript. I understood the subject of the book was sensitive to the St. Cloud area as a whole, and wanted to make sure the material came across as respectful, accurate, and relevant.

Before the book club discussion could be scheduled, Warmka left the museum for a position in another part of the state. The new book club leader contacted me in September 2014, reiterating the club's interest in hosting an author discussion. They set a date of the discussion for January 21, 2015.

I emailed Stearns County Detective Pam Jensen, the lead detective working Jacob's case, and offered her a chance to strike any information from the manuscript. She declined, saying that she had already read through it and had no objections. She asked me to provide a copy of the book when published, and wished me good luck. The original, unfinished manuscript was emailed to book club members in November 2014.

As the date of the meeting approached, the Granite City Book Club issued a press release, and the event was mentioned in several radio and newspaper briefings. Book club meetings were typically small, but they expected a large crowd would be on hand for this event due to Jacob Wetterling's significance to the local area.

I called the day before the book club event to confirm all the details. Everything was set. Then, on the day of the event, just hours before it was scheduled to start, they suddenly cancelled the meeting without citing a reason, other than they had received a couple of emails expressing concern about the meeting. A notice was posted on the door to the museum advising would-be attendees that the book discussion had been canceled.

Despite the setback, I continued work on the manuscript, finishing it in March 2015. I believed that Baker, the media, and Stearns County investigators had all been pursuing the wrong suspect in the Wetterling case—Duane Hart. They were overlooking the cycle of sexual abuse that would suggest that the abductor was more likely someone whom Duane Hart had abused.

Since I was not able to get feedback from the book club, I instead sought it from several acquaintances that were quite familiar with history of the Jacob Wetterling case. The feedback was overwhelmingly positive. The book was ultimately released as a self-published volume in April 2015. It covered the entire history of the case, and detailed what I determined to be key aspects of the case: forgotten leads, observations based on analysis of available information, and several questions that had never been addressed by a passive media.

Those forgotten leads were about to come back full circle, to the forefront of the investigation.

9

The Box

*Every case is dying to be solved. The answer is out there somewhere
… it's about going back to the basics. It's about making sure all the
'I's were dotted and 'T's crossed. The answer is out there somewhere.—*Everett Doolittle, retired BCA Cold Case Unit

John Douglas, the legendary FBI profiler based in Quantico,
Virginia, who developed the profile of Jacob's likely abductor in 1989,
has co-authored several books about his experiences and the cases
he worked on over the course of his career in law enforcement. *Mind
Hunter, Law & Disorder*, and *Journey Into Darkness* are particularly
well-written and insightful books. Douglas has noted that an interesting phenomenon rings true in almost every wide-ranging investigation of a crime: in almost all cases, investigators had likely
interviewed the individual responsible early on in the investigation.

Douglas had a reputation for consistent and remarkable accu-
racy in profiling criminals. His standard operating procedure was to
learn as much detail as possible about the crime scene itself, including
any and all physical evidence, the location, immediate surroundings,
points of access and egress, and so on. What he did not want to know
about when profiling a case was information about any potential suspects. Rather, he would use information from the crime scene to
develop a profile of the likely perpetrator. The point in all of Douglas'
efforts was to help investigators narrow down a field of likely candi-
dates to pursue as likely suspects.

Depending on the type of crime, characteristics of the victimol-
ogy, and the demographics of the victims themselves, Douglas was
able to correctly peg a range of characteristics that would often prove

to be stunningly precise. Based on crime scene analysis and behavioral science, he was able to consistently predict a criminal's approximate age, race, physical deformities or defects, education level, military experience, and occupation. Often times, Douglas was able to predict problems associated with the criminal's life history, such as their relationship with one or more parents, social interaction, and past criminal history.

Douglas explained that extensive research of serial criminals such as child molesters and murderers indicated that such persons often exhibit two other common precursors to their violent behavior: bedwetting and arson. Post-offense behavior often included a range of behavioral patterns including returning to the scene of the crime, involving oneself in the investigation, closely following the media attention to the case, accumulating newspaper clippings or videos, and moving to a new place of residence. And, in the case of murder, investigators should expect the suspect to revisit the grave on anniversaries of the crime, particularly on or around the first anniversary.

Criminal behavioral profiling also suggests that a child abductor does not just wake up one day and decide to abduct a child. Rather, the criminal builds up from a base of some lower levels of deviant behavior, such as child pornography or molesting an acquaintance. According to behavioral science, a stressor in the criminal's life most often triggers the build-up from molestation to child abduction. That stressor could come from a number of sources, including family problems, marital issues, sexual dysfunction, financial woes, the loss of a job, and so forth.

Going back to the beginning of the Wetterling investigation, John Douglas offered the following psychological profile of Jacob's likely abductor[1]:

A white male

Age 25 to 35 years old

Very low self-image

May have some form of physical deformity such as acne or scars

Probably employed in a low-skilled occupation with little contact with the public

May have had a recent stressful event in his life which influenced the high-risk approach to the abduction

High-risk crime scenario and the threat of a gun indicates abductor may have attempted an abduction previously and failed

People familiar with the individual would likely notice a heightened sense of anxiety or stress since the abduction

Abductor probably committed a similar crime in the past

As noted above, in any wide-ranging criminal case, it is more likely than not that within two weeks of the commencement of the investigation, the person responsible for the crime is already known to investigators, and probably has already been interviewed. In the Wetterling case, the list of potential suspects who had been interviewed included several hundred individuals. In all likelihood, Jacob's abductor was already "in the box"—his name was somewhere in the files.

Many times over the years, cold case reviewers would routinely go back to the files to review the case again from the beginning. Anytime a new investigative team at the SCSO would take over the case, they would review everything again. But, as Al Garber points out in his book, *Striving To Be The Best*, a cold case review from outside agencies would sometimes be met with reluctance from the primary investigative agency, the Stearns County Sheriff's Office. This is a natural phenomenon, and as Garber further suggests, each generation of investigators has a tendency to develop leads that have been generated on their own watch. Unfortunately, that means that older leads and information may be overlooked in favor of more recently developed theories of the case.[2]

Detectives are human, and human nature dictates that when pursuing a particular theory of a case, an investigator may tend to process information in a manner that reflects their bias toward a particular theory. This natural tendency may explain why second and third generation teams in the Wetterling case drifted away from an original working theory of the crime to something altogether different over the course of time.

By the fall of 2014, there seemed to be a desperate but unspoken air of oblivion hanging over the case. With no solution after a quarter-century, it seemed the mystery risked drifting off the landscape altogether. Some suspects had already died, and other suspects and witnesses were not getting any younger. If something was going to be done to break the case open, it had to be done soon.

In August, Patty Wetterling asked Sheriff John Sanner and Captain Pam Jensen to take another look at the case from the beginning.[3] Such a request from the family alone would not be enough to prompt another complete review, but apparently they found sufficient reason to do just that. Soon after, a meeting was held in Stearns County including representatives from the FBI, SCSO, and the Minnesota Bureau of Criminal Apprehension.

FBI Special Agent Shane Ball later presented a proposal to form a cold case unit to take one more crack at the Wetterling case.[4] He would bring in an FBI CARD (Child Abduction Rapid Deployment) team.[5] He would bring in FBI agents who were mostly unfamiliar with the details of the investigation. They would take a truly fresh approach.

The primary purpose of the CARD teams is to provide field investigative, tactical, and resource assistance to state and local investigators in cases of non-family child abductions. The program was established in 2005 and consists of five regionally based teams comprising a total of 60 members. The teams work with the FBI's Behavioral Analysis Unit, the National Center for the Analysis of Violent Crime coordinators, and Child Exploitation Task Force members.

Ball had recently been given information about a man who was suggested as a suspect in 1990, Danny Heinrich. It was a name that had never surfaced publicly, but had certainly been connected to the case early on. In an unlikely twist, the source of that information was none other than a man who was once investigated himself as a suspect in the Wetterling case, Duane Allen Hart, who was at that very moment, in 2014, under heavy scrutiny by the SCSO and the BCA.

As the twenty-fifth anniversary of the Wetterling kidnapping passed, there would be one more cold case review of the case files as FBI Agent Shane Ball directed investigative efforts "back to the box."

10

The Forgotten Man

We searched his house because we were looking for Jacob Wetterling.[1]—Janelle Kendall, Stearns County Attorney

When investigators raided the small white house located at 55 Myrtle Avenue South in the central Minnesota town of Annandale on July 28, 2015, they came away with a computer and several binders filled with images of child pornography, several bins of children's clothing, and photographs of known victims of child exploitation— a plethora of evidence to support charges against the owner of the home, Daniel James Heinrich.

What they came looking for, but were unable to find, was Jacob Wetterling.

After the search of his home, Danny Heinrich told some of his neighbors that investigators had seized pornography from his home, but not to worry because none of the pictures were of their children. While some of his neighbors later learned of the truth about the search, they quietly kept to themselves what the rest of the world would soon learn.[2]

Danny Heinrich was someone few people knew well, and even fewer had any inkling he had been a suspect in the Wetterling case, or that he had long been a suspect in the Paynesville cases and Jared's case.

To better understand the significance of Heinrich as a suspect in the Wetterling case, and the culmination of decades of investigation, it is necessary to go back to the early days of Heinrich himself. The raid on his home and the information that was discovered thereafter shed new light on a number of incidents that occurred prior to October 22, 1989.

Daniel James Heinrich was born at Paynesville Hospital on March 21, 1963. His parents were Howard and Corrine Heinrich. He grew up in the family home on Lake Koronis, along with his older brother David and younger brother Tommy. His father worked in the construction trades, building bridges for Lunda Construction Company. It was a job that demanded a lot of travel and often took him away from his family.[3]

Danny dropped out of high school during his junior year in 1981, but his troubles began long before. In 1977, when he was 14, a neighbor's cabin on Lake Koronis burned down. "There was a fire back in the cabin over there," a neighbor said. "They said there's two boys in there. I didn't know who they were until later on they identified Danny Heinrich as one of them. Everything burned."[4]

Howard and Corrine Heinrich divorced in 1978, when Danny was 15. That event had a significant impact on his life and he had a hard time coping. Danny's mother soon began dating Duane Allen Hart. Court records indicate that Danny spent time as a patient at the Willmar Regional Treatment Center, a hospital known for its treatment programs for chemical dependency and mental illness.[5]

Heinrich had several minor run-ins with law enforcement in the years that followed, but ultimately committed more serious crimes. He was arrested for burglary in Stearns County in 1984. He also had trouble with drinking and driving, with DWI convictions in 1982 and 1986. Burglary convictions stemmed from his arrest inside a business in Paynesville, although he claimed that he did not steal anything.[6]

Stearns County Deputy Dennis Pooler was on patrol duty near Paynesville in the early morning hours of March 30, 1984, when a VARDA alarm indicated a probable burglary in progress at the Twice's Nice store, where other recent burglaries had occurred. Pooler, along with Paynesville Police Department Sergeant Bill Drager, responded to the call.[7]

When they arrived, they found that the front door glass had been broken. Pooler and Drager searched the building with a canine and found Danny Heinrich hiding inside a pile of boxes. "I don't know what got into me," Heinrich told Pooler. "I don't know why I do these things."[8]

After being taken to the Paynesville police station, Heinrich admitted he had also broken into the Minnegasco building earlier in the night. Sergeant Drager investigated and found a broken window at the Minnegasco building. Heinrich told Pooler he had entered the buildings in search of money, but that he took nothing from either business.[9]

During court proceedings on the burglary cases, Heinrich, then 21, acknowledged he was having a difficult time dealing with his parents' divorce. He said he had also lost money due to a gambling habit, and the combination of these troubles led him to steal from a Paynesville area business.[10]

Heinrich's defense attorney, Phil Prokopowicz, spoke of Danny's personal problems when he addressed the court. "Danny still doesn't know why he did this," Prokopowicz told the court. "He was lonesome, bored with his life. He had some family problems…."[11]

Heinrich pleaded guilty to two counts of third-degree burglary. He was sentenced to 30 days in jail with work release privileges, and was placed on probation for five years. Heinrich was also ordered to pay restitution for the property damage.

On the night of August 30, 1986, Paynesville Police Officer Stephen Lehmkuhl was escorting the manager of a liquor store to the First State Bank to make his nightly deposit. As Lehmkuhl pulled his squad car up to the front of the bank, he heard tires squealing on a nearby street. He saw a maroon colored car run a stop sign and gave chase.[12] The pursuit ended behind a feed plant, where Lehmkuhl apprehended Daniel Heinrich. His breath smelled of alcohol and he was verbally abusive and combative, at one point damaging the squad car with a wild swing of his leg.

Seaching Heinrich's vehicle, Lehmkuhl found a handheld police scanner that was set to monitor transmissions of the SCSO. The scanner was confiscated and Heinrich was taken to the Paynesville police station, where a breathalyzer registered his blood-alcohol level at 0.17 percent—over the legal limit for operation of a motor vehicle.[13]

Heinrich was charged with a DWI and fifth degree assault against a police officer, and also for having a scanner in his car. He pleaded guilty to the DWI and the other charges were dropped. He was sentenced on February 2, 1987, to 90 days in jail and was required to attend weekly Alcohol Anonymous meetings.

Heinrich had an earlier DWI conviction in 1982, in the city of Willmar. He was charged with having an open container of alcohol in the car in that incident. Heinrich seemed to find alcohol-related trouble quite often. Chris Larsen, a former neighbor, remembered, "The guy did drink a lot. There was a couple of times in the car … one time the cops pulled us over and confiscated all the beer."[14]

By 1986, Daniel Heinrich was living at the Plaza Hotel building located at 121 Washburne Avenue in downtown Paynesville. His apartment was located near the epicenter of a string of attacks on juvenile boys that occurred from 1986 through 1988. The incidents were reported in the *Paynesville Press*, and Paynesville police warned the public to keep their children home after dark. In nearly all the cases, the boys had been downtown and were heading home when the incidents occurred.

According to an article published in the *Paynesville Press* in April 1986, a 12-year-old boy reported that on March 6, 1986, a man driving an older, dark blue, four-door car approached him as he was walking near G&T Foods in Paynesville. The man attempted to coax the boy into his car, offering to take him to "Toyland." The boy was able to get away. Of all the incidents that would follow in the town of Paynesville over the next two years, this was the only one that reportedly involved a vehicle. It may have been a sign of things to come.

In August of 1986, a boy was bicycling through an alley behind Papa's Pizza at 108 West Hoffman Street in downtown Paynesville, when a white male attacked him. A man jumped out at him and knocked him off his bike. He punched the boy in the nose without saying a word. The boy fled and later described his assailant as a husky, white male about 5'9" tall. He wore a mud-like substance on his face.[15]

On August 21, 1986, two juvenile boys were heading home from Papa's Pizza when a heavy-set man hit one of the boys in the back of the head, knocking him to the ground. Once the boy was on the ground the man groped his front pockets. When the boy's friend came to his defense, the assailant took off running. The man didn't say a word during the assault. The boys described him as being 5'6" to 5'8" tall, wearing a long sleeve sweater and gloves.[16]

Another Paynesville incident occurred November 30, 1986. A boy reported that a heavy-set man wearing a nylon windbreaker attacked him in the area of 603 Augusta Avenue. The man darted out from the bushes in an alley and put his hand over the boy's mouth, then dragged him into a patch of trees and told him not to speak or he would kill him. His voice was low and filled with an eerie static and his hands smelled like cigarette smoke. The assailant rubbed the boy's testicles over his clothing as well as under his clothing. He removed the boy's stocking cap and used a knife to cut off a lock of his hair. He asked the boy his name and age, and upon leaving ordered him to "keep laying down for five minutes or I'll blow your head off."[17]

The *Paynesville Press* reported on the August 21 and November 30 incidents in their December 9, 1986, edition. Police hadn't definitively connected the two crimes, and there were no clear suspects at the time, but they noted that in both cases the victims were attacked from behind.[18]

On Valentine's Day 1987, a boy had just left Papa's Pizza and went into an apartment building at 122 West James Street. A heavy-set man attacked him as he entered the stairwell, grabbing him and throwing him down the steps. When the boy started to scream the man threatened to kill him if he did not keep quiet. The attacker grabbed the boy's penis, again both over and under the boy's clothing. The man spoke in a deep, low whisper as he asked the boy what grade he was in. He stole the boy's wallet and left on foot. The boy described him as being about 5'6" tall and wearing a dark colored, quilted jacket with a mask covering his face.[19]

On May 17, 1987, the same boy was riding his bicycle on Main Street in Paynesville when he was attacked again, by a man who had about the same build as the earlier assailant. The man grabbed the boy off his bike and groped his testicles. The boy screamed, telling the man that he had already gotten him before. The attacker fled on foot, but this time he left behind something that would later help identify him—a baseball cap. The boy described him as a pudgy, with a dark face and dark colored clothing. The man said nothing during the attack but the boy believed this assailant and the previous one were the same man.[20]

On the front page of its May 26, 1987, edition, the *Paynesville Press* reported on the February 14 and May 17 assaults, along with the three prior incidents. Sergeant Bill Drager said that police were taking the assaults very seriously, noting that in all five cases the boys were between 12 and 16 years old. "After this guy grabs the boys," Drager said, "he tells them 'Don't turn around or I'll blow your head off,' and in at least one instance he used a knife."[21]

Drager further noted that in all instances the boys had been downtown just prior to the assaults. "I think he's picking them out downtown and then following them home," said Drager, "or lying in wait for them to go home."[22]

Nearly a year passed before the next reported incident occurred in late summer of 1988. A small group of boys was camping in a wooded area near 200 West Railroad Avenue in Paynesville. The boys were thirsty, so two of them went off to get drinks from a nearby vending machine. A man came out of nowhere and tackled one of the boys and sat on him forcefully. The boy screamed, and as he did, the attacker held a knife to his throat and threatened, "Shut up or I'll kill you." The boy was able to get away without being groped by the attacker. The man was described as a white male with a husky build. He spoke in a raspy voice and was wearing a pantyhose mask, black gloves, and black boots. He was also wearing camouflage pants and what looked like an army jacket.[23]

The last of the reported incidents in Paynesville occurred in the fall of 1988. A boy was delivering newspapers on his bicycle near 512 West Minnesota Street, when he stopped briefly to drop off a paper and was attacked by a husky male. The man charged out from a treed area and knocked the boy off his bicycle. He then fled the area. The boy described him as being about 5'6" tall and wearing a dark ski mask, dark stocking cap, black shirt, black pants, and black gloves.[24]

Although the Paynesville incidents had been reported on multiple times over the previous two years, many city residents were generally unaware of the string of assaults on juveniles. If the Paynesville police were suspecting Daniel James Heinrich in those assaults, it was a well-kept secret.

Serial pedophiles, much like serial killers, often escalate their behavior over time. FBI profilers cite a number of factors that contribute to this, but chief among them is the criminal's growing confidence and increasing need to satisfy the urges that drive their behavior. When the string of incidents in Paynesville seemed to have come to a stop in 1988, it was likely not because the assailant had ceased his activities, but because he had moved away, been jailed on some other offense, or was preparing to move on to the next level.

On Friday, January 13, 1989, 12-year-old Jared was abducted from the streets of Cold Spring, Minnesota. If the kidnapper was the same man involved in the Paynesville cases, he indeed had escalated his criminal behavior to the next level.

Jared had been in the park area hanging out with friends, and later on they went for an evening snack at the Side Cafe in the downtown area of Cold Spring. Shortly before 9:45 p.m., he was walking alone toward his home just a few blocks down the street, when a man in a dark blue four-door car pulled up alongside him and asked for directions to the Kraemer home. It seemed like a normal request. Here was a man who seemed to be a bit lost but had a general idea of where he was going. As Jared started giving directions, the man got out of his car and grabbed him by the shoulders, and then shoved him into the back seat.[25]

The doors in the back of the car were equipped with child safety locks, so there was no way for Jared to escape, even if he was able to overcome the initial shock of being abducted. The man displayed no weapon but he threatened the boy, saying that he had a gun and wasn't afraid to use it. The man drove the car away from the abduction location and told the boy to cover his face with his stocking cap. He then ordered Jared to lay down in the back seat. Despite being down in the back seat as the man drove them out of town, Jared was able to recognize several landmarks along the way. He noted passing the John Paul apartment building in the 200 block of 8th Avenue North. From there the kidnapper followed County Highway 158 to the west, going up Bell's Hill and then a bit south to State Highway 23. Highway 158 ended at Highway 23, and he noted that the man turned right, toward the town of Richmond. Jared paid close attention to details as the man drove him to a rural area just north of Richmond. He would later recall passing by the ballpark in Richmond, and once the driver finally stopped the car, he could see the distinctive city lights of Richmond.[26]

Jared's attention to detail would later help investigators narrow down likely suspects in his case. For example, he noticed that the man had a hand-held police radio with an antenna sitting on the front passenger seat. The radio had duct tape on it and it was scratched. He heard two voices on the radio as the man started driving, but the man soon turned the radio off. There were many other things that he picked up on during the ten-minute drive to the gravel road where the man finally stopped the car. He described the car as a newer, four-door, dark blue car with a console between the front seats. It had an automatic transmission with the shift lever located in the center console area, a luggage rack on the trunk, and a light-blue cloth interior with darker vinyl trim.

After he stopped the car the man got into the back seat with the boy and assaulted him. Jared wiped his mouth on his sweatshirt sleeve several times during the incident, and in doing so, secured the evidence that one day would positively identify his abductor.

When the assault was over the man returned to the front seat by way of the center console. He took the boy's snowsuit, wiped it off, and then returned it to the boy. He kept his size 14 stonewashed Lee jeans and his underwear on the front seat. The driver drove off back toward Cold Spring and dropped the boy off near Bell's Hill on Highway 158. He threatened Jared on the way back to town, warning him that he was lucky to be alive, and that if the police received a good lead on him as a suspect he would "get him after school and shoot him."[27]

When the man stopped the car near Cold Spring, he ordered Jared to get out and roll around in the snow to wipe his snowmobile suit off. After that, he ordered him to run home and to not look back or he would be shot. As soon as Jared got home and walked in the door, his mother could see something was terribly wrong.

She called the police and an investigation began immediately. Jared was able to give investigators a full description of the vehicle and his abductor. He estimated the man to be in his thirties, a white male, standing about 5'6" to 5'7" tall, and weighing about 170 pounds. He had dark medium-length hair, brown eyes, fat ears that stuck out a little, a fat nose, bushy eyebrows, and rough, dark skin. He had a bit of a "beer belly" and spoke in a deep raspy voice. The man was wearing camouflage fatigues, black Army boots, a military-style watch, a dark-colored zippered vest, and a brown baseball cap.[28]

Three days after Jared's abduction, on the morning of January 16, 1989, Stearns County Deputy Zieglmeier contacted Detective Doug Pearce and advised him that he had gained information about a possible suspect in the kidnapping. Zieglmeier identified the possible suspect as Danny James Heinrich, of nearby Paynesville. He informed Pearce that Heinrich drove a 1987 dark blue, four-door Mercury Topaz. Other descriptive factors of the car were consistent with the vehicle that Jared had described. What was unclear was how Detective Zieglmeier came across the information about Heinrich, but it is believed to have originated from the Paynesville Police Department, as they had apparently identified Heinrich as a suspect in the Paynesville assault cluster.[29]

Zieglmeier contacted Pearce again that day to notify him that he had learned that Heinrich was in the National Guard unit based in Willmar, Minnesota, and that he was known to frequently wear military fatigues. Heinrich's physical description at the time was that he was 5'5" tall, weighed 160 pounds, and had brown eyes and brown-colored hair. Detective Pearce was later able to confirm that Danny Heinrich was indeed a member of the National Guard unit based in Willmar.

There is no published information about where Heinrich attended meetings that were mandated following his 1986 DWI conviction, but it is interesting to note that there was an AA meeting in downtown Cold Spring on January 13, 1989, just a couple blocks away, and an hour and a half before the abduction and assault of Jared.

On January 17, 1989, Detective Pearce gathered six photographs of various men whose physical builds and characteristics were similar to what Jared had described. One of the photographs was a current photo of Daniel Heinrich. Pearce asked Jared to view the photographs and asked him to identify anyone from the photos who looked like his attacker. He identified Heinrich and one other man as resembling his abductor.[30]

Danny Heinrich was employed at Master Mark Industries at the time of Jared's abduction. On January 18, 1989, five days after the incident, Detectives Pearce and Leland drove to Master Mark and looked at Heinrich's vehicle, a 1987 Mercury Topaz. The detectives matched up the license plate number with motor vehicle records to confirm the car belonged to Heinrich. They noted that the interior of the car appeared to be gray-colored and found there was no luggage rack on the trunk of the vehicle. That was a detail that represented a significant difference from Jared's account of his abductor's car. Despite the strong circumstantial evidence that Heinrich was involved in Jared's kidnapping, and the suggestion from law enforcement that Heinrich should be looked at as a suspect, investigators in Jared's case apparently failed to question Danny Heinrich.[31]

Cold Spring Police and Stearns County investigators continued to seek information to identify Jared's abductor. There was a pair of published stories in the *Cold Spring Record* about Jared's assault in February 1989, an article in the *Paynesville Press*, and a front-page story in the *St. Cloud Times*. All the articles featured a sketch of the abductor, a physical description of the car he drove, a physical description of the man, and also announced a Crimestoppers reward for information leading to the man's conviction. Although the case remained very active, there was no additional information released for several months.

In July or August 1989, more than six months after Jared's abduction, a man in a light tan van attempted to abduct a nine-year old boy, Andrew, in the Township of St. Joseph, near Kraemer Lake. The incident occurred just off of County Highway 2, which links Cold Spring to St. Joseph. The man in that case was described as a white male in his late twenties, with dark brown hair, dark eyes, a slender build and a fair complexion. The man had a mole on his forehead, and in a manner similar to the assailant's behavior in the Paynesville incidents, he asked Andrew to tell him his age.

Nineteen eighty-nine was a very stressful year for Danny Heinrich. He was having financial problems and lost his 1987 Mercury Topaz to repossession in March. Knowing that he had problems dealing with his parents' divorce a few years earlier, the news of his mother's engagement to another man would have been an understandable source of significant stress to Heinrich. His mother remarried in May 1989. Heinrich lost a grandmother in July.

To cap it all off, he lost his job at Fingerhut in St. Cloud on October 8, 1989. The company was just finishing up a high technology distribution center, but was facing several market-based challenges simultaneous to their rapid expansion. The facility had announced the layoff of several white-collared workers in September, and the dismissal of blue-collar workers would soon follow.

In 1989, Heinrich had split time between living in his mother's apartment in Paynesville and his father's home on Lake Koronis, three miles east of Paynesville. On October 12, 1989, the home of one of Howard Heinrich's neighbors caught fire. It was the home of Roger and Kathy Larsen, and it was just down the road from Heinrich's place on State Highway 55. The fire was investigated as an arson fire.

On the night of October 22, 1989, just ten days after the Larsen fire and exactly two weeks after Heinrich lost his job at Fingerhut, Jacob Wetterling was kidnapped from a dark, dead-end road just south of the small town of St. Joseph.

On the morning after Jacob's abduction, investigators used a bloodhound to track Jacob's scent up the Rassier driveway. At that point, Jacob's last footprints were found adjacent to tire tracks and another set of unknown footprints. Plaster casts of the tire and shoe prints were made. Investigators keyed on those tire tracks, and there was enough detail in the tread prints that they were able to exclude a suspicious car that had been abandoned near Lake Owasso, on the basis of that car's tire tread prints not matching those left behind at the scene of Jacob's abduction.

Recalling that Stearns County Deputy Robert Zieglmeier had suggested that Danny Heinrich be considered a suspect in Jared's abduction and assault in January, Stearns County jailers came forward to Stearns County investigators immediately after Jacob Wetterling's abduction, reiterating their belief that Heinrich should be looked at for Jacob's case. One jailer cited Heinrich's unusual behavior during the times he was in and out of the Stearns County jail for prior offenses. Heinrich was noted as a loner and acted very strange when other prisoners or jail officers attempted to interact with him.[32]

Wetterling investigators revealed very early on that they had made an unspecified connection between Jacob's abduction and Jared's abduction and assault in January 1989. The "sure link" between the cases that investigators often referred to vaguely, without mentioning specifics, was that in both cases the abductor had grabbed the boys' penis over their clothing. That had also been a common element of most of the Paynesville cases between 1986 and 1988.

There were many differences between Jacob's and Jared's abduction. The most paramount of those differences, of course, was that Jacob was never seen or heard from again. The other key variations between the incidents were that the man in Jacob's case wore a nylon mask, used a gun, and left witnesses behind—Aaron Larson and Trevor Wetterling. They were able to give a basic description of Jacob's abductor. He was said to be about 5'9" to 5'10" tall, weighing approximately 180 pounds and spoke in a low, rough voice, as though he had a cold or was a smoker. He was wearing dark pants, a dark coat, and dark shoes.

Danny James Heinrich started a new job working at North Star Mailing in St. Cloud on November 12, 1989. It had been exactly three weeks since Jacob Wetterling's abduction, and five weeks since Heinrich's last day of work at Fingerhut. Coincidentally, an arsonist struck another Lake Koronis area home that same day—November 12, 1989. It was the home of Wayne and Arlene Jude that burned down that day. The family had been away from home for the weekend. The fire was investigated as an arson and it was determined that the fire started in the basement. The home showed evidence of being burglarized prior to being set on fire. In an unusual twist, the Jude home was located right next door to the Larsen home, which had burned on October 12, 1989, exactly one month earlier.[33]

Two FBI agents interviewed Danny Heinrich on December 16, 1989. Heinrich admitted to investigators that he had been arrested a couple of times for burglary and had two DWI convictions. He was not able to provide an alibi for either January 13, 1989, or October 22, 1989, but he did suggest to the investigators that he was probably doing laundry or visiting a friend. Investigators learned that Heinrich had moved out of his mother's apartment in Paynesville and had been living in his father's home on Lake Koronis since November 30, 1989. He said that he had been driving a 1975 gray-colored Ford Granada since losing his Mercury Topaz in March 1989, and when he bought his then-current car, a blue, two-door 1982 Ford EXP, he sold the Granada to his mother. Heinrich told the investigators he had no knowledge of the abductions of Jared or Jacob Wetterling. He also denied ever wearing his military fatigues or Army boots when he wasn't on Guard duty. He said the Guard frowned upon wearing that gear while off duty.[34]

Paynesville Police Chief Robert Schmiginsky told Wetterling Task Force investigators on January 8, 1990, that the city of Paynesville had experienced a period of molestation incidents in the late 1980s, and that he believed Danny Heinrich should be considered a suspect in those cases. He told the Wetterling investigators that there had been several incidents of an adult male fitting Heinrich's description groping or chasing juvenile boys. Paynesville police had never made an arrest in those cases but Heinrich appeared to have been a prime suspect.[35]

The FBI interviewed Heinrich again on January 12, 1990. He was wearing a pair of tennis shoes during the interview and admitted to investigators that it was the only pair of tennis shoes he owned and that he had purchased them at *Sears* about a year before. He gave his shoes to the investigators so they could perform tests on them. Three days later, on January 15, 1990, Heinrich surrendered the rear tires on his blue 1982 Ford EXP. He told the investigators he had purchased the Ford EXP in September 1989, a month before the abduction.

On January 15, 1989, Detective Pearce obtained documents that indicated Heinrich had purchased the 1987 Mercury Topaz on March 10, 1988. The car had been repossessed on March 15, 1989.[36]

Detective Pearce was able to track down and contact the people who had bought the 1987 Mercury. The new owners of the car voluntarily drove it to the Stearns County Sheriff's Office on January 16, 1990. Pearce brought Jared into the Sheriff's office to view the vehicle. Jared sat inside the Topaz for a few minutes and agreed that the car "felt like" the car he had been kidnapped in, and he said he "wouldn't change a thing about the car's interior." When asked to rate the Topaz on a scale of 1 to 10, with a 10 being the most similar to the car he was taken in, he rated it as an 8 or a 9.[37]

Detective Pearce collected back seat and carpet fiber samples from the Mercury Topaz formerly owned by Heinrich on January 18, 1990. The samples were retained for testing against fibers from the clothing Jared wore during the January 13, 1989, assault.

On January 24, 1990, investigators executed a search warrant on the home owned by Howard Heinrich, located at 16021 County Road 124, east of Paynesville. Danny's younger brother, Tommy, had told investigators that Danny had been living in the basement of his father's house since November 30, 1989. Officials seized a number of items from Heinrich's home including a black portable police scanner carrying case, lists of police scanner frequencies and user manuals, a pair of black lace-up boots, two brown caps, a Radio Shack scanner frequency book, and a pay stub from Fingerhut dated October 8, 1989. They also confiscated a brown vest, a Regency programmable handheld scanner, and a six-channel Regency scanner.

Danny Heinrich was interviewed during the January 24 search. He was again unable to provide an alibi for the night of October 22, 1989, telling investigators that he was probably at his mother's apartment on Washburne Avenue in Paynesville. He told them that he would typically spend his Sundays driving around town, doing laundry, or watching a movie. He denied being in St. Joseph that night or any time that weekend. It was noted that Heinrich's bottom row of teeth had black spots in the front due to many years of chewing tobacco. Heinrich produced six photographs of children during the search. Three of the photos appeared to be of school-age children and were marked with the name "Wurm." Heinrich claimed that the photos were of youths from the Twin Cities, and that he had met them while he was a patient at the Willmar Regional Treatment Center. Two of the other photos were of young males in various states of undress, and the last photo was of three fully clothed children.[38]

Officers intended to seize the photos but Heinrich objected, stating they shouldn't be taking photographs solely on the basis that "they just don't look right." The photos were left at the home, but in subsequent interviews with investigators Heinrich said that he burned the photos because they "looked bad" and were "no kind of pictures to have anyway."[39]

It is interesting to note that January 24, 1990, the day the search warrant was executed at the Heinrich home, was also the same date that Duane Allen Hart was arrested and charged with several counts of sexually assaulting juvenile boys.

FBI agents returned to the Heinrich home the next day, January 25, 1990. This time, Danny's father, Howard, was also present. Danny agreed to come to the SCSO the next day to pick up the rear tires that had been removed from his 1982 Ford EXP ten days earlier. Heinrich arrived at the sheriff's office on January 26, 1990, and agreed to participate with five other white males in a physical lineup for Jared to view.

When Jared viewed the lineup, more than a year had passed since he had been kidnapped and assaulted, and he was unable to positively identify any of the men as being the man who had assaulted him. He did identify Heinrich and one other person as being similar to his kidnapper, but he rated Danny as just a 4 on a scale of 1 to 10, and the other man was rated a 7.[40] Photographs of Heinrich demonstrate that his physical appearance fluctuated significantly, even over relatively brief periods of time. It is unknown how significantly Heinrich's appearance changed in the year that passed between the date of Jared's assault and his viewing of the lineup.

On January 26, 1990, the FBI Laboratory called Wetterling investigators and told them that the tires from Heinrich's 1987 Mercury Topaz were consistent with tire impressions that were left at the scene of Jacob Wetterling's abduction. The consistencies were specific to the tread design and size of Heinrich's *Sears Superguard* tires. However, the tires could not be considered a perfect match because there were no distinguishing characteristics or defects in either the tires or the tread marks in the sandy gravel driveway to provide enough evidence to call them a match.[41]

The January 30, 1990, issue of the *Paynesville Press* carried a front-page article about the arrest of Duane Allen Hart. The article again referenced the ongoing investigation of the assaults of the young boys in Paynesville. That issue marked the fifth time that the *Paynesville Press* had published an article about the assaults or attempted kidnappings of young boys in town.

Soon after searching the Heinrich home, investigators began making a connection between Heinrich and the fires that had been set in the neighborhood after Jacob's abduction. FBI Special Agent Eric Odegard interviewed James Wurm on February 5, 1990. The name had appeared on at least one photograph that was found in Danny Heinrich's possession during the January 24, 1990, search. Wurm told the investigator that two of his sons would often visit the home of Wayne and Arlene Jude, whose home had burned on November 12, 1989. Arlene Jude was James Wurm's sister. Wurm recalled that Tommy Heinrich would sometimes play football with his sons while visiting the Jude home. Danny Heinrich would be there also, but would only watch the boys playing, according to Wurm. He also noted that the Jude home had been burglarized in about 1984 or 1985, and again on the day of the house fire. Wurm showed Agent Odegard some photographs of his sons from 1980. It was then that Odegard realized the boys in the photos resembled boys that were seen in the photographs that were in Danny Heinrich's possession.[42]

The information about the photographs led investigators to more carefully consider the arson fire at the Jude home, and a possible tie to Jacob Wetterling's kidnapping. However, the relevance of the arson fires at the Jude and Larsen homes were likely of more value from a behavioral analysis standpoint than they would be in terms of evidence in Jacob's case. If Heinrich had burned Jacob's body in the Jude home, as some suspected, evidence of a body would probably have been found during the subsequent arson investigation.

FBI investigators arrested Danny Heinrich for probable cause for the kidnapping and assault of Jared, on February 9, 1990, more than a year after the January 1989 incident. The consistency between the fibers found in Heinrich's car, and on the snow pants that Jared wore the night of his assault, was the basis for the arrest. As described in Al Garber's book, *Striving To Be The Best*, the interview room was staged with furniture, special lights, and a flag. Heinrich told the investigators that he was not guilty of Jared's assault and that he was being framed. Heinrich demanded an attorney and refused to speak to investigators any further. He was subsequently released without being charged.

Of significant interest with regard to Heinrich's 1990 arrest was the apparent dissent between investigating agencies. The FBI moved forward with the arrest without consulting with the BCA and against advice from the Stearns County Attorney's office. Garber notes that the Stearns County district attorney was furious that Heinrich had been arrested prematurely.[43]

One day short of the anniversary of Danny Heinrich's arrest, on February 8, 1991, investigators returned to Heinrich all of the property that had been seized during the January 24, 1990, execution of the search warrant on his father's home.

On April 2, 1991, Paynesville police officer Stephen Lehmkuhl requested assistance from the SCSO. City residents had complained about a strange man driving a tan-colored vehicle that had been witnessed following boys on their newspaper delivery routes. A Stearns County deputy was dispatched to perform surveillance and he observed a tan-colored 1984 Buick driven by Danny Heinrich. Heinrich appeared to be following a paperboy through the downtown area. The deputy noted that although it appeared that Heinrich was stalking newspaper boys, he did not have probable cause to pull him over. The deputy wrote a report but no further action was taken.[44]

According to court records, there was no further contact between Wetterling investigators and Danny Heinrich for more than twenty years. It was as if he had disappeared from the investigative radar with regard to the Jacob Wetterling kidnapping.

The only references to Heinrich that would come in the years to follow came from media sources, and those sources never mentioned Heinrich by name. The first reference to Heinrich came in

1995, when WCCO reported on search warrants that had been executed on several Wetterling suspects during the early days of the investigation. Stearns County officials thought the warrants were sealed but those seals had unknowingly expired. One of those warrants was apparently for Danny Heinrich, a man who had not been cleared in the case.

The second media reference to Heinrich came a year later when WCCO interviewed him. Heinrich was not identified, nor is his face seen in the video, but his voice can be heard denying he had anything to do with Jacob's abduction. He recounted that investigators had confronted him, saying, "We know it's you, it's you, it's you!" Heinrich said that he countered with "No it isn't, no it isn't, no it isn't."[45]

Heinrich told WCCO that he had failed a lie detector test when questioned about Jacob Wetterling's abduction in 1990, and that he refused to take a second test. He told the reporter that he didn't keep track of where he was the night of Jacob's abduction but that he was probably at home. Heinrich said that he was aware that he was under surveillance for months following Jacob's abduction.

"It was pure hell," Heinrich said as he described the pressure on him while under surveillance. "There is nothing I can tell them. I have no information whatsoever. That's the truth."[46]

The drinking incidents from the mid–1980s as described by Chris Larsen, and the possible link between Heinrich and the Larsen home arson in October 1989, were not the last times that Heinrich and the Larsens would cross each other's paths. Larsen's parents bought Heinrich's dark blue 1982 Ford EXP from his driveway for $1,000 a few years later. The Larsens scrapped the car in 2007 after it was involved in an accident. Little did they know that that car would draw some unwanted attention decades later, as Wetterling investigators would zero in once again on Danny Heinrich.[47]

On July 18, 2012, a Minnesota BCA report revealed that a DNA profile had been obtained from Jared's snow pants, sweatshirt, and t-shirt. The DNA results showed the presence of a DNA mixture of two or more individuals. Jared could not be excluded as a contributor to the DNA mixture, and that would naturally be expected since Jared had worn the clothing that was tested. What investigators were most interested in was the presence of a predominant male profile that did not match Jared's DNA. The results were solid—99.5 percent of the general population could be excluded from the profile, meaning whoever had left that DNA was Jared's abductor. If investigators could match that profile to a suspect they would have their man.[48]

What is particularly interesting about the July 2012 DNA report, is that it is indicative that investigators had been actively looking at Jared's case in connection to Jacob's, long before Robert Dudley or Joy Baker had begun researching Jared's case or the Paynesville incidents in 2013. In fact, there are references in court documents that appear to suggest that investigators had been making an effort to obtain the DNA profile for some time.

Nearly two years later, on March 5, 2014, investigators received laboratory DNA profiling results for samples taken from the blue hat that had been left behind after the May 17, 1987, Paynesville incident. The results indicated a mixture of DNA from three or more individuals on the baseball cap.[49]

Hair samples had been taken from Danny Heinrich during the execution of a January 1990 search warrant. On May 12, 2015, the FBI submitted those hair samples to the BCA for evaluation. The BCA laboratory determined the samples were suitable for nuclear DNA testing. The results came back on July 10, 2015. The DNA results from Heinrich's hair samples were a match to the previously unknown male DNA profile that had been found on Jared's clothing. For the first time, investigators had indisputable proof of the identity of Jared's abductor, as the DNA results excluded all persons other than Danny Heinrich.[50]

In July of 2015, Heinrich's DNA was also tested against the hat from the May 17, 1987, Paynesville assault. Heinrich could not be excluded as a contributor to one of the three DNA profiles that were recovered from the hat. While not conclusive, the results indicated that 80.5 percent of the general population could be excluded as being contributors to the DNA.

Investigators used the DNA results as the basis to obtain a search warrant for Danny Heinrich's home in Annandale. The "sure link" between Jacob Wetterling's kidnapping and Jared's kidnapping and assault appeared to be more certain than ever once investigators had the combination of Heinrich's tire and shoe prints in the Rassier driveway, and evidence that Heinrich's DNA was present on Jared's clothing.

With a search warrant in hand, investigators raided the home of Danny Heinrich at 55 Myrtle Avenue South in the city of Annandale, Minnesota on July 28, 2015. The application for a search warrant, filed with the Tenth District Court of Minnesota, gave significant insight as to what investigators were hoping to find when they searched Heinrich's home. The most substantial items related to the Jacob Wetterling kidnapping listed in the warrant application included Jacob himself, alive or dead, and including any bones, dental work, hairs, or biological samples. Also listed were the items of clothing that Jacob was known to be wearing at the time of his abduction.

The application also listed any indications of residence or the whereabouts of Heinrich for January 13, 1989, and/or October 22, 1989. They were looking for human hair, a wallet, knives, a silver gun, hand-held police scanners, clothing, a military style watch, computers and computer files, electronic devices, email files, and deleted computer files. In short, investigators were looking for anything and everything that could link Heinrich to Jacob Wetterling, Jared, or the Paynesville assault cases. They were also looking for any evidence of possession or distribution of child pornography.

Stearns County Attorney Janelle Kendall left no doubt as to what investigators were seeking when they entered Danny Heinrich's home on July 28, 2015.

"We searched his house because we were looking for Jacob Wetterling," Kendall declared. "The search warrant that we used to search the house is a fully public document, and that's everything there is to know. That's it. The good news and the bad news is, that's all of it."[51]

Among other things, investigators found nineteen three-ring binders filled with pages of child pornography during the search. Although they were looking primarily for items related to Jacob Wetterling's abduction, they were also seeking anything they could find related to Jared's assault and the Paynesville cluster of assaults from the late 1980s. Due to statutes of limitations laws, those cases could never be tried even if clear evidence linking Heinrich to those crimes was found. However, investigators knew that prosecutors would be able to use evidence in those crimes as consideration during any future sentencing hearings related to other charges.

A three-page receipt and inventory of items removed from Heinrich's home included a total of 55 itemized pieces of evidence. Some of the more interesting items included several keys to unidentified locks, a State of Minnesota driver's license of Heinrich's that had expired in 1991, sixteen photographs of children in a plastic tote, boxes of film negatives, a Huawei cell phone, two handheld scanners, dozens and dozens of VHS tapes and DVDs, two Ambico super telephoto lenses, military camouflage pants and shirt, and four clear totes of boys' athletic clothing.[52]

One item of note that had been on the inventory list originally was a pair of blue sweatpants, size 32 × 34. That item was crossed off the inventory list and included a notation that the sweatpants were sent to the BCA on July 28, 2015. Perhaps the pants and other items were sent in for laboratory testing?

Several other items were found during the search but were not listed on the inventory of materials confiscated from Heinrich's home. There were knives, Nazi memorabilia, a pair of silver handcuffs, and duct tape. Investigators were not able to find the silver handgun they were looking for, but one of Heinrich's homemade videos appeared to have been a video tour of his home. In the video Heinrich is shown opening the door to a safe, and inside the safe was a gun. The video focused on the gun, which appeared to be loaded.[53]

Videotapes found in Heinrich's home indicated that Heinrich had recorded hours of video footage of young boys delivering newspapers, riding bicycles, playing on public playgrounds, and participating in sports activities. In some of the videos, Heinrich could be seen putting money on the ground with the video camera positioned in such a way that when a boy bent over to pick up the money the camera would be pointing at the boy's buttocks. Investigators noted that Heinrich sexualized the subjects in the homemade videos in several ways. For example, the videos would focus and zoom in on the buttocks and genital areas of the boys that were videotaped. Other photos in Heinrich's possession were converted into still images and had sexually charged phrases superimposed on them. Most of the images were of boys, but Heinrich's collection did include some photos of juvenile girls as well.[54]

Investigators also found recordings of news reports about Jacob Wetterling's abduction as well as reports about other missing children. FBI behavioral analysis suggests that violent criminals such as child molesters often keep close tabs on the investigation and tend to keep newspaper clippings and videos as precious mementos.

The three-ring binders that were seized from Heinrich's home contained multiple images of prepubescent children that appeared to fit the definition of child pornography. Some of the photos were printed from online websites and included the source website's URL information. Some of the images seemed to be labeled with phrases that indicated an interest in blond-haired boys. A review of what Agent Ball described as "only a small portion of the binders" was compared against a national database of known victims of sexual abuse and it was determined that some of the pictures were identified as known victims of child exploitation.[55]

Investigators found images in Heinrich's collection that indicated he engaged in the practice of morphing, whereby images of children are converted into child pornography through the use of computer technology. An example of morphed images that were found included copying the head of a child from a non-sexual image and superimposing that image onto another image that portrays child pornography. From information contained within the criminal complaint, it was alleged that Heinrich morphed several images of boys from Paynesville High School yearbooks from the 1970s. The complaint specifies that 1970s images of a juvenile boy, identified only as "Victim K," were morphed onto several pornographic images. An examination of Heinrich's computer revealed that Heinrich had made online searches for "Victim K." Investigators were able to identify at least three other juvenile boys whose photos had been morphed into child pornographic images found in Heinrich's possession.[56]

Further examination of Heinrich's computer usage found that he had used Internet search terms such as "1976 7th grade class photos," "Kids Christmas photos 1978," "2013 7th grade wrestling photos," "Boys in Toughskins jeans photos," "Paynesville Minnesota school photos," and more.[57]

Heinrich was present for the July 28, 2015, search of his home and he spoke with investigators during the search. He admitted that he had "child porn" and suggested that investigators would find materials that would be "pretty damning." When confronted about pictures of juvenile boys in the three-ring binders, he told investigators that he might have downloaded the pictures from the Internet "years ago" when he had Internet access. He said he printed the images to conserve storage capacity on his computer hard drive. He proclaimed himself to be "addicted" to child pornography when he had Internet access and referred to himself as a "dirty old man."[58]

Shortly after the search of Heinrich's home, investigators were able to recover Heinrich's silver handgun that they had been looking for. It was a snub-nose .38 caliber Smith & Wesson.

On October 27, 2015, St. Cloud-based FBI Special Agent Shane Ball filed a criminal complaint in United States District Court for the arrest of Daniel James Heinrich. In the criminal complaint, Agent Ball noted that statements in the affidavit were based on his investigation and information provided from other FBI special agents. He also noted that the affidavit did not include all the known facts concerning the investigation, but only those facts necessary to establish probable cause for Heinrich's arrest. Ball's wording in the complaint seemed to suggest a contradiction to Janelle Kendall's statement that the warrants contained all there was to know about Heinrich.

Daniel James Heinrich was arrested at home on Wednesday October 28, 2015, and a news conference announcing Heinrich's arrest was held at 2:00 P.M. on Thursday October 29, 2015—26 years and one week after Jacob Wetterling's abduction. The news conference was a joint effort between the U.S. Attorney's Office, the FBI, the Minnesota BCA, and the SCSO.

The press conference provided a summary of five counts of child pornography charges that had been filed against Danny Heinrich. While authorities stated that Danny Heinrich had been identified as a person of interest in Jacob's abduction, they repeatedly cautioned that Heinrich had not been charged with any crime related to Jacob's case, and that the investigation remained open and active. U.S. Attorney Andrew Luger said that Danny Heinrich had denied any involvement in Jacob Wetterling's kidnapping.

"Let me be very clear," Luger told the media. "The defendant has denied any involvement in the disappearance of Jacob Wetterling and is not charged at this time with any crime related to that disappearance."[59]

Luger added that investigators were actively pursuing Heinrich and encouraged the public to contact police with any information.

"I would strongly encourage anyone with knowledge of Danny Heinrich's activities during the late 1980s or early 1990s to make contact with our investigators," Luger said. "Even if you don't believe that information is relevant, please let our investigators make that determination."[60]

When the press conference was opened to questions from reporters, the first question asked was whether it was true that Danny Heinrich was known in 1989 to drive a dark-colored four-door car, wear camouflage clothing, owned handheld police scanners, and spoke in a deep, raspy voice. The question was strikingly similar to how Duane Hart had described Danny Heinrich in the Hart Notes that had been drafted by a private investigator in February 1990. Those same notes indicated that Hart had abused Danny Heinrich when he was a minor. Multiple media reports in November 2015 confirmed that Duane Hart did abuse Danny Heinrich. If Danny Heinrich was indeed the man responsible for Jacob's and Jared's abduction, and for the Paynesville incidents, then it would seem that Heinrich had continued the cycle of abuse. Ironically, that is the very same cycle of abuse that had been the bedrock of the teachings of the Jacob Wetterling Foundation for years.

The criminal complaint against Heinrich clearly stated that investigators went to Heinrich's home in July 2015 looking for evidence relating to Jared's kidnapping and assault, and Jacob Wetterling's abduction. The complaint summarized Jared's abduction and assault as well as Jacob's abduction. It confirmed that investigators had found a set of shoe impressions that were similar to shoes worn by Jacob at the time of his abduction. The complaint further detailed the consistency between the tire tread pattern and tire size found at the scene of the crime and the rear tires from Danny Heinrich's car. Heinrich's right shoe corresponded in size and design to an impression found at the abduction site. Agent Ball explained that the consistent tire and shoe prints could not constitute an exact match because such a match would require the presence of a unique scuff, wear mark, or divot in the items themselves, and no such unique markings were present. Ball concluded, however, that the non-unique "class characteristics" of size, shoe pattern and tread pattern of each appeared to be the same.[61]

Agent Ball's criminal complaint also referenced the January 24, 1990, search of Howard Heinrich's home. He specified the items of Danny Heinrich's clothing that were consistent with what Jared had described his assailant wearing. The complaint also referenced photos of a boy dressed in underwear and a boy coming out of the shower wrapped in a towel.

Following Danny Heinrich's arrest, Stearns County Attorney Janelle Kendall confirmed what few media outlets had acknowledged prior to Heinrich's arrest, and what most of the general public had been unaware of, that the Paynesville cases had been investigated since the beginning, well before those incidents became publicized again in 2014.

"The Paynesville cluster, as we've referred to it for years," Kendall said, "there isn't proof beyond a reasonable doubt who did that."[62]

The Paynesville cases could never be prosecuted even if the search of Heinrich's home turned up evidence of his involvement in those incidents because the statute of limitations on those cases had expired years earlier. In fact, despite the 100 percent DNA match linking Danny Heinrich to Jared's assault, that case could not be prosecuted either, again due to statute of limitations established by legislation. The statute in Jared's case expired in 1998. The statute of limitations was extended in 2000 due to advancements of modern DNA technology being reflected in new legislation. However, that new legislation could not bridge the gap between the 1998 expiration of the statute of limitations and the law change in 2000.[63]

Despite the fact that Jared's case and the Paynesville cases could never be prosecuted, Kendall pointed out that it was still relevant for investigators to find evidence of Heinrich's involvement in those cases. If investigators could prove that Heinrich was involved in any or all of those incidents, that evidence could be used when considering sentencing of Heinrich for any other crimes he would be convicted of during future court proceedings.[64]

Kendall's comments about the Paynesville cases being investigated for years echoed what Stearns County Sheriff John Sanner had said several times since the renewed interest in the Paynesville cases, that the Paynesville cluster of assaults had been investigated many times over the years.

"That's not new," Sanner said of the Paynesville cases and their possible connection to Jacob Wetterling's abduction. "That's been looked at many, many different times."[65]

Sanner also seemed to downplay the significance of the Hart Notes that had resurfaced in the summer of 2014. He said investigators had the notes years ago, and added that "they don't tell us anything we didn't already know."[66]

Media speculation from May 2014 and through 2015 implied that the Paynesville cases had never been investigated, and many in the general public seemed to buy into that speculation. While it's true that the media frenzy about the Paynesville cases led to more victims coming forward to tell their stories, none of that changed the fact that the Paynesville cluster had been investigated by the Paynesville Police Department since 1986, and by the SCSO since at least January 1989, and by the Minnesota BCA and the FBI immediately after Jacob Wetterling's kidnapping. In fact, investigators had identified Danny Heinrich as a suspect in those cases, as well as Jared's and Jacob's cases, more than twenty-six years before investigators arrested him on October 28, 2015.

Stearns County officials repeatedly said that all of these stories that had come out during the latter half of 2014 and 2015 had been known all along by investigators. Heinrich, the Paynesville cluster of assaults, the Hart Notes—all of it was known to Stearns County for many years. The *Paynesville Press* had run no less than a handful of front-page stories about the Paynesville assaults. The very first article, in 1987, directed tipsters to call Crimestoppers, a Stearns County crime program, with information. That is a strong indication that the Paynesville Police Department had enlisted the help of Stearns County from the very beginning of those cases.

All of this further suggests that it was the FBI's involvement in the case that finally propelled the decades-old case toward resolution.

Danny Heinrich made a court appearance on November 4, 2015. Federal Magistrate Judge Tony Leung listened to prosecutors and witnesses who described the evidence found in Heinrich's home on July 28, 2015. During the testimony of FBI Agent Shane Ball, Judge Leung halted proceedings to ask Ball why investigators were focused on Danny Heinrich. Ball explained that investigators had decided to review the entire Wetterling case a year ago, and by November they had decided to focus their attention on Heinrich.

"When we got into Mr. Heinrich, it wasn't clear why we weren't still looking at him as a suspect," Ball told Judge Leung.[67]

Judge Leung ordered Heinrich to remain in custody at the Sherburne County Jail pending trial. Leung relied on FBI Agent, Shane Ball's testimony and concluded that Heinrich represented a danger to the community. The evidence "creates a chilling context and a gravity of danger to the community," Judge Leung said of Daniel Heinrich. "(He has a) long history of attraction and fixation on young boys."[68]

Although it would take several months for the information to surface, Danny Heinrich apparently mentioned another man's name while being transported by U.S. Marshals between the courthouse and the Sherburne County Jail. The man, who was about Heinrich's age, had lived in Hawick, Minnesota at the time of Jacob's abduction. While some media speculated behind the scenes that this unnamed man might have been an accomplice of Heinrich's, the man had an alibi for the night that Jacob was kidnapped. It was more likely that the man may have had information about Heinrich, or perhaps he unknowingly held evidence in the case.

On December 16, 2015, U.S. Attorney Andrew Luger announced

an indictment against Danny James Heinrich, amending the original charges to include an additional twenty counts of child pornography. That brought the total number of federal charges against Heinrich to twenty-five.

Heinrich's trial on the federal pornography charges was scheduled for July 11, 2016, in Minneapolis. He pleaded not guilty to the child pornography charges during a February 22, 2016, court appearance. Heinrich continued to deny involvement in the kidnapping of Jacob Wetterling. Investigators were presumably continuing to interview Danny Heinrich and working to get him to confess to the kidnapping of Jacob Wetterling. A criminal conviction on the substantial slate of child pornography charges facing Heinrich would likely mean that Heinrich would spend at least twenty years in prison. Getting a confession from Heinrich would be problematic for prosecutors because Heinrich would have no incentive to confess, unless the prosecution agreed to a reduction of charges, or perhaps offered immunity in Jacob's case. Since the pornography charges were filed in federal court, prosecutors' only other source of leverage may be in negotiating a more favorable prison site, should Heinrich be convicted on the pornography charges.

Pam Jensen, who had been Stearns County's lead detective on the Wetterling investigation since 1999, retired in January 2016. Long-time Sheriff Deputy Bruce Bechtold replaced Jensen as the lead investigator on the case. That change in leadership brought Bechtold full circle, as he was the first officer on the scene of when Jacob Wetterling was taken.

11

Answers in the Sand

I just remember generally that he was a strange type person. But there were a lot of strange type people around.[1]—Al Garber, following the arrest of Danny Heinrich

A substantial volume of information was released to the public following the October 2015 arrest of Danny Heinrich. But none of it was new information to investigators. What the world came to know soon after Heinrich's arrest, investigators had known all along. Did subsequent generations of investigators simply forget about Heinrich and the strong circumstantial evidence of his connection to all these crimes? How else could investigators leave him behind as a suspect in favor of Dan Rassier or anyone else? How could Heinrich be left free to walk the streets for all these years?

It is quite understandable that, in 1990, there was not sufficient evidence to arrest, charge, and convict Danny Heinrich with any of these crimes. Heinrich was one of several individuals who garnered the attention of the Wetterling Task Force. Former FBI supervisor of the Wetterling investigation, Al Garber, remembered that Heinrich was one of several suspects in Jacob's abduction case.

"I just remember generally that he was a strange type person," Garber said. "But there were a lot of strange type people around. We watched that guy for weeks, 24/7. Really good surveillance team and techniques in hopes of seeing him do something that would make us believe we could get evidence and he never did."[2]

As for why investigators in 1990 could not bring charges against Heinrich, Garber explained they simply didn't have sufficient evidence to do so.

"In my whole career investigating crimes, evidence is what counts," Garber said. "Whatever else that people see—emotions, logic, common sense—that's good, but it's not evidence. So I'm hoping that this is their (Wetterling investigators) first step. They proved other crimes. I'm hoping that they're going to be able to find the evidence that either he (Heinrich) did it, or he didn't do it."[3]

Other legal experts weighed in on the Fall 2015 developments. Former U.S. Attorney Rachel Paulose appreciated that investigators had never stopped in their pursuit of justice in Jacob's case, but she noted that the tire and shoe prints were not enough to bring charges against Heinrich.

"You have to prove your case beyond a reasonable doubt to a jury," Paulose said. "And those two pieces of evidence, clearly the government decided in its own judgment that that would not be sufficient to prove a crime, but secondly we have this question of federal jurisdiction."[4]

Paulose explained that Heinrich would have to have taken Jacob Wetterling across state lines to charge him with the kidnapping in federal court. There were no indications of that happening in court documents.

"The best evidence," Paulose added, "is always a defendant's own incriminating statement or physical evidence. Or, if a witness comes forward with something Heinrich allegedly said or did that would incriminate him. Even if the government doesn't have sufficient evidence to convict, they seem to be painting a picture of evidence to connect Mr. Heinrich to Jacob Wetterling's abduction."[5]

The October 22, 1989, kidnapping case of Jacob Wetterling went viral across the Midwest, the country, and throughout the world. It is a case that has remained on the minds and in the hearts of many, many people ever since. With the widespread and rapid access to instant information that the Internet has brought to the modern world, perhaps future generations will not appreciate the magnitude and depth to which Jacob's story resonated without the aid of the Internet.

"I think people's fascination and horror with this case is it could have happened anywhere," said Stearns County Attorney Janelle

Kendall. "It is very stereotypical of this area of the state, and really the entire country, that if you live in a small town and these sort of things are going on, you know where is safe, and you know where isn't ... that people don't jump out of the bushes and take children. They do ... they did ... and the world is a different place because of that."[6]

But for Dan Rassier, the newly revealed information about Danny Heinrich would surely spur wonder as to why his own name had ever come up at all, if indeed Stearns County had their finger on the pulse of what otherwise appeared to have been long-forgotten evidence. Rassier had been publicly named as a person of interest in Jacob's kidnapping in July 2010, although he had been treated as a suspect by Stearns County for much longer.

When federal investigators released detailed information about Danny Heinrich in November 2015, the most alarming evidence that stood out in Jacob's case was the information about Heinrich's shoeprints and tire prints found in the driveway where Jacob Wetterling was abducted. Jacob's last shoeprint was found right next to Heinrich's shoeprint and tire prints. That information immediately raised questions about how investigators had lost track of Heinrich for so many years. But there was another question, a question about how the disclosure by Kevin Hamilton changed the focus of the Wetterling investigation to abduction on foot, rather than by car.

Investigators knew that Kevin Hamilton only stopped once in the Rassier driveway, at the very end by the paved road, where his headlights were pointing toward the bicycles in the ditch. The car Kevin was driving had new tires that had been purchased locally at a *Goodyear* tire center. The *Goodyear* store was a company store, meaning it only sold *Goodyear* branded tires, which at the time may have included *Goodyear* subsidiaries *Dunlop* and *Kelly* tires. The tires on Danny Heinrich's Ford Exp were known to be *Sears Superguard* tires. Even if the *Sears* tires on Heinrich's car and the tires available at *Goodyear* had matching treads, and that may well be a stretch, their sizes would have had to match as well.

It had been established from the very beginning of the investigation, that the detail in the tire prints left in the Rassier driveway on the night of Jacob's abduction were sufficient enough to rule out specific vehicles in 1989. For example, the abandoned 1987 red Mercury car that was reported at Lake Owasso in October 1989 was ruled out in the case because its tire treads did not match those left at the scene of Jacob's abduction. For the information from Kevin to lead investigators to negate the tires from Heinrich's car, they would have to have determined the treads from the tires of both cars matched.

It should be noted that Kelly Tire did manufacture some models of Sears Superguard tires, so it's reasonable to understand how the tread patterns of Heinrich's Ford EXP might possibly be matched to those of the Grand Prix that Kevin was driving. A match of treads between Kevin's tires and Heinrich's tires is possible, but only if Heinrich's Sears Superguard tires had been manufactured by Kelly Tire. There is, however, another significant point about why the tires stand out, and it has to do with tire size.

The 1982 Ford EXP was equipped with tires sized at 165/80/R13. When matching tire print sizes, the most important number in that description is the first number, 165. It is a measurement of tire width in millimeters. Kevin was driving a Pontiac Grand Prix. Although he could not recall with certainty the year of that car, all model years of the body style of the Grand Prix he was driving were fitted with size 195/75/R14 tires. That difference in tire width is 30 mm, or 1.18 inches—a substantial difference. Absent further explanation from the SCSO, this difference calls into more serious question how Kevin coming forward in 2003 propelled a change in the theory of Jacob's abduction to abduction on foot. To further the point, the difference in wheelbase, or the distance between the tires, between Heinrich's EXP and the Grand Prix is more than 6 inches.

Kevin did not step outside of his car at any time while in the gravel driveway. That detail further calls into question how his presence in the driveway gave investigators reason to eliminate the use of a car in Jacob's abduction. They knew that the footprints that had been found next to Jacob's last known prints were likely those of his abductor. Investigators had long known of a strong link between the tire prints and footprints found at the abduction scene to Daniel James Heinrich.

Another question that had yet to be addressed by investigators or the media had to do with the pursuit of Dan Rassier as a suspect in Jacob's kidnapping, in light of the fact that investigators had long argued that Jacob's and Jared's cases were related. From the very beginning investigators consistently reported their belief that Jacob's abduction and the abduction and assault of Jared in Cold Spring were related crimes. After Dan Rassier was named as a person of interest in the Wetterling case in July 2010, investigators suggested that Rassier had been considered in the investigation all along. Rassier has acknowledged publicly that investigators questioned him many times over the years. His first interrogation was at his place of employment the morning after the abduction. He was questioned again the following Saturday as investigators spent three hours searching his bedroom.

Rassier, however, had a solid alibi for the night that Jared was assaulted, and he has said that he was never questioned about Jared's sexual assault case. Knowing that investigators had connected the two cases from the beginning, and knowing that Rassier was investigated since immediately after Jacob's kidnapping, why wouldn't investigators have questioned him about Jared's case? If Rassier was not considered a top suspect in the beginning, then what was the impetus for investigators to break the "sure link" between the cases, the "sure link" they had maintained from the beginning of the investigation?

People will likely debate the Wetterling investigation for years to come. They'll focus on the mistakes made by investigators over the years. They'll wonder how Danny Heinrich slipped away from the investigative crosshairs for more than two decades.

Again, it is not difficult to understand that back in 1990, there simply was not enough evidence to charge, try, and convict Danny Heinrich. But there was more than enough information and strong circumstantial evidence to not forget Danny Heinrich, and that's exactly what happened.

For all the ups and downs that accompanied the Wetterling investigation over the twenty-six years leading up to Heinrich's arrest, it turned out there were answers in the sand the entire time. But there was an uncomfortable hurdle in the way of justice in the disappearance of Jacob Wetterling, and it's that blurry divide that lies between knowing and proving.

Danny Heinrich's lawyers filed a series of appeals over the summer of 2016. They asked for a change of venue. They asked for statements to be dismissed. They asked for evidence to be dismissed. But as Labor Day weekend quietly approached, Heinrich was ready to talk about what happened on the night of October 22, 1989.

There was only one thing prosecutors could do to finally get answers: they had to offer to drop all but one of the counts of child pornography against Heinrich. And although many among the public would cry foul, and say that they had made a deal with the devil, prosecutors also had to grant him immunity from prosecution for the murder of Jacob Wetterling. In exchange, Heinrich would be required to give a detailed confession of what happened to Jacob Wetterling. He would face a maximum of twenty years in prison, with an opportunity to get out early on good behavior. Upon release, he would be subject to detention in a sex offender treatment facility. He would probably never again walk the world as a free man.

An agreement was reached between prosecutors and Heinrich, but the Wetterling family would have to sign off on it before a court date could be scheduled, and that's what they did.

On September 6, 2016, Heinrich signed the plea agreement in United States District Court in Minneapolis, Minnesota. Then, as agreed upon, Heinrich confessed to a courtroom packed full of Wetterling family, friends, supporters, investigators, lawyers, and reporters.

12

Closure

I told Jacob to turn around, I had to go to the bathroom. He didn't know what I was doing.—Danny Heinrich, during his courtroom confession

Sometime on the evening of October 22, 1989, Danny Heinrich left his apartment at 121 Washburn Avenue in Paynesville, Minnesota. He climbed into his car and headed out of town. He drove northeast on old Highway 23. It had been unseasonably warm that Sunday, so it was a bit unusual that he had with him a long, dark-colored, puffy coat. He probably didn't give much thought to that. He just knew that he had to get out of town that night.

As Heinrich drove out of Paynesville he passed the 400-acre farm that belonged to Arthur Voss. The farm was on the left side of the road, sprawled out along what was known as the pond road. The farm and the surrounding area were covered with a disorganized array of heavy vegetation, jagged tree lines, water, and tall prairie grass. Heinrich knew this area well, for it was this place just north of town along the Crow River that he had often gone to hang out and party with the few friends that he had. He probably didn't plan for it at that moment, but he would be returning to that farm area again that night.

It was October 22, 1989. Heinrich had just lost his job at Fingerhut in St. Cloud two weeks earlier. He had lost his previous car, a dark blue, four-door 1987 Mercury Topaz to repossession in March. During the summer of 1989, his mother, Corrine, had remarried. His grandmother died. It had been a stressful year. He had to get out of Paynesville for the night.

Danny Heinrich was on a mission that night—a mission that he didn't dare attempt to accomplish in Paynesville. The small city had experienced a period of sexual assaults and attempted assaults dating back three years, to 1986. The assaults had been well publicized in the Paynesville Press, and the Paynesville police had been actively investigating those cases. Danny knew that he was suspected of involvement in those assaults, and for that very reason he knew it would be foolish of him to complete tonight's mission in town.

That long, dark, puffy coat wasn't the only unusual item that Danny Heinrich had with him in the car on the night of October 22, 1989. His evil-minded mission compelled him to bring along a flashlight, a mask, a gun, and a pair of silver handcuffs.

As he continued to drive northeast on Highway 23, the road pulled him through the towns of Richmond and Cold Spring. Danny Heinrich knew those towns as well, as he had driven through them daily on his way to and from his job at Fingerhut. But he wouldn't dare complete his mission that night in those places either. His blue-colored 1982 Ford EXP looked too much like his previous car, the blue 1987 Mercury Topaz that he had been driving in Cold Spring on the night of January 13, 1989. That was the car Danny Heinrich owned when he abducted 12-year-old Jared and drove him to a secluded area near Richmond. There, he assaulted the boy before returning him to the cold winter night on the outskirts of Cold Spring. Danny kept the boy's pants and underwear as a souvenir.

Immediately following Jared's abduction, the local newspapers in Cold Spring, St. Cloud, and Paynesville carried articles describing in great detail the car that his abductor had been driving, and the man who had been driving it. The articles included a sketch of the kidnapper, and it looked very much like Heinrich. Within three days of Jared's abduction, Stearns County Detective Doug Pearce was given a tip by a fellow Stearns County deputy, that Danny Heinrich should be considered a suspect in Jared's case. Indeed, detective Pearce followed up on the lead. Pearce and another investigator went to Heinrich's place of employment, Master Mark Industries in Paynesville. They noted that Heinrich's car looked very much like the car that Jared had described. They showed Jared a picture of Heinrich, and he indicated that his kidnapper looked like the man in the picture.

But they didn't talk to Heinrich about the crime. No one interviewed him or put him in a lineup. Danny Heinrich had gotten away with abducting and assaulting a 12-year-old boy.

As Heinrich pulled into Cold Spring, he likely turned left onto Stearns County Highway 2, the shortest route to St. Joseph. Highway 2 passes near Kraemer Lake, where a nine-year-old boy, Andrew, had nearly been abducted just three months earlier. In that case, a man who fit Danny Heinrich's general description, driving a tan-colored van, had asked Andrew his age before trying to force him into the van. Andrew was lucky enough to get away. There were other incidents in the Kraemer Lake area that summer, involving a tan-colored van and a man fitting Danny Heinrich's description. Jared's kidnapping case was just six months past when someone tried to abduct Andrew, but apparently that case was not fresh enough in mind to pique the interest of Stearns County investigators. There was no mention made of Andrew's case in any media, and no warnings issued to Cold Spring or St. Joseph police.

Just about the time that Heinrich was driving into the small, peaceful town of St. Joseph on Highway 75, Jacob Wetterling, Aaron Larson, and Trevor Wetterling were setting out from the Wetterling home for an innocent ride to the Tom Thumb store to rent a movie. Heinrich was a stranger on a mission of evil, and three little boys were on a mission of innocence. In a matter of minutes those two missions would come to a horrific intersection, a fateful and devastating crossing of two worlds.

It was about 9:00 p.m. when Heinrich turned off of Highway 75 in St. Joseph, and headed south on 91st Avenue. He was driving his blue-colored 1982 Ford EXP. It was a small, dark-colored car with headlights close together. Somewhere along that dark, dead end road he met a group of three young boys that were riding into town on a pair of bikes and a scooter. Knowing that the boys would likely be returning the same way, Heinrich turned left onto a sandy gravel driveway. He followed the driveway about 300 yards or so up a gentle hill, and then around to the left as the driveway made a gradual 90-degree turn to the north, and finally down a gentle hill to a cluster of farmhouse buildings. When he got to the end of the driveway up by the house he made a 180-degree turn to the left and drove back out the driveway toward the road.

Dan Rassier was home alone in the farmhouse, working on organizing his record collection. Smokey, the family dog, began barking and alerted him to something going on outside. When Rassier looked out his upstairs bedroom window, he saw a small, dark car, perhaps blue, turning around in his driveway. Smokey stopped barking. Rassier went back to his record collection.

Danny Heinrich parked his car on the sandy gravel driveway, about 75 yards short of 91st Avenue. He lay there in wait, anticipating that the three boys would be biking back soon, from his right hand side. He waited for about twenty minutes and then saw the glimmer of light coming from the flashlight that Trevor Wetterling was carrying. Heinrich put on a pair of gloves, and then a mask. He grabbed the flashlight and his gun, and then walked out to the end of the driveway to confront the three boys.[1]

Jacob Wetterling, Aaron Larson, and Trevor Wetterling were riding back home with a video rental—*The Naked Gun*. They approached the portion of the road where Aaron Larson had heard a rustling in the grass a few minutes before. But now, Aaron heard the shuffle of feet against the gravel driveway instead, and a strange man in black stepped out from the dark.

"Stop! I have a gun," shouted the strange man.

The boys stopped immediately. Both Trevor and Aaron initially thought it was a joke. Trevor pointed his flashlight at the man, and that's when the boys saw that the man had a gun and was wearing a mask. They knew then that this was no joke, that the man was serious. They offered to give him the videotape.

"No, don't do that," Heinrich said, ordering Trevor to shut off the flashlight.

Heinrich knocked the videotape to the ground, and ordered the boys to put their bicycles in the ditch. He told them to lie down on the ground. They complied. He asked them their ages.

Aaron Larson was eleven, Trevor Wetterling said he was ten, and Jacob Wetterling was eleven.

With that, the man ordered Trevor to run off into the woods to the west. "Don't look back, or I'll shoot," he warned. Trevor did as he was told.

Danny Heinrich groped Aaron and Jacob by placing his hand over his clothing, grasping his genitals. He told Aaron to run to the woods, and repeated the same warning he had given to Trevor. Aaron did as he was told.

Heinrich then grabbed Jacob Wetterling by the shoulder and led him up the Rassier driveway to his car. They approached the car on the passenger side, with the car facing 91st Avenue. The abductor opened the car door, put Jacob's hands behind his back, and secured them with the silver pair of handcuffs.[2]

"What did I do wrong?" Jacob asked of his abductor.[3]

Heinrich shoved Jacob into the passenger seat of his car. In stepping into the car against his will, Jacob Wetterling left a clear shoeprint in the sand, perpendicular to the tire prints left by his abductor's car. That shoeprint was the last anyone else would see of Jacob Wetterling for the next twenty-seven years.

After securing Jacob in the car, Heinrich removed his mask, got back into the driver's seat, and drove out of the Rassier driveway. He turned right onto 91st Avenue, and followed it about a mile north to Highway 75. As he turned left on Highway 75, his handheld Regency 50-channel scanner quickly filled the air with the sounds of police activity. The other two boys had called for help, and the SCSO and St. Joseph Police were on their way to the abduction scene. Heinrich ordered Jacob to lean forward in his seat and to put his head down out of view of the windows as they drove through town.

Once they were out of the town of St. Joseph, Heinrich told Jacob he could sit back up. He continued driving northwest, merging onto Interstate Highway 94 West near Collegeville. Within fifteen minutes of kidnapping Jacob Wetterling, Heinrich was fifteen miles away, in Albany, Minnesota. There, he exited the Interstate and headed south on Highway 10, to Roscoe, another fifteen miles away. At Roscoe, Heinrich turned right and headed back toward Paynesville on Highway 23. About a mile north of Paynesville, Heinrich made a right hand turn onto the pond road by the Voss farm. He proceeded a little ways to the west and then turned left into an approach entrance to a field.

Heinrich drove his car up close to a grove of trees. He parked the car, shut off its lights, and got out. He let Jacob out of the passenger side door and removed his handcuffs. Then, he led Jacob over to the line of trees and ordered him to remove his clothing. Jacob did as his abductor ordered. Danny Heinrich also removed his clothing, and assaulted Jacob for twenty to thirty minutes.[4]

"I'm cold," Jacob said, fighting through tears.

"Okay. You can get dressed," Heinrich told Jacob.

Jacob put his clothing back on, and so did his abductor. Heinrich began to lead Jacob back toward the car.

"Are you taking me home?" Jacob asked his abductor.

"I can't take you all the way home," Danny Heinrich explained. "You live a town or so away."

With that, Jacob started to cry.

"Don't cry," the man said.[5]

They were almost back to the car when an awful fate intervened. A police cruiser went speeding out of Paynesville toward the northeast, its emergency lights flashing, but its siren silent. Heinrich got scared and he panicked. The unseasonably warm day suddenly turned very cold. He pulled the silver-colored .38 caliber Smith & Wesson revolver out of his pocket and loaded two bullets into the chamber. Then Heinrich told Jacob to turn around so he could go to the bathroom. Jacob did as he was told.

With Jacob Wetterling facing the away from him, Heinrich raised the gun to the back of Jacob's head and looked away. He pulled the trigger.

Click. Nothing.

The first bullet in the chamber had not lined up with the hammer. Danny Heinrich pulled the trigger a second time. This time the gun went off, but when Danny looked back again he saw that Jacob was still standing. He pulled the trigger a third time, and that second bullet sent Jacob to the ground. He was dead.[6]

Heinrich got back into his car and drove back to his apartment in Paynesville. He waited in his apartment for about two hours, then decided to go back to bury Jacob. He grabbed a collapsible shovel and starting walking along Washburne Avenue, then up along Highway 23.

It was just past midnight when he returned to Jacob's body. He dragged Jacob about 100 yards to the northeast, and tried in vain to dig a hole with his small shovel, but the rocky soil was too difficult to penetrate. Danny remembered that there was a construction company right down the road, so he walked over there to look for a bigger shovel. Instead, he climbed into a Bobcat skid loader, found the keys, and drove it to Jacob's body. The lights were kept turned off as he drove it down the pond road, but he turned them on for a moment to find Jacob's body. He dug a grave with the bucket of the skid loader, then dragged Jacob's body into the grave and covered him with dirt. Jacob was still wearing the red jacket, the blue sweat pants, and the reflective safety vest that he had put on before biking into St. Joseph just a few hours earlier.

Heinrich returned the Bobcat skid loader to where he had found it, and then walked back to Jacob's burial site. He camouflaged the grave with grass and brush, and then noticed that Jacob's Nike tennis shoes had fallen off his feet. He grabbed the shoes and threw them into a ravine as he walked back to his apartment. Jacob Wetterling's killer had buried him in a location that was familiar, a place where he felt comfortable.

About one year later, Heinrich returned to Jacob's grave. He brought with him a garbage bag and a military entrenching tool. Once again, he walked to the site instead of driving. When he arrived he noticed that Jacob's red jacket was sticking out of the ground, and there was Jacob's skull and other bones lying there on the ground too. He picked up all the bones and Jacob's jacket and put them into the garbage bag. He carried the bag across the road and dug a new two-foot deep grave with the entrenching tool. He removed Jacob's jacket from the bag and set it aside. Then he took the bones and put them into the hole, covering them with Jacob's jacket. He covered the grave with dirt.[7]

The next time Heinrich visited Jacob's grave was Wednesday, August 31, 2016. This time, he was wearing a pair of handcuffs, as he led authorities to the location where he had buried Jacob Wetterling.

Authorities found the grave almost immediately, as Heinrich was able to pinpoint the location to within a few feet. They found Jacob's red jacket, but the "St. Cloud Hockey" lettering had decomposed over time. They found bones. Laboratory testing performed the following day revealed that the bones were animal bones. Long sought answers would have to wait one more day.

Investigators returned to the grave on Friday, September 2, 2016. They expanded the search area and found more bones and a skull. Dental records confirmed that the skull was Jacob Wetterling's. On Saturday, authorities would announce that they had confirmed the identity of the remains.

After nearly twenty-seven years, the world finally knew what had become of Jacob Wetterling—an 11-year-old whose heartbreaking story made the world a safer place for children.

Afterword

There are watershed moments in time, enduring events in every person's life, when something happens that is so significant or meaningful, so tragic or heartbreaking, or so uplifting or endearing—that those such moments become engrained in one's memory for all time. These "flashbulb memories" are moments that every member of every generation experiences. They are moments upon which a person will reflect back, and with an indelible mark in time they'll recall exactly where they were and what they were doing when the moment happened.

Perhaps it was the shock that came on the day of the assassination of John F. Kennedy, or the terror of 9/11, or the unexpected loss on the day Elvis died. Maybe it was the news that a loved one is sick or has passed. Or maybe it's something overwhelmingly beautiful, such as the birth of child, a wedding, or a hero's homecoming. Maybe it was a child's first day of school, waiting at the bus stop with a backpack over his shoulder and lunch bag clutched in his hand.

Since the publication of the original edition of this book, I have heard from countless readers who have told me their story, either as a parent or as a youngster, that the abduction of Jacob Wetterling on October 22, 1989, was such a watershed moment for them. For parents, it was the biting reality that something so horrific, so terrible, could happen in a small Midwestern town like St. Joseph, Minnesota. It did happen there. How could they protect their own children from this seemingly new and mysterious danger? How could they balance the need to protect their children, yet allow them to thrive in the innocence and freedom of their youth?

For those who were children at the time of Jacob's abduction, many recall the sudden imposition of strict rules against being outside after dark, or bicycling to a friend's house, or to a local store. Some have told me about how they grew up not understanding the sudden layers of restrictions applied by their parents in a seemingly sudden and irrational fashion. It was a fear that many did not fully come to understand until they had grown up and had children of their own, and they are now seeing things from their parents' perspectives for the first time, and after all these years it finally made sense.

I cannot say that I remember distinctly the day that Jacob Wetterling was abducted. I do remember quite well the aura of fear which came afterward, the fear that spread through the air of my own neighborhood, and reports of suspicious vans and strangers. Jacob's story truly had an impact on how I raised my own children, and I was always cognizant of the apparent dangers that lurked behind unknown cover. Those feelings stuck with me even after my children had grown into young adults, and I know they will still be there when I have grandchildren.

As an amateur sleuth, I spent more than five years of spare time researching newspaper archives, books, magazines, and online videos—anything I could get my hands on. I quickly recognized that there was a plethora of information about Jacob's case, and much of it had seemed to slip by the wayside, forgotten in time. I also came to discern that for every question that had been answered along the way, there begged other, more mysterious questions. It seemed that answers were so close, yet so far away. At some point I began reaching out to investigators, old and new, to television and newspaper reporters from the past and present, bloggers, librarians—anyone who I thought represented an opportunity to help bring answers to Jacob's case.

Countless hours of research yielded a large volume of interesting and potentially meaningful information, but I seemed to be gaining little traction with reporters or investigators. Anniversary after anniversary had passed, and I eventually came to understand that the only way to truly help make a difference would be to get Jacob's story out there for anyone and everyone to see. If all pertinent information could be brought together in one place, I thought, and put into the hands of the right person, perhaps the case could be solved. And maybe, just maybe, I would come across some information through my research efforts that could make a difference too. As fate would have it, that's exactly what happened.

I started writing this book in 2013. It was a start that I was determined to finish, for a case that I believed could be solved. When authorities arrested Danny Heinrich in October 2015, the possibility of finally finding the answers to what happened to Jacob Wetterling appeared to be more promising than ever before. Regardless of how or why investigators had finally come to the brink of finding them, it was the promise of answers that was truly important. When Heinrich confessed to abducting and murdering Jacob Wetterling, it appeared that the answers had been lying there in the sand the whole time.

Timeline of the
Investigation

Aug 30, 1986 Daniel Heinrich is arrested for driving a vehicle while intoxicated. He is also charged with possessing a police scanner set to monitor Stearns County Sheriff's Office communications.

Mar 15, 1988 Daniel Heinrich purchases a 1987 Mercury Topaz, dark blue in color with 4 doors.

Summer, 1988 A juvenile boy reports being attacked by a man with a husky build near 200 West Railroad Avenue in Paynesville. The man spoke in a raspy voice and wore pantyhose over his head. He was dressed in camouflage pants, a green Army jacket, black boots, and black gloves. A group of boys had been camping when 2 of the boys left to get beverages. The suspect grabbed one of the boys, sat on him, and held a knife to his throat. The boy escaped without being groped.

Fall, 1988 A juvenile boy reports that he was attacked while delivering newspapers in Paynesville. The attacker was described as about 5'6" tall with a husky build. He was wearing a ski mask, a dark colored stocking hat, black shirt, black pants, and black gloves. The man knocked the boy off his bicycle and then fled the area. It was the last of eight reported assaults on boys in Paynesville since 1986.

Jan 13, 1989 Jared is abducted from downtown Cold Spring, MN, at about 9:45 p.m. He is driven out into the country, assaulted, and returned to Cold Spring at about 11:00. Jared described the car as a dark blue 4-door car, fairly new. The abductor had a handheld police scanner and used the threat of a gun. He was described by Jared as a white male, age 35–40, 170 lbs. He was wearing camouflage pants, a gray vest, a cap, and black boots. The man had a deep, raspy voice.

Jan 16, 1989 SCSO Deputy Zieglmeier contacts detective Doug Pearce to identify Daniel Heinrich of Paynesville as a possible suspect in Jared's

171

kidnapping. Zieglmeier said that Heinrich drove a 1987 dark blue Mercury Topaz. He further reported that Heinrich was in the National Guard or Army Reserves and was regularly observed wearing military fatigues.

Jan 17, 1989 Doug Pearce showed Jared a photograph lineup of 6 similarly built males including Daniel Heinrich. Jared indicated that Heinrich and another male somewhat resembled his attacker. Pearce confirms that Heinrich is a member of the National Guard unit based in Willmar, MN, and that the Guard unit did not have any meetings on the weekend of January 13, 1989.

Jan 18, 1989 SCSO detectives Doug Pearce and Lou Leland observe a 1987 blue Mercury Topaz owned by Daniel Heinrich parked at Master Mark Plastics where Heinrich is employed.

Feb 24, 1989 Stearns County investigators release a sketch of the man wanted in Jared's abduction.

Mar 15, 1989 Daniel Heinrich's 1987 Mercury Topaz is repossessed. He begins driving a 1975 gray-colored Ford Granada.

June 1989 Daniel Heinrich is now driving a blue 1982 Ford EXP. He reports selling his Ford Granada to his mother.

July 1989 A woman in St. Joseph Township, near Kraemer Lake, reports to Stearns County investigators that her son, Andrew, was the victim of an attempted abduction by a man in a light tan-colored van.

Oct 8, 1989 Daniel Heinrich's last day of employment at Fingerhut Corporation in St. Cloud, MN.

Oct 22, 1989 Jacob Wetterling, Trevor Wetterling, and Aaron Larson bike from the Wetterling home to the Tom Thumb store. At about 9:15, on their way back home, they are stopped by a masked gunman. Trevor and Aaron are released and the man grabs Jacob by the shoulder and leads him up the Rassier driveway. At 9:25 Trevor and Aaron arrive back at the Wetterling home and Merle Jerzak calls 911 at 9:32 to report Jacob's abduction. At 9:40 SCSO Deputy Bruce Bechtold arrives at the Wetterling home. The boys describe the man as about 5'10", weighing 180 lbs, and wearing a nylon facemask, dark coat, dark pants, and dark shoes. He had a silver handgun and spoke in a rough voice like he had a cold. Local FBI agent Al Catello calls his supervisor Al Garber in St. Paul, MN. By the end of the night the number of law enforcement officers on the scene expands to 35. At 10:00 they begin a local search. At 11:00 a Minnesota State Patrol helicopter arrives and aerial search begins. At 11:23 Dan Rassier calls 911 to report intruders with flashlights near the firewood pile along the driveway to the Rassier farm. He goes outside to meet law enforcement officers and offers to search the farm buildings.

Oct 23, 1989 A bloodhound tracks Jacob's scent up the Rassier driveway, east of the abduction site. Detective Steve Mund makes plaster casts of footprints and tire tracks found in the driveway. Dan Rassier tells *St. Cloud Times* about the small dark car he saw in his driveway at about the time of the abduction. The ground and air search are called off that evening—officers had searched a 25 square mile, including a door-to-door search of neighboring homes.

Oct 25, 1989 Investigators establish a link between Jacob's abduction and the Jan 13 abduction of Jared in Cold Spring.

Oct 26, 1989 The FBI releases a psychological profile of Jacob's likely abductor. It indicates a white male, 25–35 years old, employed in a low-skilled job with little public contact, with probable facial acne or scars. His high-risk approach suggests he may have attempted another abduction recently and failed. Acquaintances would likely notice an increased level of anxiety in the man.

Oct 27, 1989 Minnesota State Attorney requests the neighboring states of Wisconsin, Illinois, Iowa, North Dakota, and South Dakota to upgrade their investigations to "extremely high alert" status.

Oct 28, 1989 Investigators release a sketch of a man who attempted to abduct a boy named Andrew in the Township of St. Joseph in July or August 1989. They consider the possibility that Jacob's abductor had failed with Andrew, leading him to use a gun in Jacob's kidnapping.

Oct 30, 1989 The National Guard search ends after scouring hundreds of buildings and thousands of acres across a 36 square mile area.

Nov 2, 1989 FBI announces they have cleared as many as 100 suspects but have at least 100 more to investigate.

Nov 3, 1989 The ground search for Jacob is called off. The FBI indicates they believe Jacob's abductor is a local man familiar with the area.

Nov 6, 1989 Authorities release a sketch of a man who had been seen acting strangely at the Tom Thumb store at about the time of the abduction. He was described as being in his fifties, about 6 feet tall, weighing about 200 lbs. A store clerk reported that the man later man came back to the store laughing that Jacob would never be found. He drove away in a dark-colored car.

Nov 12, 1989 Daniel Heinrich's first day of employment at North Star Mailing in St. Cloud, MN. The home of Wayne Jude is burglarized and set on fire by an arsonist. The Jude home is located on Hwy 55 about 3 miles southeast of Paynesville, and very near the home of Roger Larson which was set on fire a month earlier.

Nov 22, 1989 The Minnesota Bureau of Criminal Apprehension removes 6 of the 8 officers working Jacob's case as leads dwindle. The FBI reduces its staff as well.

Nov 30, 1989 Daniel Heinrich moves out of his mother's residence at 121 Washburne Avenue, to his father's home at 16021 County Road 124, Paynesville.

Dec 14, 1989 Authorities reiterate that Jacob's abduction is likely related to the January 1989 abduction and assault of Jared in Cold Spring. Another, more detailed sketch of Jared's abductor is released, producing a significant number of leads.

Dec 16, 1989 FBI agents interview Daniel Heinrich, who informs them he has a couple of prior arrests for burglary and a DWI. He does not remember where he was on the dates that Jared and Jacob were kidnapped but speculates he may have been washing laundry or visiting a friend. He denies wearing camouflage clothing or Army boots except when he was on Guard duty.

Jan 8, 1990 Paynesville Police Chief Robert Schmiginsky briefs Wetterling investigators on Paynesville's year of molestation reports and that Daniel Heinrich should be considered a suspect in those cases.

Jan 10, 1990 The Wetterling Task Force compiles a database of 5,000 known sex offenders in the state of Minnesota—the first of its kind.

Jan 12, 1990 Investigators interview Daniel Heinrich, who volunteers his shoes for examination. He provides body hair samples to SCSO Detective Steve Mund and FBI agent Pete Cunningham.

Jan 15, 1990 Heinrich authorizes investigators to remove the rear tires from his 1982 Ford EXP.

Jan 16, 1990 Jared sits inside the 1987 Mercury Topaz Heinrich owned in January 1989. He reports that it "feels like" the car he had been assaulted in.

Jan 18, 1990 Stearns County Detective Pearce obtains samples from the back seat and carpet from the Mercury Topaz.

Jan 24, 1990 Duane Allen Hart is arrested and charged in incidents involving multiple boys in the Belgrade and Paynesville areas from 1987 through 1989. Investigators execute a search warrant at Danny Heinrich's residence at 16021 County Road 124 in Paynesville. Investigators seize one handheld Regency programmable scanner, one six channel Regency scanner, a list of scanner frequencies and operating manuals, a Radio Shack scanner frequency book, a pair of black lace-up boots, two brown caps, a camouflage shirt and a pair of camouflage pants, and one vest. Interviewed during the search, Heinrich cannot recall his whereabouts on October 22, 1989, but denies being in St. Joseph.

Jan 25, 1990 FBI agent Eric Odegard retrieves the rear tires from Heinrich's 1982 Ford EXP. Heinrich agrees to participate in a lineup of 6 white males. Jared is unable to positively identify any of the men as his attacker. He rates Heinrich a 4 in similarity and another man a 7.

Jan 26, 1990 The FBI finds that Heinrich's tires are consistent with tire impressions at the scene of the Wetterling kidnapping, but not an exact match.

Feb 9, 1990 Daniel Heinrich is arrested for probable cause in the kidnapping of and sexual assault of Jared. Stearns County refuses to press charges and he is released.

Feb 16, 1990 In a jail cell interview with a private investigator, Duane Allen Hart implicates Heinrich in Jared's abduction. Hart's description closely matches the description of Jared's abductor.

Mar 5, 1990 The FBI finds that the gray synthetic fibers found on Jared's snowmobile suit are consistent with samples taken from from the 1987 Mercury Topaz formerly owned by Heinrich.

Apr 13, 1990 The FBI reports that it cannot conclusively determine whether the shoe impression at the abduction scene was made by Heinrich's right shoe, though the impression does correspond in design and size.

May 4, 1990 Sheriff Charlie Grafft announces that the reward for Jacob's safe return had been quadrupled to $200,000.

Feb 8, 1991 Investigators return all property seized from Danny Heinrich's home on January 24, 1990.

Apr 1991 Paynesville residents report a man in a tan colored vehicle following newspaper boys on their delivery routes. An SCSO deputy investigates and identifies a tan 1984 Buick belonging to Danny Heinrich following a newspaper boy.

May 1996 A WCCO report reveals that search warrants investigators thought were sealed were actually open records. One of the warrants was for a January 1990 search of the home of a Paynesville area man. Part of the warrant was inexplicably blacked out as Stearns County investigators scrambled to get the records resealed.

Oct 2003 Kevin Hamilton comes forward to inform investigators that he had driven up the Rassier driveway minutes after Jacob's abduction.

They quietly begin changing their theory of the crime and focusing on local suspects.

Jan 2004 SCSO Captain Pam Jensen and BCA agent Ken McDonald review the November 1989 video tape of Dan Rassier's interview, and the 911 call made by Merle Jerzak on October 22, 1989. In light of the information from Kevin Hamilton, they develop the theory that Jacob's abductor was on foot.

Feb 7, 2004 Jensen and McDonald interview Dan Rassier, hoping to eliminate the car he had witnessed in his driveway. They repeatedly accuse Rassier of kidnapping Jacob, but he insists that the abductor must have been driving the car that he saw that night.

Feb 2004 Sheriff Sanner reports that investigators had questioned a neighbor of the Wetterlings as a possible suspect. It was learned later that a search warrant was served on the home of Dan Rassier. Sanner announces that investigators now believe that someone on foot, someone local, abducted Jacob, though he does not rule out the use of a vehicle. He also discounts the link between Jacob's and Jared's cases, which earlier investigators had long maintained to be all but certain.

Jul 30, 2004 Jared comes forward to tell his story publicly for the first time, detailing his January 1989 abduction and assault in a televised interview on KARE 11. He believes that his case is related to Jacob's. Sheriff Sanner acknowledges that he could not rule out a connection.

October 2007 Law enforcement officers monitor Dan Rassier from October 15 through October 19 to better understand his daily activities.

Nov 7, 2007 BCA agent Ken McDonald applied for a mail cover to intercept U.S. Postal Service delivery to Rassier.

Oct 20, 2009 Stearns County investigators orchestrate a "chance encounter" between Patty Wetterling and Rassier. Patty wears a recording device to document the meeting. Investigators later use the recoding for probable cause to obtain a search warrant for the Rassier farm.

Mar 19, 2010 Patty and Jerry Wetterling visit the Rassier farm and speak to Robert and Rita Rassier. Dan Rassier had not mentioned the October 20, 2009 meeting with Patty to his parents.

Jun 30, 2010 A team of investigators including the SCSO, the BCA, the FBI, and the National Center for Missing and Exploited Children descends on the Rassier farm and serve a search warrant. They develop probable cause to obtain additional search warrants for the property, including the home and outbuildings. The search lasts for 2 days. Investigators remove a number of items, including 6 truckloads of dirt, a cedar chest, an umbrella stand, Dan Rassier's journal, and a box of information about the Wetterling case.

Jul 3, 2010 Sheriff Sanner names Dan Rassier a person of interest in the abduction of Jacob Wetterling. In subsequent television and newspaper interviews, Rassier acknowledges that investigators had searched his property in 1989, in 2004, and again in 2010, and that he voluntarily submitted to a DNA test, a lie detector test, hypnosis, and multiple questionings over the years. Rassier maintained that he had been cooperative with authorities since the beginning of the case and that he was a witness to what had happened.

September 29, 2010 Sheriff Sanner announces that testing on items and soil taken during the search of the Rassier property yielded no significant findings.

Jul 8, 2012 A BCA report indicates that a DNA profile was obtained from Jared's snowmobile suit, sweatshirt, and shirt. Results indicated the presence of DNA from an unknown male on the sweatshirt.

Aug 2, 2012 Dan Rassier sends a five-page letter to 14 different local and state agencies complaining of violation of his civil rights in being named a person of interest in Jacob's kidnapping.

Aug 9, 2013 Amateur sleuth Robert Dudley finds articles about Duane Hart and the Paynesville assault cluster in the online archives of the Paynesville Press. Dudley shares the information with blogger Joy Baker.

Aug 2013 Joy Baker contacts Stearns County about the Paynesville assaults, and begins a push to publicize those assaults, and tie them together along with Duane Hart to Jared's assault, and to Jacob Wetterling's abduction.

Dec 2013 Stearns County Captain Pam Jensen and BCA agent Ken McDonald interview Duane Hart at the sex offender treatment facility in Moose Lake, Minnesota. Hart denies involvement in Jacob's case, Jared's case, and the Paynesville assault cluster. He denies knowledge of the baseball cap left behind in one of the Paynesville cases. Hart voluntarily provides a DNA sample.

Mar 5, 2014 A BCA laboratory report indicates that DNA profiling was performed on a sample collected from a baseball cap that the suspect had left behind during the May 17, 1987, attack on a juvenile boy in Paynesville. Results indicate the presence of DNA from 3 or more individuals.

Mar 2014 DNA results indicated that Duane Hart cannot be excluded as a contributor to DNA found on the baseball cap left behind during the May 17, 1987, Paynesville attack.

Apr 22, 2014 Robert Dudley sends email to SCSO suggesting that a man was arrested for Jared's assault in 1990, per Al Garber's book, *Striving To Be The Best*.

May 15, 2014 In a televised interview on WCCO, Jared reiterates his belief that his case is related to Jacob's, and suggests it may also be related to the cluster of assaults in Paynesville 2–3 year prior.

Aug 2014 BCA agent Ken McDonald once again goes to Moose Lake to interview Duane Hart.

The Wetterlings meet with Stearns County Sheriff John Sanner Captain Pam Jensen, and they ask that Jacob's case be reviewed from the beginning.

Aug 22, 2014 BCA agent Ken McDonald secures a search warrant to monitor phone calls, visitor logs, and patient records for Duane Hart. The phone calls and visitor logs to be monitored date back to July 2013.

Aug/Sep 2014 The FBI later proposes to assemble a task force to take another look at the Jacob Wetterling abduction case. The FBI, BCA, and Stearns County agencies meet to determine a course of action to follow up on the FBI's proposal, and prepare for a surge in tips expected from an upcoming television program featuring the Wetterling case. No specific suspects are discussed during the meeting. An FBI agent who worked the Wetterling case in 1989/1990, currently stationed in Oklahoma, brings up Danny Heinrich's name to the local FBI in St. Cloud.

Sep 6, 2014 Robert Dudley sends Hart Notes to SCSO, and offers to meet to discuss the notes. There was no reply.

Dudley sends Hart Notes to Joy Baker. Baker then forwards the documents to Patty Wetterling.

Sep 10, 2014 Robert Dudley sends a copy of the Hart Notes to local FBI agent Shane Ball. The Hart Notes are a 25-page set of handwritten notes made by a private investigator working on behalf of Duane Allen Hart's defense Team. The notes were written in February 1990 and were thought by the investigator to have been lost many years earlier in an office purge of files. In the notes, Hart appears to be assisting investigators in identifying likely suspects in Jacob's and Jared's cases. The notes include particular emphasis on Daniel Heinrich as a suspect. The notes also contain references to other unsolved cases in the area including the 1976 bombing of the Post Office in Kimball, MN and the 1983 murder of Scriver Olson from rural Belgrade, MN.

Sep 13, 2014 FBI agent Shane Ball contacts Robert Dudley requesting the source of the Hart Notes. Informant responds with detailed information about the source.

Sep 14, 2014 Robert Dudley follows up with email to FBI agent Ball that the private investigator's impression was that Hart was indicating Daniel Heinrich as a likely suspect due to his car, camouflage clothing, fascination with police scanners, rough and raspy voice when excited, and that he had been arrested in early 1990.

Nov 2014 An FBI CARD (Child Abduction Rapid Deployment) team is implemented by FBI Agent Shane Ball and begins work to review the Wetterling case. FBI Agent Shane Ball concludes that it is unclear why Daniel Heinrich was not the prime suspect in the kidnapping of Jacob Wetterling.

May 12, 2015 Hair samples that had been collected from Daniel Heinrich on January 12, 1990, are submitted to the BCA for nuclear DNA testing.

Jul 10, 2015 DNA samples from Jared's sweatshirt are found to match the DNA of Daniel Heinrich. Heinrich's DNA was found to be an 80.5 percent match to DNA found on the cap that was recovered from the May 17, 1987, assault in Paynesville.

Jul 28, 2015 Law enforcement officers execute a search warrant on the home of Daniel Heinrich located at 55 Myrtle Avenue South, in Annandale, MN. They were looking for a wide range of items related to the abduction of Jacob Wetterling. Investigators seize 19 three-ring binders containing child pornography, home video footage of children delivering newspapers, news reports about the abduction of Jacob Wetterling and other missing children, a set of military-style camouflage pants and shirt, and several bins of children's clothing. Heinrich spoke with investigators during the search, acknowledging that they would find child porn and things that are "pretty damning," and that he was a "dirty old man."

Oct 28, 2015 Following a criminal complaint filed by FBI agent Shane Ball, Heinrich is arrested by investigators and charged with multiple federal counts of possession of child pornography.

Nov 4, 2015 In Federal Court in St. Paul, Judge Tony Leung rules that Heinrich be held without bail. Agent Ball testifies that investigators decided to review the Wetterling case about a year earlier and by November 2014 it was unclear why Heinrich was no longer considered a suspect.

Dec 16, 2015 Additional child pornography charges are added to the federal indictment against Heinrich, bringing the total to 25.

Feb 22, 2016 Heinrich pleads not guilty in federal court to all 25 charges. A trial is scheduled for July 11, 2015.

Jun 27, 2016 Heinrich's lawyers request additional time to prepare a change of venue appeal and to seek suppression of evidence seized at his home in July 2015.

Jul 11, 2016 Granting the request of Heinrich's legal team, U.S. District Court Judge John Tunheim postpones the trial until October 11, 2016.

Aug 31, 2016 Striking a plea deal with prosecutors on the child pornography charges, Heinrich tells investigators he will lead them to the location where he buried Jacob Wetterling. Jacob's red jacket and some bones are found. The bones are tested and determined to be animal bones.

Sep 2, 2016 Heinrich returns to the burial area and investigators expand the search for Jacob's remains. His remains are found and positively identified.

Sep 3, 2016 Authorities publicly confirm that Jacob Wetterling's remains were found in a field north of Paynesville.

Sep 6, 2016 Daniel Heinrich confesses in federal court to the kidnapping and murder of Jacob Wetterling. In a plea agreement, he pleads guilty to one count of child pornography in exchange for immunity from prosecution in Jacob's murder. Sentencing is scheduled for Nov 21, 2016.

Chapter Notes

Chapter 1

1. DuBois, A Year Without Jacob—Big Brother, Who Made Everything OK, Still Missing, 1990.
2. DuBois, A Year Without Jacob—Dad Runs on Spiritual Energy, 1990.
3. *Ibid.*
4. *Ibid.*
5. *Ibid.*
6. *Ibid.*
7. *Ibid.*
8. *Ibid.*
9. Dalman, Search for One Child Becomes Search for All, 1999.
10. DuBois, A Year Without Jacob—Dad Runs on Spiritual Energy, 1990.
11. Petrie K., 2009.
12. Haukebo K., "Jacob Needs Me to Be Strong Now"—Mom, Family Hope, Wait, 1989.
13. DuBois, A Year Without Jacob—Dad Runs on Spiritual Energy, 1990.
14. *Ibid.*
15. Haukebo K., Jacob's Buddy Struggles with Kidnap's Aftermath, 1989.
16. DuBois, A Year Without Jacob—Big Brother, Who Made Everything OK, Still Missing, 1990.
17. *Ibid.*
18. *Ibid.*
19. Petrie K., 2009.
20. DuBois, A Year Without Jacob—Big Brother, Who Made Everything OK, Still Missing, 1990.
21. *Ibid.*
22. *Ibid.*

Chapter 2

1. DuBois, A Year Without Jacob—Dad Runs on Spiritual Energy, 1990.
2. DuBois, A Year Without Jacob—Patty Will Never Give Up—Life Has Become Exhaustive Search, 1990.
3. Hawkins, 2009.
4. *Ibid.*
5. Behme T. J., A Year Without Jacob—"Nothing … Has Hit Me Like This Case," 1990.
6. Merryhew, 1999.
7. Behme T. J., A Year Without Jacob—"Nothing … Has Hit Me Like This Case," 1990.
8. *Ibid.*

Chapter 3

1. Larson T., A Year Without Jacob—Friend Fueled Media Blitz, but Work Took Toll, 1990.
2. Larson T., A Year Without Jacob—"I Became Part of the Family"—Story Drains Reporter, 1990.
3. *Ibid.*
4. Larson T., A Year Without Jacob—Friend Fueled Media Blitz, but Work Took Toll, 1990.
5. *Ibid.*
6. *Ibid.*
7. *Ibid.*
8. *Ibid.*
9. *Ibid.*
10. *Ibid.*
11. *Ibid.*
12. Larson T., A Year Without Jacob—

"I Became Part of the Family"—Story Drains Reporter, 1990.
13. *Ibid.*
14. *Ibid.*
15. *Ibid.*
16. *Ibid.*
17. *Ibid.*
18. *Ibid.*
19. *Ibid.*
20. *Ibid.*
21. *Ibid.*
22. *Ibid.*
23. *Ibid.*
24. Lowe S., Sketch Concerns Kidnapping Officials, 1989.
25. Lowe S., Jacob Rumours Untrue, FBI Says, 1989.
26. *Ibid.*
27. Behme T. J., Image of Jacob at Age 15 Could Help Solve Case—Investigators: Case Remains High Priority, 1991.
28. Goldschen, TV Newscasts Reveal Police Files on Leads in Jacob Wetterling Case, 1992.
29. *Ibid.*
30. Behme T. J., 1992.
31. Lanpher, 1997.

Chapter 4

1. Peterson, "Unprecedented" Community Response, 1989.
2. *San Jose Mercury News* Staff Report, 1990.
3. Haukebo K., So Many People Have Offered to Help, Boy's Father Says, 1989.
4. DuBois, Experience Touches Jacob's Class, 1993.
5. Larson T., Counselors Help Local Parents Find Ways to Explain Tragedy to Children, 1989.
6. Goldschen, Police Chief Answers Children's Questions on Abduction, 1989.
7. Lowe S., Town Prays Abductor "Comes to His Senses," 1989.
8. Board S. C., Editorial—Our Midwestern Roots are Showing, 1989.
9. Haukebo K., Alert Public Becomes Key in Search—Volunteers Will Gather Tonight, 1989.
10. Lowe S., A Year Without Jacob—Massive Effort Took Seasoned Search Organizer by Surprise, 1990.

11. Nistler, Jacob Gets "Line of Love"—5,000 Link Hands to Show Jacob's Hope, 1989.
12. Bodette, 1989.
13. Haukebo K., Pope John Paul Shares Wetterlings' Pain, Hope, 1989.

Chapter 5

1. Hawkins, 2009.
2. Garber, 2009.
3. Behme T. J., A Year Without Jacob—"Nothing … Has Hit Me Like This Case," 1990.
4. Hawkins, 2009.
5. *Pioneer Press* Staff Report, 1989.
6. *Star Tribune* Staff Report, 1989.
7. Haukebo K., Ground Search Ends—Police Think Gunman, Boy No Longer in St. Joseph, 1989.
8. *Pioneer Press* Staff Report, 1989.
9. *Ibid.*
10. *Star Tribune* Staff Report, 1989.
11. Doyle P., Officials Seek 100 Potential Suspects in Hunt for St. Joseph Boy's Abductor, 1989.
12. Haukebo K., Ground Search Ends—Police Think Gunman, Boy No Longer in St. Joseph, 1989.
13. Baker, *JoyThe.Curious* "Dan's Story, 2013.
14. *Ibid.*
15. Stearns County, 2010.
16. *Ibid.*
17. Murphy, For 1st Time, "Person of Interest" Goes Through Day of Wetterling Abduction, 2013.
18. Nelson, Julie Nelson Interviews Dan Rassier, Part 1, 2010.
19. Murphy, For 1st Time, "Person of Interest" Goes Through Day of Wetterling Abduction, 2013.
20. Baker, *JoyThe.Curious* "The Next Day," 2013.
21. Dalman, "Person of Interest" Says He Witnessed "Things," 2010.
22. Hawkins, 2009.
23. Lowe C., 2015.
24. Cook M., 1989.
25. Garber, 2009.
26. Haukebo K., Police Searching for Red Car—Kidnap Case Gets New Lead, 1989.

27. Cook M., 1989.

28. Haukebo K., National Guard Joins Search—Red Car a False Lead in St. Joseph Kidnap Case, Police Say, 1989.

29. *La Crosse Tribune* Staff Report, 1990.

30. Doyle P., Officials Seek 100 Potential Suspects in Hunt for St. Joseph Boy's Abductor, 1989.

31. Chapman, KARE 11 Investigates: Coincidence in Wetterling Case, 2004.

32. *Cold Spring Record* Staff Report, 1989.

33. Ibid.

34. Wright County, State of Minnesota, 2015.

35. *Ibid.*

36. *Ibid.*

37. Newton, 1994.

38. Associated Press, 1989.

39. *Star Tribune* Staff Report, 1989.

40. Goldschen, Van Still Haunts St. Joseph Residents, 1990.

41. *Ibid.*

42. *Ibid.*

43. *Ibid.*

44. Haukebo K., FBI Profiles Boy's Abductor—White Man with Deformity; Loner; Low Skills, Self-Image, 1989.

45. Lowe S., A Year Without Jacob—Families Stunned by Stolen Innocence, 1990.

46. *Pioneer Press* Staff Report, 1989.

47. Haukebo K., Horses Added to Search—Kidnap Probe Gets Hundreds of Tip Calls, 1989.

48. Stearns County, 2010.

49. *Ibid.*

50. Larson T., 1989.

51. Larson and Haukebo, Roadblocks Net Few Clues—200 Troops to Search Sauk River Shoreline.

52. Larson T., 1989.

53. Haukebo K., Searchers Move into Hector Area—Investigators Turn Focus to White Car, 1989.

54. *Ibid.*

55. Haukebo K., Ground Search Called Off—Richmond Lions Offer $100,000 Reward for Jacob, 1989.

56. Garber, 2009.

57. *Star Tribune* Staff Report, 1989.

58. *Ibid.*

59. Lowe S., Another Suspect Sought in Kidnap—FBI Appeals to Public for Help in Finding Man, 1989.

60. *Star Tribune* Staff Report, 1989.

61. Haukebo K., Man with Piercing Stare Sought, 1989.

62. *Star Tribune* Staff Report, 1989.

63. Haukebo K., Minot Lead on Jacob is Soft, FBI Says—Probe Focuses on Man Seen at Store, 1989.

64. Haukebo K., Louisiana Suspect Ruled Out in Jacob Case, 1989.

65. *Star Tribune* Staff Report, 1990.

66. Haukebo K., FBI Chases New Kidnap Leads, 1989.

67. *Star Tribune* Staff Report, 1989.

68. *Ibid.*

69. Haukebo K., FBI Probes Attempted Abduction, 1989.

70. *Ibid.*

71. *Ibid.*

72. Lewis, 1989.

73. Haukebo K., Number of Kidnap Case Officers Cut—BCA Chief: "It Was One of Those Tough Decisions," 1989.

74. *Ibid.*

75. Haukebo K., Escaped Mental Patient Killed Himself Five Years Ago, 1989.

76. Haukebo K., Authorities Release Revised Sketch of Abduction Suspect, 1989.

77. *Ibid.*

78. *Star Tribune* Staff Report, 1989.

79. Haukebo K., FBI Seeks Tips on 3 Drivers—Cars Were Seen Near Jacob's Home, 1989.

80. *Ibid.*

81. *Ibid.*

82. *Ibid.*

83. *Star Tribune* Staff Report, 1989.

84. Nistler, Candles Burn for Jacob—Wetterlings, Supporters Hold Vigil, 1989.

85. Haukebo K., St. Joseph Man Hospitalized After Standoff with Deputies, 1989.

86. *Ibid.*

87. Haukebo K., Monticello Kidnap Attempt Fails—FBI Appeals for Witnesses, 1989.

88. *Ibid.*89. *St. Cloud Times* Staff Report, 1989.

89. *Ibid.*

90. Haukebo K., Two Abductions May Be Linked—Cold Spring Assault May Offer Jacob Clues; Sketch Given, 1989.

91. Doyle P., New Lead Reported in Wetterling Case, 1989.

92. *Ibid.*
93. St. Paul *Pioneer Press* Staff Report, 1989.
94. Lowe S., Sketch of Abduction Suspect Prompts Flood of Phone Calls, 1989.
95. *Ibid.*
96. *St. Cloud Times* Staff Report, 1989.
97. *Ibid.*
98. *Ibid.*
99. Haukebo K., Jacob Case Haunts Officers—Focus Narrows, Few Leads After 81 Days, 1990.
100. Hood, 1990.
101. Douglass, Belgrade Man Arrested—Charged with Assaulting Boys, 1990.
102. *Paynesville Press Staff* Report, 1986.
103. *Ibid.*
104. Thyen, Local Police Seek Help in Accosting Incidents, 1987.
105. *Ibid.*
106. *Ibid.*
107. Doyle P., Bail Set at $100,000 for Suspect in Child Sex Case, 1990.
108. Haukebo K., Man Arrested in Sexual Assaults—No Known Link to Wetterling Case, FBI Says, 1990.
109. Douglass, Belgrade Man Arrested—Charged with Assaulting Boys, 1990.
110. Anonymous, 2014.
111. Associated Press, 1990.
112. Annette, 1990.
113. Unze D., Private Investigator's Notes 1990 Notes Mention Heinrich, 2015.
114. Schugel, 2012.
115. Unze D., Private Investigator's Notes 1990 Notes Mention Heinrich, 2015.
116. Garber, 2009.

Chapter 6

1. Haukebo K., Patty: "I Didn't Believe it Was Jacob"—Body Found Near St. Paul Dam Still Unidentified, 1990.
2. *Pioneer Press* Staff Report, 1990.
3. *Ibid.*
4. Goldschen, Local Boy Frightened by Stranger, 1990.
5. *St. Cloud Times* Staff Report, 1990.
6. *Ibid.*
7. Lowe S., Wisconsin Suspect Questioned on Jacob, 1990.
8. *St. Cloud Times* Staff and Wire Report, 1990.
9. St. Joseph Newsleader Staff Report, 1990.
10. Lowe S., $200,000 Reward for Clues on Jacob, 1990.
11. Goldschen, Investigators Feel Jacob's Out There—Wetterlings Back Seclusion Theory, 1990.
12. *Ibid.*
13. *Ibid.*
14. *Ibid.*
15. Associated Press, 1990.
16. Goldschen, Phone Call Raises Jacob's Hope—Illinois Woman Sees Boy Who Might Be Jacob, 1990.
17. Goldschen, Patty Wetterling: "I Never Lost Hope"—Illinois Incidents Among Many in Search for Jacob, 1990.
18. Stelling, 1990.
19. Behme T. J., Detectives Pursue New Lead—Officials Cautious, but Suspect Looks Good on Paper, They Say, 1990.
20. Behme T. J., Jacob's Birthday Sunday; Case Still Priority, 1991.
21. *Ibid.*
22. Behme T. J., Mother's Mailing Pleads for Clues on Jacob, 1991.
23. *St. Cloud Times* Staff Report, 1991.
24. Urseth, 2010.
25. Behme T. J., Jacob Searchers Drain Pond—Marker Found with "Jacob" Carved on It, 1991.
26. Bergquist, Photo of Jacob to Be Mass-Mailed, 1992.
27. Van Pilsum, Investigators: Feeney Fascinated with Wetterling Case, 2013.
28. Van Pilsum, Investigators: In Feeney's Words, 2013.
29. Van Pilsum, Investigators: Feeney Fascinated with Wetterling Case, 2013.
30. *Ibid.*
31. *Ibid.*
32. Goldschen, TV Newscasts Reveal Police Files on Leads in Jacob Wetterling Case, 1992.
33. Associated Press, 1992.
34. Welsh, Man Claims Sex Ring Took Jacob—Authorities Unconvinced; Jerry Wetterling Wants More Information, 1994.
35. *Ibid.*
36. Welsh, Warrants Reveal Early Wetterling Suspects—but New Information

Doesn't Center on top Suspects, Police Say, 1996.
37. Haukebo K., St. Joseph Man Hospitalized After Standoff with Deputies, 1989.
38. Welsh, Warrants Reveal Early Wetterling Suspects—but New Information Doesn't Center on top Suspects, Police Say, 1996.
39. Horwich, 2002.
40. *Ibid.*
41. *Pioneer Press* Staff Report, 1997.
42. *Ibid.*
43. Wright, 2009.
44. Associated Press, 1998.
45. Unze D., Media Still Drawn to Wetterling Case—As 10th Anniversary of Son's Abduction Nears, Mother Holds Hope He'll Be Found, 1999.
46. Unze D., Unsolved Case Investigators Ask About Blom, 1999.
47. *Star Tribune* Staff Report, 1999.
48. *St. Cloud Times* Staff Report, 1990.
49. Unze D., Man May Be Linked to Wetterling Case—Child Pornography Allegations, Sketch Similarity Prompt Background Check, 2001.
50. Ghere, 2001.

Chapter 7

1. *Star Tribune* Staff Report, 2004.
2. Scott, Investigators Explore New Path in Wetterling Case—Kidnapper May Have Been on Foot, Not in Car, 2004.
3. Winkels, 2003.
4. *Ibid.*
5. *Ibid.*
6. *Ibid.*
7. *Ibid.*
8. Hawkins, 2009.
9. Winkels, 2003.
10. *Ibid.*
11. *Star Tribune* Staff Report, 2004.
12. Stearns County, 2010.
13. *Ibid.*
14. *Ibid.*
15. Scott, Investigators Explore New Path in Wetterling Case—Kidnapper May Have Been on Foot, Not in Car, 2004.
16. Scott, Sheriff's Officials, Wetterlings Discuss New Twist, 2004.
17. *Ibid.*
18. Scott, Answers in Wetterling Case Elude, but Hope Doesn't—Reminders of the Boy Taken 14 Years Ago Remain, Inspire Those Hunting for Closure, 2004.
19. Chapman, KARE 11 Investigates: News in the Wetterling Case, 2004.
20. *Ibid.*
21. Scott, Answers in Wetterling Case Elude, but Hope Doesn't—Reminders of the Boy Taken 14 Years Ago Remain, Inspire Those Hunting for Closure, 2004.
22. Doyle P., From the Start, Wetterling Case Drew Range of Tips, 2004.
23. Scott, Answers in Wetterling Case Elude, but Hope Doesn't—Reminders of the Boy Taken 14 Years Ago Remain, Inspire Those Hunting for Closure, 2004.
24. *Ibid.*
25. Simons A., 2010.
26. Meryhew, Hope Keeps Search for Jacob Going, 1999.
27. Nelson, Julie Nelson Interviews Dan Rassier, Part 2, 2010.
28. Murphy, For 1st Time, "Person of Interest" Goes Through Day of Wetterling Abduction, 2013.
29. *Ibid.*
30. *Star Tribune* Staff Report, 2004.
31. Chapman, KARE 11 Investigates: Coincidence in Wetterling Case, 2004.
32. Stearns County, 2010.
33. Garza, 2009.
34. *Ibid.*
35. *Ibid.*
36. Welsh, His Pal Lives Jacob's Football Dream—"I Always Wish That He Will Come Home," Friend Says, 1993.
37. Vezner T., 2010.
38. State Fire Marshal Division, 2009.
39. Petrie K., Enduring Hope—Family, Friends, Investigators Reflect on the Night the 11-Year-Old Was Kidnapped, 2009.
40. Petrie K., Investigators Learned from Wetterling Case, 2009.
41. Petrie K., Case Still Gets Leads—Investigation Has Shifted to Focus on Local Suspects, 2009.
42. Nelson, Julie Nelson Interviews Dan Rassier, Part 2, 2010.
43. Murphy, For 1st Time, "Person of Interest" Goes Through Day of Wetterling Abduction, 2013.
44. Stearns County, 2010.

45. Petrie K., Site Near Wetterling Abuction Searched—Authorites Expected to Return to Scene Today, 2010.

46. *Ibid.*

47. *Ibid.*

48. *Ibid.*

49. Petrie K., Investigation Near Abduction Site Moves into Second Day—Crews Dig Up Field, 2010.

50. Petrie K., Wetterling Investigation—Sheriff: Rassier "Person of Interest"—Man Says He Will Do What He Can to Help Investigators, 2010.

51. *St. Cloud Times* Editorial Board, 2010.

52. *Ibid.*

53. Kampshroer, 2010.

54. Petrie K., Wetterling Investigation—Sheriff: Rassier "Person of Interest"—Man Says He Will Do What He Can to Help Investigators, 2010.

55. Dalman, "Person of Interest" Says He Witnessed "Things," 2010.

56. *Ibid.*

57. Petrie K., Wetterling Investigation—Sheriff: Rassier "Person of Interest"—Man Says He Will Do What He Can to Help Investigators, 2010.

58. *St. Cloud Times* Staff Report, 2010.

59. Petrie K., 2010.

60. *Ibid.*

61. *St. Cloud Times* Staff Report, 2010.

62. Kampshroer, 2010.

63. *Ibid.*

64. *Ibid.*

65. Nelson, Julie Nelson Interviews Dan Rassier, Part 2, 2010.

66. Forliti, 2012.

67. *Ibid.*

68. Rassier, 2012.

69. *Ibid.*

70. *Ibid.*

71. *Ibid.*

Chapter 8

1. Haukebo K., Ground Search Ends—Police Think Gunman, Boy No Longer in St. Joseph, 1989.

2. Stearns County, 2010.

3. Baker, *JoyThe.Curious*, "An Early Suspect," 2014.

4. Murphy, Neighbors Discuss Paynesville Family and Possible Wetterling Connection, 2014.

5. Murphy, Are Paynesville Father and Son Connected to Wetterling Case, 2014.

6. Murphy, It Got Frustrating: Blogger, Survivor Pushed Investigators to Re-Examine Wetterling Case, 2016.

7. State of Minnesota, 2015.

8. *Ibid.*

9. *Ibid.*

10. Unze D., Private Investigator's Notes 1990 Notes Mention Heinrich, 2015.

11. *Ibid.*

Chapter 9

1. Haukebo K., FBI Profiles Boy's Abductor—White Man with Deformity; Loner; Low Skills, Self-Image, 1989.

2. Garber, 2009.

3. Furst, 2015.

4. Smith, 2015.

5. Hult, 2105.

Chapter 10

1. Caldwell, 2015.

2. Ross, 2015.

3. Collin, Heinrich's Strange Connection to Another Wetterling Case Suspect, 2015.

4. *Ibid.*

5. *Ibid.*

6. Divine, Jacob Wetterling "Person of Interest" Ordered Held Without Bail, 2015.

7. Stearns County, State of Minnesota, 1984.

8. *Ibid.*

9. *Ibid.*

10. Blume, 2015.

11. Divine, Jacob Wetterling "Person of Interest" Ordered Held Without Bail, 2015.

12. Stearns County, State of Minnesota, 1986.

13. *Ibid.*

14. Blume, 2015.

15. Wright County, State of Minnesota, 2015.

16. *Ibid.*

17. *Ibid.*

18. *Ibid.*

19. *Ibid.*

20. *Ibid.*

21. Thyen, Local Police Seek Help in Accosting Incidents, 1987.

22. *Ibid.*

23. Wright County, State of Minnesota, 2015.

24. *Ibid.*

25. *Ibid.*

26. *Ibid.*

27. *Ibid.*

28. *Ibid.*

29. *Ibid.*

30. *Ibid.*

31. *Ibid.*

32. Collin, Former Jail Worker and Author Speak Out on Heinrich's Alleged Connection to Wetterling, 2016.

33. Collin, An In-Depth Look into Heinrich's Life Before, After Wetterling Abduction, 2015.

34. Wright County, State of Minnesota, 2015.

35. *Ibid.*

36. *Ibid.*

37. *Ibid.*

38. *Ibid.*

39. *Ibid.*

40. *Ibid.*

41. *Ibid.*

42. *Ibid.*

43. Garber, 2009.

44. Lyden, 2015.

45. Murphy, WCCO Spoke with Wetterling Abduction "Person of Interest" In 1996, 2015.

46. *Ibid.*

47. Blume, 2015.

48. Wright County, State of Minnesota, 2015.

49. *Ibid.*

50. *Ibid.*

51. Caldwell, 2015.

52. Kern, 2015.

53. Wright County, State of Minnesota, 2015.

54. United States Attorney Office, Shane Ball, 2015.

55. *Ibid.*

56. *Ibid.*

57. *Ibid.*

58. *Ibid.*

59. Divine, Wetterling Case Takes Fresh Turn, 2015.

60. *Ibid.*

61. United States Attorney Office, Shane Ball, 2015.

62. Caldwell, 2015.

63. *Ibid.*

64. *Ibid.*

65. Unze D., Hope Rises with Wetterling Billboard Campaign, 2014.

66. Unze D., Private Investigator's Notes 1990 Notes Mention Heinrich, 2015.

67. Divine, Jacob Wetterling "Person of Interest" Ordered Held Without Bail, 2015.

68. *Ibid.*

Chapter 11

1. Blume, 2015.

2. *Ibid.*

3. Mayerle, Original FBI Investigator on Wetterling Case Speaks Out, 2015.

4. Mayerle, What Do Prosecutors Need to Charge Heinrich in the Wetterling Case?, 2015.

5. *Ibid.*

6. Caldwell, 2015.

Chapter 12

1. United States of America verus Daniel Heinrich, 2016.

2. *Ibid.*

3. *Ibid.*

4. *Ibid.*

5. *Ibid.*

6. *Ibid.*

7. *Ibid.*

Bibliography

Aeikens, D. (1997, August 14). Suspect, Wetterling May Be Connected. *St. Cloud Times*, 1A.

Aekins, D. (2010, August 28). Concerns Unfold Around Teacher in Wetterling Case. *St. Cloud Times*, 1A, 7A.

Annette, H. M. (1990, January 26). County Attorney: Hart Likely to Face Additional Charges. *West Central Tribune*, A1.

Anonymous. (2014, January 8). 25 Years Later ... Embracing the Past. *Paynesville Press*, 4.

Application for Search Warrant and Supporting Affadavit—Duane Hart, Search Warrant Application (Carlton County, August 22, 2015).

Application for Search Warrant and Supporting Affadavit (Dan Rassier), Rassier Farm (Stearns County, June 28, 2010).

Associated Press. (1989, October 29). Attempted Kidnapping May Uncover New Leads. *St. Paul Pioneer Press*, unknown.

Associated Press. (1989, December 10). Authorities to Create Sketch of Man in Monticello Incident. *St. Cloud Times*, 1B.

Associated Press. (1990, August 9). Call Sends Wetterling Searchers to Illinois. *St. Paul Pioneer Press*, unknown.

Associated Press. (1991, July 22). Credibility of Abduction Informant Questioned. *St. Cloud Times*, 3A.

Associated Press. (1992, October 22). FBI Questioned Priest About Jacob. *St. Cloud Times*, 9A.

Associated Press. (1990, January 31). FBI Reduces Number on Wetterling Task Force. *Minneapolis Star Tribune*, unknown.

Associated Press. (2013, November 19).

Lawsuit: Priest Admitted Abuse but Stayed Active. Retrieved September 14, 2014, from Minnesota.cbslocal.com: www.minnesota.cbslocal.com/2013/11/19/lawsuit-priest-admitted-abuse-but-stayed-active.

Associated Press. (1989, November 10). Man Arraigned in Ohio Abduction. *St. Cloud Times*, 5A.

Associated Press. (1989, October 24). National Alert Issued for Boy, Kidnapper. *St. Paul Pioneer Press*, unknown.

Associated Press. (1998, November 1). Patty Wetterling's Letter Spurs New Leads—A Half-Dozen Tips Deemed Significant. *St. Cloud Times*, 4C.

Associated Press. (1997, August 15). Police Doubt Car Bombing, Weiss Linked—Explosion Occurs on Street of Accused Child Molester. *St. Paul Pioneer Press*, unknown.

Associated Press. (2012, May 25). *Priest Admitted to Abuse, but Was Never Prosecuted*. Retrieved March 17, 2014, from bishop-accountability.org: www.bishop-accountability.org.

Associated Press. (1989, October 27). Searchers Find No Trace of Abducted Boy. *Wisconsin State Journal*, 3A.

Associated Press. (1989, December 26). Wetterling Kidnapping Voted top Story in State. *St. Cloud Times*, 3A.

Associated Press. (2007, February 2). Wetterling on Missouri Radar—Task Force Probes Links. *St. Cloud Times*, 3B.

Associated Press. (1992, October 22). Wetterlings Make Plea for Son's Safe Return. *St. Cloud Times*, 1C.

Baker, J. (2013, February 23). *JoyThe.Curious*, "Dan's Story." Retrieved April 22,

2014, from joybaker.com: www.joybaker.com/2013/02/23/dans-story-2.

Baker, J. (2014, December 27). *JoyThe.Curious*, "An Early Suspect." Retrieved January 25, 2015, from joybaker.com: www.joybaker.com/2014/12/27/an-early-suspect/.

Baker, J. (2013, August 11). *JoyThe.Curious*, "Jared's Story." Retrieved June 15, 2014, from joybaker.com: www.joybaker.com/2013/08/11/jareds-story/.

Baker, J. (2013, March 20). *JoyThe.Curious*, "The Next Day." Retrieved April 22, 2014, from joybaker.com: www.joybaker.com/2013/03/20/the-next-day.

Behme, T. J. (1990, October 16). A Year Without Jacob—"Nothing … Has Hit Me Like This Case." *St. Cloud Times*, 1A, 10A.

Behme, T. J. (1991, January 24). CBS Show to Spotlight Jacob Abduction. *St. Cloud Times*, 3A.

Behme, T. J. (1992, May 31). Changes Left Former Director "Flabbergasted." *St. Cloud Times*, 1A, 7A.

Behme, T. J. (1990, October 20). Detectives Pursue New Lead—Officials Cautious, but Suspect Looks Good on Paper, They Say. *St. Cloud Times*, 1A.

Behme, T. J. (1990, October 11). Grafft Says Latest Lead Not Unusual. *St. Cloud Times*, 1A.

Behme, T. J. (1991, October 20). Image of Jacob at Age 15 Could Help Solve Case—Investigators: Case Remains High Priority. *St. Cloud Times*, 6A.

Behme, T. J. (1992, April 8). Inmate Sentenced for Trying Extortion. *St. Cloud TImes*, 1C.

Behme, T. J. (1991, October 23). Jacob Searchers Drain Pond—Marker Found with "Jacob" Carved on It. *St. Cloud Times*, 1A.

Behme, T. J. (1992, May 13). Jacob Wetterling Foundation Plans Summer Hiatus. *St. Cloud Times*, 1A, 10A.

Behme, T. J. (1991, February 16). Jacob's Birthday Sunday; Case Still Priority. *St. Cloud Times*, 5A.

Behme, T. J. (1991, December 17). Judge: Suppress Statements by Inmate in Wetterling Case. *St. Cloud Times*, 1A, 4A.

Behme, T. J. (1991, November 15). Lawyer Wants Statements About Wetterling Letter Erased. *St. Cloud TImes*, 1A.

Behme, T. J. (1992, January 30). Letter Writer Found Guilty of Extortion. *St. Cloud Times*, 1C.

Behme, T. J. (1992, January 4). Mass Mailings Aid Wetterling Investigation. *St. Cloud Times*, 2C.

Behme, T. J. (1991, May 3). Mother's Mailing Pleads for Clues on Jacob. *St. Cloud Times*, B1.

Behme, T. J. (1991, May 3). Praises TV Report on Pardons. *St. Cloud Times*, B1.

Behme, T. J. (1991, October 20). Two Years of Hope—Jacob's Family Yearns for Him, Fights for Others. *St. Coud Times*, 1A, 6A.

Behme, T. J. (1992, May 31). Wetterling Foundation Tries to Douse Internal Fires. *St. Cloud Times*, 1A, 7A.

Behme, T. J. (1992, June 3). Wetterling Vehicle Stolen from Parking Lot. *St. Cloud Times*, 6B.

Behme, T. J. (1992, May 13). Wetterlings Worry TV News Report May Curtail Tips. *St. Cloud Times*, 1A.

Behme, T. J. (1992, May 13). Wetterlings Worry TV News Report May Curtail Tips. *St. Cloud Times*, 1A.

Bergquist, K. (1990, October 21). Club Dedicates Run to Jacob. *St. Cloud Times*, 8A.

Bergquist, K. (1992, January 4). Photo of Jacob to Be Mass-Mailed. *St. Cloud Times*, 1B.

Bertram, J. (1992, August 4). Laws to Protect Our Children. *Paynesville Press*, 5.

Blume, (2015, November 15). *Looking into Danny Heinrich's Past*. Retrieved November 25, 2015, from fox9.com: www.fox9.com/news/49649710-story.

Board, E. (1990, October 22). "Jacob's Hope" Lives in All of Us. *St. Cloud Times*, 8A.

Board, E. (1999, October 22). Jacob's Hope Remains Strong at 10-Year Mark. *St. Cloud Times*, 12.

Board, S. C. (1989, October 25). Editorial—Missing Boy Bonds Community. *St. Cloud Times*, 12A.

Board, S. C. (1989, November 3). Editorial—Our Midwestern Roots are Showing. *St. Cloud Times*, 7A.

Bodette, J. (1989, October 28). Jacob, We're

with You, Wherever You Are—Editor's Note. *St. Cloud Times*, 7A.

Bush, G. (1990, June 8). President Remembers Missing Children. *St. Joseph Newsleader*, 11.

Bushey, S. (2010, July 9). Farm Investigation Still Remains "Mystery." *St. Joseph Newsleader*, 1, 4.

Caldwell, J. (2015, December 9). Janelle Kendall Talks About Danny Heinrich. (J. Caldwell, Interviewer).

Capacio, S. a. (2013, October 22). *Patty Wetterling: Miracles Can Happen*. Retrieved November 15, 2014, from Myfox twincities.com: www.myfoxtwincites. com/story/23760683/patty-wetterling-miracles-can-happen.

Chapman, C. (2004, July 30). *Kare 11 Investigates: Coincidence in Wetterling Case*. Retrieved May 7, 2014, from kare11.com: www.kare11.com/news/article/63324/26-kare-11-investigates-coincidence-in-wetterling-case.

Chapman, C. (2004, July 30). *Kare 11 Investigates: News in the Wetterling Case*. Retrieved November 12, 2015, from Kare11. com: archive.kare11.com/news/news_article.aspx?storyid=63364.

Cintron, D. (2010, July 4). St. Joseph Reflects on Renewed Search—Community Hopes for Closure in Probe. *St. Cloud Times*, 1A, 2A.

Cintron, D. (2010, July 2). St. Joseph Watches, Waits for Wetterling Information. *St. Cloud Times*, 1A, 6A.

Clark, D. M. The Abduction of Jacob. *Rosholt Review*. Rosholt, SD, USA.

Cold Spring Record Staff. (1989, January 10). Cold Spring Police Dept / Stearns Co. Sheriff's Dept to Fingerprint Children. *Cold Spring Record*, 1.

Cold Spring Record Staff. (1989, January 17). Cold Spring Youth Abducted Recently. *Cold Spring Record*, 1.

Cold Spring Record Staff. (1989, February 07). Crime Stoppers Needs Public's Information. *Cold Spring Record*, 1.

Cold Spring Record Staff Report. (1989, January 10). Rocori Band Boosters to Host Fun-d Night. *Cold Spring Record*, 3.

Cold Spring Record Staff. (1989, January 10). Rocori Band Boosters to Host Fun-d Night. *Cold Spring Record*, 3.

Collin, L. (2015, November 25). *An In-Depth Look into Heinrich's Life Before, After Wetterling Abduction*. Retrieved December 21, 2015, from Minnesota. cbslocal.com: www.minnesota.cbslocal. com/2015/11/25/investigators-take-an-in-depth-look-into-heinrichs-life-before-after-wetterling-abduction/.

Collin, L. (2016, February 24). *Former Jail Worker and Author Speak Out on Heinrich's Alleged Connection to Wetterling*. Retrieved September 16, 2016, from Minnesota.cbs.local.com: www.min-nesota.cbs.local.com/2016/02/24/fmr-jail-worker-and-author-speak-out-on-Heinrich's-alleged-connection-to-Wetterling.

Collin, L. (2015, November 13). *Heinrich's Strange Connection to Another Wetterling Case Suspect*. Retrieved December 13, 2015, from Minnesota.cbslocal.com: www.minnesota.cbslocal.com/2015/11/13/heinrichs-strange-connection-to-another-wetterling-case-suspect.

Cook, M. (1989, October 26). FBI Kidnapper Profile Suggests White Loner. *St. Paul Pioneer Press*, unknown.

Cook, R. (1995, June 30). Jacob's Hope Cars Make the Circuit. *St. Cloud Times*, 1C, 2C.

Dalman, D. (1999, October 15). "Jacob's Hope" Remains Alive 10 Years After Abduction. *St. Joseph Newsleader*, 1, 8.

Dalman, D. (2010, July 9). "Person of Interest" Says He Witnessed "Things." *St. Joseph Newsleader*, 1.

Dalman, D. (1999, October 22). Search for One Child Becomes Search for All. *St. Joseph Newsleader*, 1, 8.

DeCamp, J. (1994, February 13). Letters—Story Laden with Lies, Half-Truths, Subject Claims. *St. Cloud TImes*, 12A.

DeLand, D. (2014, October 18). Wetterlings Still Coping with Heartbreak. *St. Cloud Times*, 1A.

Divine, M. (2015, November 4). *Jacob Wetterling "Person of Interest" Ordered Held Without Bail*. Retrieved November 24, 2015, from Twincities.com: www.twincities.com/localnews/ci_29070515/jacob-wetterling-person-interest-appears-court.

Divine, M. (2015, October 30). Wetterling

Case Takes Fresh Turn. *St. Paul Pioneer Press*, 1.

Douglass, T. (1990, January 30). Belgrade Man Arrested—Charged with Assaulting Boys. *Paynesville Press*, 1.

Douglass, T. (1984, February 22). Local Agent Offers Unique Crime Assistance Policy. *Paynesville Press*, 3.

Douglass, T. (1989, November 14). "Somewhere Out There"—Middle School Students Help with Public Awareness Campaign. *Paynesville Press*, 1B.

Doyle, a. (2004, February 29). From the Start, Wetterling Case Drew Range of Tips. *Minneapolis Star Tribune*, unknown.

Doyle, a. (2004, February 25). New Theory in Kidnap Case—Wetterling Abductor May Have Been on Foot. *Minneapolis Star Tribune*, unknown.

Doyle, (1990, January 26). Bail Set at $100,000 for Suspect in Child Sex Case. *Minneapolis Star Tribune*, unknown.

Doyle, (1990, January 25). Man Held in Molestation Cases; Police Seek Wetterling Link. *Minneapolis Star Tribune*, unknown.

Doyle, (1989, December 15). New Lead Reported in Wetterling Case. *Minneapolis Star Tribune*, unknown.

Doyle, (1989, October 25). Officials Seek 100 Potential Suspects in Hunt for St. Joseph Boy's Abductor. *Minneapolis Star Tribune*, 1A.

DuBois, J. (1990, October 15). A Year Without Jacob—Big Brother, Who Made Everything OK, Still Missing. *St. Cloud Times*, 1A, 8A.

DuBois, J. (1990, October 14). A Year Without Jacob—Dad Runs on Spiritual Energy. *St. Cloud Times*, 1A, 12A.

DuBois, J. (1990, October 21). A Year Without Jacob—Patty Will Never Give Up—Life Has Become Exhaustive Search. *St. Cloud Times*, 1A, 8A.

DuBois, J. (1990, October 15). Dad Hopes Appearance in Race Rejuvenates Search. *St. Cloud Times*, 8A.

DuBois, J. (1993, October 22). Experience Touches Jacob's Class. *St. Cloud Times*, 1A, 16A.

DuBois, J. (1990, October 23). Family Rekindles Jacob's Hope—First-year Ceremony Radiates Optimism. *St. Cloud Times*, 1A.

Duchschere, K. (1989, November 21). FBI Cites Similarities in Wetterling Case, Attempted Abduction of Wisconsin Boy. *Minneapolis Star Tribune*, unknown.

Ebben, R. (2015, October 18). Telephone Interview with Kevin Hamilton.

Fogarty, S. (1989, November 1). Minnesota Connection Discounted. *Elyria Chronicle—Telegram*, A-1, A-6.

Forliti, A. (2012, August 2). Man Called Person of Interest in Wetterling Case Airs Complaints. *Minneapolis Star Tribune*, unknown.

Furst, R. a. (2015, October 31). *25th Anniversary Sparks Fresh Look at Jacob Wetterling Mystery.* Retrieved November 24, 2015, from Startribune.com: www.m.startribune.com/person-of-interest-named-in-1989-jacob-wetterling-disappearance-/338852902/.

Gabbert, J. (1989, November 6). Vikes, Fans Line Up to Help Find Jacob. *St. Cloud Times*, 1A.

Garber, A. (2009). *Striving to Be the Best—A Memoir.* Minneapolis: Quinn Publishing.

Garza, J. (2009, January 06). Dead Barber's Home Yields Creepy Stash. *Milwaukee Journal Sentinal*, 1.

Ghere, E. (2001, February 1). Man Cleared in Wetterling Case. *St. Cloud Times*, 1B.

Goldschen, S. (1990, October 26). Abducted Children Dependent on Abductor for Life Support—Kids Not Likely to Come Forward. *St. Joseph Newsleader*, 7.

Goldschen, S. (1989, November 11). All the World Around—I Know Jacob Because My Child Is He. *St. Joseph Newsletter*, 2.

Goldschen, S. (1989, December 22). All the World Around—We're Advocates for Jacob Wetterling. *St. Jospeph Newsleader*, 4.

Goldschen, S. (1990, January 5). Anoka Veterans March 65 Miles for Jacob. *St. Joseph Newsleader*, 1, 3.

Goldschen, S. (1990, July 6). Apple Donates $20,000 Computer System to Wetterling Foundation. *St. Joseph Newsleader*, 3.

Goldschen, S. (1989, November 24). Betram Supports Stronger Laws Against Child Abduction. *St. Joseph Newsleader*, 4.

Goldschen, S. (1990, February 2). Busy Wetterlings "Doing Well, but It's So Hard." *St. Joseph Newsleader*, 2.

Goldschen, S. (1990, February 2). Campaign May Spur Stronger Child Protection Laws. *St. Joseph Newsleader*, 1, 12.

Goldschen, S. (1990, January 5). Dear Santa: All I Want Is Jacob. *St. Joseph Newsleader*, 2.

Goldschen, S. (1993, February 5). Dennis Green to Carry the Ball for Jacob Wetterling and Missing Children at Celebrity Banquet Feb. 19—Vikings Coach and Jacob Share Birthdays Feb. 17 When Jacob Turns 15. *St. Joseph Newsleader*, 1, 12.

Goldschen, S. (1990, January 19). FBI Steadfast in Jacob Investigation. *St. Joseph Newsleader*, 1.

Goldschen, S. (1990, February 2). Foundation Created for Jacob. *St. Joseph Newsleader*, 3.

Goldschen, S. (1989, November 24). Hands Keep Flame Alive. *St. Joseph Newsleader*, 1, 6.

Goldschen, S. (1992, October 9). Hope Holds for Jacob Wetterling—Name Still Synonymous with Missing Children After Three Years. *St. Joseph Newsleader*, 1, 5.

Goldschen, S. (1989, November 24). Inmates Show Compassion. *St. Joseph Newsleader*, 3.

Goldschen, S. (1990, February 2). Investigation Leaves No Stone Unturned. *St. Joseph Newsleader*, 5.

Goldschen, S. (1990, July 6). Investigators Feel Jacob's Out There—Wetterlings Back Seclusion Theory. *St. Joseph Newsleader*, 1.

Goldschen, S. (1990, October 26). Jacob Among Highway 94 Victims?—FBI Pursues Theory of "Corridor" Case. *St. Joseph Newsleader*, 7.

Goldschen, S. (1990, April 13). Jacob Foundation Seeks $900,000. *St. Joseph Newsleader*, 2.

Goldschen, S. (1989, November 10). "Jacob Wetterling Office" To Coordinate Volunteer Effort. *St. Joseph Newsleader*, 12.

Goldschen, S. (1989, December 22). Jacob's Face Melts Heart of St. Louis Volunteer. *St. Joseph Newsleader*, 4.

Goldschen, S. (1989, December 22). Jacob's Hope Burns Ever Brighter—Pope's Letter "Like Big Prayer Answered." *St. Joseph Newsleader*, 1, 12.

Goldschen, S. (1989, December 22). Jacob's Hope Candle Aflame on City Hall. *St. Joseph Newsleader*, 1, 12.

Goldschen, S. (1989, December 8). Jacob's Hope to Rise Atop City Hall. *St. Joseph Newsleader*, 12.

Goldschen, S. (1989, November 24). Letters, Friends, Hope Fill Wetterling Home. *St. Joseph Newsleader*, 1, 12.

Goldschen, S. (1990, March 30). Local Boy Frightened by Stranger. *St. Joseph Newsleader*, 1,8.

Goldschen, S. (1993, Unknown Unknown). "New Kids" Speak Out for Child Safety—Pop Group to Do TV, Theater Spots. *St. Joseph Newsleader*, Unknown.

Goldschen, S. (1989, November 24). North Community Joins "Hands." *St. Joseph Newsleader*, 6.

Goldschen, S. (1990, January 5). Old Friends Miss Jacob at VA Hospital. *St. Joseph Newsleader*, 5.

Goldschen, S. (1993, October 15). Patty Wetterling Won't Say Uncle—as Committed as Ever to Search for Jacob After Four Years—Investigation Still Active; Leads Still Being Investigated. *St. Joseph Newsleader*, 1, 4.

Goldschen, S. (1990, August 17). Patty Wetterling: "I Never Lost Hope"—Illinois Incidents Among Many in Search for Jacob. *St. Joseph Newsleader*, 4.

Goldschen, S. (1990, July 20). Perpich in Town for Joe and Jacob. *St. Joseph Newsleader*, 1, 11.

Goldschen, S. (1990, August 17). Phone Call Raises Jacob's Hope—Illinois Woman Sees Boy Who Might Be Jacob. *St. Joseph Newsleader*, 4, 10, 11.

Goldschen, S. (1989, October 27). Police Chief Answers Children's Questions on Abduction. *St. Joseph Newsleader*, 1, 12.

Goldschen, S. (1990, March 30). President, Barbara Bush Express Hope for Jacob—Wetterlings Await Personal Message. *St. Joseph Newsleader*, 2,5.

Goldschen, S. (1989, November 10). Quadraplegic Tells Wetterlings, Others Not to Give Up Hope. *St. Joseph Newsleader*, 9.

Goldschen, S. (1992, November 6). St. John's Abbey Statement on Sex Abuse, Exploitation. *St. Joseph Newsleader*, 12.

Goldschen, S. (1989, October 27). St. Joseph Steps Forward for Jacob Wetterling. *St. Joseph Newsleader*, 1, 12.

Goldschen, S. (1989, November 24). St. Joseph Still "Wonderful Community" for Wetterlings. *St. Joseph Newsleader*, 12.

Goldschen, S. (1990, April 13). Suspicious Van Sighted Again—Woman Says Sheriff "Sloughs Off" Report. *St. Cloud Times*, 1,12.

Goldschen, S. (1990, January 19). Teacher Preparing Scrapbook Album for Jacob's Hope. *St. Joseph Newsleader* .

Goldschen, S. (1989, November 24). Teacher, Principal Say Jacob Model Student. *St. Joseph Newsleader*, 6.

Goldschen, S. (1991, October 11). Threatening Phone Calls Jar Wetterling Foundation Office—Latest Scare from Man with BB Gun in Jerry Wetterling's Albany Office. *St. Joseph Newsleader*, 4.

Goldschen, S. (1992, May 22). TV Newscasts Reveal Police Files on Leads in Jacob Wetterling Case. *St. Joseph Newsleader*, 5, 11.

Goldschen, S. (1990, January 19). Van Still Haunts St. Joseph Residents. *St. Joseph Newsleader*, 1.

Goldschen, S. (1990, July 20). Wetterlings Campaign Again—New SAFE Program Educates Families. *St. Joseph Newsleader*, 6.

Goldschen, S. (1989, December 8). Wetterlings Receive Gift of Music. *St. Joseph Newsleader*, 11.

Goldschen, S. (1989, November 24). "Where is Jacob?"—Trevor Wants to Know. *St. Joseph Newsleader*, 12.

Hasson, J. (1989, December 23). Experts: Missing Children's Visibility Hinges on Community. *St. Cloud Times*, 1, 12A.

Haukebo, K. (1989, November 19). 30 Days After Kidnapping, Officers Share Jacob's Hope. *St. Cloud Times*, 1, 12A.

Haukebo, K. (1989, November 2). Alert Public Becomes Key in Search—Volunteers Will Gather Tonight. *St. Cloud Times*, 1, 8A.

Haukebo, K. (1989, November 30). Authorities Release Revised Sketch of Abduction Suspect. *St. Cloud Times*, 1, 12A.

Haukebo, K. (1989, November 22). Escaped Mental Patient Killed Himself Five Years Ago. *St. Cloud Times*, 1B.

Haukebo, K. (1989, November 13). FBI Chases New Kidnap Leads. *St. Cloud Times*, 1, 6A.

Haukebo, K. (1989, November 20). FBI Probes Attemped Abduction. *St. Cloud Times*, 1B.

Haukebo, K. (1989, October 26). FBI Profiles Boy's Abductor—White Man with Deformity; Loner; Low Skills, Self-Image. *St. Cloud Times*, 1A.

Haukebo, K. (1989, November 24). FBI Seeks Tips on 3 Drivers—Cars Were Seen Near Jacob's Home. *St. Cloud Times*, 1A.

Haukebo, K. (1989, December 5). FBI to Question Wisconsin Boy Again About Abduction Try. *St. Cloud Times*, 1B.

Haukebo, K. (1989, November 15). FBI: Escaped Mental Patient Not Prime Suspect. *St. Cloud Times*, 1, 12A.

Haukebo, K. (1990, April 22). Fear Lingers Six Months After Jacob's Abduction. *St. Cloud Times*, 1, 7A.

Haukebo, K. (1989, November 12). Freedom Flight Prays for POW's, MIA's, Jacob. *St. Cloud Times*, 1, 12A.

Haukebo, K. (1989, November 3). Ground Search Called Off—Richmond Lions Offer $100,000 Reward for Jacob. *St. Cloud Times*, 1, 5A.

Haukebo, K. (1989, October 24). Ground Search Ends—Police Think Gunman, Boy No Longer in St. Joseph. *St. Cloud Times*, 1, 8A.

Haukebo, K. (1989, October 23). Gunman Abducts St. Joseph Boy. *St. Cloud Times*.

Haukebo, K. (1989, October 26). Horses Added to Search—Kidnap Probe Gets Hundreds of Tip Calls. *St. Cloud Times*, 1, 10A.

Haukebo, K. (1989, November 16). Inmates Share Jacob's Family's Pain. *St. Cloud Times*, 1, 3B.

Haukebo, K. (1989, November 9). Investigation Slows; Community Still Rallying. *St. Cloud Times*, 1A.

Haukebo, K. (1990, January 10). Jacob Case Haunts Officers—Focus Narrows, Few Leads After 81 Days. *St. Cloud Times*, 1, 8A.

Haukebo, K. (1989, October 29). "Jacob

Needs Me to Be Strong Now"—Mom, Family Hope, Wait. *St. Cloud Times*, 1A-5A.

Haukebo, K. (1989, November 17). Jacob Radiothon Brings in $70,000. *St. Cloud Times*, 1B.

Haukebo, K. (1989, November 11). Jacob Tragedy Stirs Hope, Fear—Workers' Give Time, Emotion at Office. *St. Cloud Times*, 1, 3B.

Haukebo, K. (1989, November 5). Jacob's Buddy Struggles with Kidnap's Aftermath. *St. Cloud Times*, 8A.

Haukebo, K. (1989, November 8). Louisiana Suspect Ruled Out in Jacob Case. *St. Cloud Times*, 1, 2B.

Haukebo, K. (1990, January 25). Man Arrested in Sexual Assaults—No Known Link to Wetterling Case, FBI Says. *St. Cloud Times*, 1, 8A.

Haukebo, K. (1989, November 11). Man with Piercing Stare Sought. *St. Cloud Times*, 1B.

Haukebo, K. (1989, November 7). Minot Lead on Jacob is Soft, FBI Says—Probe Focuses on Man Seen at Store. *St. Cloud Times*, 1, 6A.

Haukebo, K. (1990, January 28). Molester Files May Further Investigations. *St. Cloud Times*, 1A.

Haukebo, K. (1989, December 1). Monticello Kidnap Attempt Fails—FBI Appeals for Witnesses. *St. Cloud Times*, 1, 8A.

Haukebo, K. (1989, October 27). National Guard Joins Search—Red Car a False Lead in St. Joseph Kidnap Case, Police Say. 1A, 8A.

Haukebo, K. (1989, October 27). National Guard Joins Search—Red Car a False Lead in St. Joseph, Kidnap Case, Police Say. *St. Cloud Times*, 1, 8A.

Haukebo, K. (1989, November 23). New Sketch to Combine 3 Suspects. *St. Cloud Times*, 1A.

Haukebo, K. (1989, November 21). Number of Kidnap Case Officers Cut—BCA Chief: "It Was One of Those Tough Decisions." *St. Cloud Times*, 1, 2B.

Haukebo, K. (1990, February 14). Patty: "I Didn't Believe It Was Jacob"—Body Found Near St. Paul Dam Still Unidentified. *St. Cloud Times*, 1, 10A.

Haukebo, K. (1989, October 25). Police Searching for Red Car—Kidnap Case Gets New Lead. *St. Cloud Times*, 1, 9A.

Haukebo, K. (1989, November 14). Police Sketch of Suspects Prompt 300 Tips. *St. Cloud Times*, 1A.

Haukebo, K. (1989, December 6). Pope John Paul Shares Wetterlings' Pain, Hope. *St. Cloud Times*, 1, 10A.

Haukebo, K. (1989, November 1). Search for Jacob Uses Mail—Volunteers Needed to Send Fliers Nationwide; Investigation Centers on Sighting, White Car. *St. Cloud Times*, 1, 12A.

Haukebo, K. (1989, October 31). Searchers Move into Hector Area—Investigators Turn Focus to White Car. *St. Cloud Times*, 1, 12A.

Haukebo, K. (1989, October 24). So Many People Have Offered to Help, Boy's Father Says. *St. Cloud Times*, 1, 8A.

Haukebo, K. (1989, November 29). St. Joseph Man Hospitalized After Standoff with Deputies. *St. Cloud Times*, 1B.

Haukebo, K. (1989, November 28). Tips Lag in Search for Jacob. *St. Cloud Times*, 1B.

Haukebo, K. (1989, December 14). Two Abductions May Be Linked—Cold Spring Assault May Offer Jacob Clues; Sketch Given. *St. Cloud Times*, 1, 10A.

Haukebo, K. (1989, January 30). Watkins Chief Admits to Sex Abuse. *St. Cloud Times*, 1B.

Haukebo, K. (1989, December 24). Wetterlings: "Our Family Will Never Be the Same"—Christmas Eve '89: Waiting for a Child. *St. Cloud Times*, 1, 8A.

Hawkins, B. (2009, October Unknown). Without a Trace. *Minnesota Monthly*, Unknown.

Hood, D. (1990, March 30). Letters—Applicant Questioned as Kidnapping Suspect. *St. Cloud Times*, 12A.

Hoogesteger, J. (1999, October). Hope Still Alive as 10-Year Abduction Annivesary Nears. *St. Cloud Times*, 1B, 2B.

Horwich, J. (2002, July 11). As Priest Abusers Become Public, a Parish Looks at Its Past. *Minnesota Public Radio*, n/a.

Hult, K. (2105, November 9). *Patty Wetterling's Mission of Hope*. Retrieved January 14, 2016, from www.Kare11.com: www.kare11.com/news/exclusive-patty-wetterling-mission-of-hope/11630192.

In the Matter of: Duane Allen Hart, No. C9–9502057 (Minnesota Court of Appeals February 20, 1996).

Jared. (2015, February 27). Podcast Interview with Jared. (J. Baker, Interviewer).

Johnson, K. E. (1997, May 31). TV Show, Photo Renew Attention—Jacob Wetterling's Mom Appears on "Today Show" with Age-Progressed Image of Abducted Son. *St. Cloud Times*, 1A.

Jones, S. (2014, October 22). Minnesota.cbs local.com. Retrieved October 29, 2014, from Minnesota.cbslocal.com/2014/10/22/25-years-later-mom-recalls-jacob-wetterlings-abduction.

Kampshroer, C. (2010, September 30). *Web Exclusive: Interview with Jacob Wetterling "Person of Interest."* Retrieved August 26, 2014, from GreaterMinnesota.KSTP.com: www.greaterminnesota.kstp.com/news/news/56198/web-exclusive-interview-jacob-wetterling-person-interest.

Kern, D. (2015). *Receipt, Inventory and Return 1–1.* Wright County: State of Minnesota.

La Crosse Tribune Staff. (1990, October 1990). City Police Try to Link Man to Wetterling. *La Crosse Tribune*, unknown.

Lanpher, K. (1997, February 20). Belgians to Examine Wetterling Tragedy. *St. Paul Pioneer Press*, unknown.

Larson, T. (1989, October 25). Counselors Help Local Parents Find Ways to Explain Tragedy to Children. *St. Cloud Times*, 9A.

Larson, T., & Haukebo, a. K. (n.d.). Roadblocks Net Few Clues—200 Troops to Search Sauk River Shoreline. *St. Cloud Times*, 1, 6A.

Larson, T. (1989, October 30). St. Joseph Residents Launch More Efforts to Find Jacob. *St. Cloud Times*, 6A.

Larson, T. (1990, October 18). A Year Without Jacob—Friend Fueled Media Blitz, but Work Took Toll. *St. Cloud Times*, 1A, 14A.

Larson, T. (1990, October 17). A Year Without Jacob—"I Became Part of the Family"—Story Drains Reporter. *St. Cloud Times*, 1A, 12A.

Lewis, D. (1989, November 16). Inmates Join Effort to Find Jacob—Stillwater Prisoners Donate T-Shirts with Missing

Child's Picture. *St. Paul Pioneer Press*, unknown.

Lindblad, O. (2006). *Rooted in Christ, the Living Stone—the Story of St. Joseph Church, St. Joseph, MN 1856–2006.* St. Joseph, MN: Self Published.

Lowe, S. (1989, November 6). Another Suspect Sought in Kidnap—FBI Appeals to Public for Help in Finding Man. *St. Cloud Times*, 1A.

Lowe, S. (1990, February 14). Community, Friends Relieved That Boy's Body Isn't Jacob's. *St. Cloud Times*, 1, 10A.

Lowe, S. (1989, October 27). Family Reaches Out WIth Boy's Favorite Song. *St. Cloud Times*, 1, 8A.

Lowe, S. (1989, November 18). FBI: Jacob Lead Proves False—Caller Said Abducted Boy Was in St. Joseph. *St. Cloud TImes*, 1, 6A.

Lowe, S. (1989, November 2). FBI Still Investigating 100 Possible Suspects. *St. Cloud Times*, 1A.

Lowe, S. (1989, October 31). Fear Sending More to Parties for Halloween. *St. Cloud Times*, 1, 12A.

Lowe, C. (2015, November 13). *Former Police Officer Describes Dog's Role in Wetterling Case.* Retrieved November 16, 2015, from Karel1.com: karel1.com/story/news/local/2015/11/13/former-police-officer-describes-dogs-role-in-wetterling-case/75747986/.

Lowe, S. (1990, October 20). Foundation Stokes Drive to Find Jacob, Others. *St. Cloud Times*, 14A.

Lowe, S. (1989, December 23). Jacob Rumours Untrue, FBI Says. *St. Cloud Times*, 1, 12A.

Lowe, S. (1989, November 7). Kidnap Investigation Costs Stearns County $41,000. *St. Cloud Times*, 1, 6A.

Lowe, S. (1989, November 10). Sketch Concerns Kidnapping Officials. *St. Cloud Times*, 1, 8A.

Lowe, S. (1989, December 15). Sketch of Abduction Suspect Prompts Flood of Phone Calls. *St. Cloud Times*, 1B.

Lowe, S. (1989, October 31). Songwriter Visits Wetterling Family. *St. Cloud Times*, 12A.

Lowe, S. (1989, October 24). Stranger Abductions Rare, Premediatated, Expert Says. *St. Cloud Times*, 8A.

Lowe, S. (1989, Decemberr 28). $10,000 Offered for Suspect Identification. *St. Cloud Times*, 3A.

Lowe, S. (1989, October 25). Town Prays Abductor "Comes to His Senses." *St. Cloud Times*, 1, 9A.

Lowe, S. (1989, November 5). Tragedy Wrenches St. Joseph: "We Are All Scared." *St. Cloud Times*, 8A.

Lowe, S. (1990, May 4). $200,000 Reward for Clues on Jacob. *St. Cloud Times*, 1, 4A.

Lowe, S. (1989, November 3). Volunteers Mail 35,000 Fliers. *St. Cloud Times*, 1, 5A.

Lowe, S. (1989, November 1). Wetterlings Make Plea on ABC's Good Morning America. *St. Cloud Times*, 12A.

Lowe, S. (1990, May 1). Wisconsin Suspect Questioned on Jacob. *St. Cloud Times*, 1B.

Lowe, S. (1990, October 19). A Year Without Jacob—Families Stunned by Stolen Innocence. *St. Cloud Times*, 1A, 8A.

Lowe, S. (1990, October 20). A Year Without Jacob—Massive Effort Took Seasoned Search Organizer by Surprise. *St. Cloud Times*, 1A, 14A.

Lowe, S., and Larson, A. T. (1989, October 28). Sketch Released in Kidnap Case—Earlier Abduction Attempt may be Linked to st. Joe Boy. *St. Cloud Times*, 1, 5A.

Lyden, T. (2015, November 19). *Police Report Details an Incident Where Heinrich Was Observed Following Paperboys Along Their Routes.* Retrieved December 13, 2015, from fox9.com: www.fox9.com/news/51782857-story.

Mattern, (1992, October 21). Jacob's Hope Burns Through Three Years. *St. Cloud Times*, 1A, 12A.

Mattern, (1992, October 21). Task Force Focuses on Old Leads. *St. Cloud Times*, 1A.

Mattern, (1992, November 5). Wetterling Anniversary Prompts More Leads. *St. Cloud TImes*, 1A.

Mattern, (1992, October 22). Wetterling Center Grows Sturdier Through Changes. *St. Cloud Times*, 1A.

Maurice, J. (2015, January 24). *New Book Investigates the Abduction of Jacob Wetterling.* Retrieved September 18, 2016, from www.WJON.com: www.wjon.com/news-noon-new-book-investigates-the-abduction-of-jacob-wetterling.

Mayerle, J. (2015, November 12). *Original FBI Investigator on Wetterling Case Speaks Out.* Retrieved December 13, 2015, from Minnesota.cbslocal.com: www.minnesota.cbslocal.com/2015/11/12/orginal-fbi-investigator-on-wetterling-case-speaks-out.

Mayerle, J. (2015, October 30). *What Do Prosecutors Need to Charge Heinrich in the Wetterling Case?* Retrieved November 24, 2015, from Minnesota.cbslocal.com: www.minnesota.cbslocal.com/2015/10/30/what-do-prosecutors-need-to-charge-heinrich-in-the-wetterling-case.

McAllister, B. (1989, November 21). Breakfast-goers Pray for Jacob. *St. Cloud Times*, 1, 2B.

McAllister, B. (1989, October 25). Fear, Shock Likely to Grip St. Joseph. *St. Cloud Times*, 1, 9A.

Meinert, K. (1989, October 21). "Catch Me' Does Well at Box Office. *St. Cloud Times*, 1A, 14A.

Merrill, A. (1989, November 6). Rockville Hoists Huge White Ribbon for Jacob. *St. Cloud Times*, 8A.

Merrill, A. (1989, October 28). Tom Thumb Offers Wetterlings Support. *St. Cloud Times*, 5A.

Merryhew, R. (1999, October 22). Hope Keeps Search for Jacob Going. *Star Tribune*, Unknown.

Meryhew, R. (2002, May 11). Agents Reviewing Abbey's Records. *Minneapolis Star Tribune*, unknown.

Meryhew, R. (1999, October 22). Hope Keeps Search for Jacob Going. *Minneapolis Star Tribune*, unknown.

Meryhew, R. (2010, September 19). Jacob's Sheriff. *Minneapolis Star Tribune*, A1, A10.

Meryhew, R. (2002, May 26). St. John's Community Wonders About Future. *Minneapolis Star Tribune*, unknown.

Minneapolis Star Tribune Staff Report. (1990, January 31). FBI Reduces Number on Wetterling Task Force.

Minneapolis Star Tribune Staff Report. (2004, February 25). New Theory in Kidnap Case.

Minneapolis Star Tribune Staff Report.

(1999, September 16). Wetterling, Other Unsolved Cases Revisited in Documents. *Minneapolis Star Tribune* Staff Report.

(1992, May 14). The Wetterling Stories Bring Charges of Politics at WCCO. *Minneapolis Star Tribune*, unknown.

Minnesota Board of Psychology. (1999, May 7). In the Matter of Renee Fredrickson, Ph. D., L.P. License No. LP2653. *n/a*. St. Paul, MN, USA: Minnesota Board of Psychology.

Murphy, E. (2013, May 14). Retrieved October 23, 2014, from Minnesota.cbslocal.com: Minnesota.cbslocal.com/2013/5/14/for-1st-time-person-of-interest-goes-through-day-of-wetterling-abduction.

Murphy, E. (2014, May 15). *Abuction Victime Speaks Out on Wetterling Case*. Retrieved September 12, 2014, from Minnesota.CBSlocal.com: www.minnesota.cbslocal.com/2015/05/15/abduction-victim-speaks-out-on-wetterling-case.

Murphy, E. (2014, May 21). *Are Paynesville Father & Son Connected to Wetterling Case*. Retrieved September 14, 2014, from Minnesota.CBSlocal.com: www.Minnesota.cbsloca.com/2014/05/21-are-payneville-father-&-son-connected-to-wetterling-case.

Murphy, E. (2013, May 14). *For 1st Time, "Person of Interest' Goes Through Day of Wetterling Abduction*. Retrieved June 12, 2014, from Minnesota.CBSlocal.com: www.minnesota.cbslocal.com/.

Murphy, E. (2016, September 13). *It Got Frustrating: Blogger, Survivor Pushed Investigators to Re-Examine Wetterling Case*. Retrieved September 26, 2016, from www.WCCO.com: www.minnesota.cbslocal.com/2016/09/13/jared-scheierl-joy-baker-wetterling/.

Murphy, E. (2014, May 23). *Neighbors Discuss Paynesville Family & Possible Wetterling Connection*. Retrieved September 14, 2014, from Minnesota.CBSlocal.com: www.minnesota.cbslocal.com/2014/05/23/neighbors-discuss-paynesville-family-&-possible-wetterling-connection.

Murphy, E. (2014, May 14). *New Developments Revealed in Jacob Wetterling Case*. Retrieved August 25, 2014, from Minnesota.CBSlocal.com: www.minnesota.cbslocal.com/2014/05/14/new-developments-in-jacob-wetterling-case.

Murphy, E. (2015, November 9). *WCCO Spoke with Wetterling Abduction "Person of Interest' in 1996*. Retrieved November 22, 2015, from Minnesota.cbslocal.com: www.minnesota.cbslocal.com/2015/11/09/wcco-spoke-with-wetterling-abduction-person-of-interest-in-1996/.

Nelson, J. (2010, October 6). *Julie Nelson Interviews Dan Rassier Part 1*. Retrieved October 15, 2013, from Karell.com: www.karell.com/video/6253870480 01/0/julie-nelson-interviews-dan-rassier-part-I.

Nelson, J. (2010, October 6). *Julie Nelson Interviews Dan Rassier Part 2*. Retrieved October 15, 2013, from Karell.com: www.karell.com/news/article/875817/14/part-2-julie-nelsons-conversation-with-dan-rassier.

Newton, E. M. (1994, October 22). Five Years After an Abduction..Central Minnesotans Share What They Were Robbed of—Family Nearly Lost Son to Abductor Few Months Earlier. *St. Cloud Times*, 1A.

Nistler, M. (1989, November 19). Candles Burn for Jacob—Wetterlings, Supporters Hold Vigil. *St. Cloud Times*, 1, 12A.

Nistler, M. (1989, November 11). Eden Valley Self-Defense Class Revived. *St. Cloud Times*, 1B.

Nistler, M. (1989, November 5). FBI Gives Van Sketch to Spark New Clues. *St. Cloud Times*, 1, 8A.

Nistler, M. (1989, December 31). FBI to Pull Agents Off Jacob Case. *St. Cloud Times*, 1A.

Nistler, M. (1989, November 5). Jacob Gets "Line of Love"—5,000 Link Hands to Show Jacob's Hope. *St. Cloud Times*, 1, 8A.

Nistler, M. (1989, October 29). Jacob's Friends Haven't Given Up. *St. Cloud Times*, 5A.

Nistler, M. (1989, October 29). More Troops Join Search—but Few New Clues Found. *St. Cloud Times*, 1, 5A.

Norman R. Larson, Appellant v. State of Minnesota, Respondent, Kandiyohi County, Defendant, 19900206 (Kandiyohi County February 6, 1990).

Olson, R. (2012, October 10). *KMSP-TV MyFox9.com/Allegations of Sexual Misconduct Bring Two Monks Under Investigation.* Retrieved December 13, 2014, from MyFoxTwinCities.com: www.myfoxtwincities.com/story/19809508/alleged-sexual.

Owen, D. D. (1990, November 3). Letter to the Editor—TV Has Turned Tragedy into Crass Media Event. 7A.

Parker, T. (1990, August 9). Police Quiz Witness Who Spotted Boy. *The Pantagraph*, A2.

Paynesville Press Staff Report. (1986, December 09). Assault Incidents Reported—Local Man Charged. *Paynesville Press*, 1.

Paynesville Press Staff Report. (1955, September 8). Jackie Theel Disappeared 11 Years Ago. *Paynesville Press*, 1.

Paynesville Press Staff Report. (1965, June 3). John Scott Administers Oath to Duane Hart. *Paynesville Press*, 1.

Paynesville Press Staff Report. (1965, June 03). John Scott Adminsters Oath to Duane Hart. *Paynesville Press*, 1.

Paynesville Press Staff Report. (1944, September 14). Mystery of Jackie Theel Unsolved. *Paynesville Press*, 1,4.

Paynesville Press Staff Report. (1986, March 8). Police News. *Paynesville Press*, 8.

Perez, I. (2013, June 28). myFoxTwinCities.com. Retrieved September 14, 2014, from myFoxTwinCities.com/story/22711576/matthew-feeney-sentenced-for-child-sex-abuse.

Peterson, J. (1990, February 2). Campaign May Spur Stronger Child Protection Laws. *St. Joseph Newsleader* .

Peterson, J. (1989, November 10). Community Keeps Jacob's Hope Alive. *St. Joseph Newsleader*, 1, 12.

Peterson, J. (1990, November 23). Conference Alerts All to Dangers of Abduction. *St. Joseph Newsleader*, 1, 8.

Peterson, J. (1990, November 9). National Abduction Conference to Be Held—Wetterling Foundation Sponsors Event Saturday at St. Cloud Civic Center. *St. Joseph Newsleader*, 1, 12.

Peterson, J. (1990, March 2). Top Priorities for Jacob Wetterling Foundation—Public Awareness and Education. *St. Joseph Newsleader*, 4–5.

Peterson, J. (1989, December 8). "Unprecedented' Community Response. *St. Joseph Newsleader*, 2–3.

Petrie, K. a. (2010, July 2). Investigation Near Abduction Site Moves into Second Day—Crews Dig Up Field. *St. Cloud Times*, 1A, 6A.

Petrie, K. a. (2010, September 29). Jacob Wetterling Case—No Clues in Items Removed from Site. *St. Cloud Times*, 1A, 4A.

Petrie, K. a. (2010, July 1). Site Near Wetterling Abuction Searched—Authorites Expected to Return to Scene Today. *St. Cloud Times*, 1A, 8A.

Petrie, K. a. (2010, July 3). Wetterling Investigation—Sheriff: Rassier "Person of Interest"—Man Says He Will Do What He Can to Help Investigators. *St. Cloud Times*, 1A, 6A.

Petrie, K. (2009, October 18). Case Still Gets Leads—Investigation Has Shifted to Focus on Local Suspects. *St. Cloud Times*, 6A.

Petrie, K. (2009, October 18). Enduring Hope—Family, Friends, Investigators Reflect on the Night the 11-Year-Old Was Kidnapped. *St. Cloud Times*, 1A.

Petrie, K. (2009, October 22). Investigators Learned from Wetterling Case. *St. Cloud Times*, 4A.

Petrie, K. (2009, October 18). Larsons Recall Finding Healing in Daily Routines. *St. Cloud Times*, 9A.

Petrie, K. (2009, October 18). Moving Forward—Larson Kept Waiting for His Friend to Come Home. *St. Cloud Times*, 1A, 7A.

Pioneer Press Staff. (1989, November 1). Authorities Seek Jacob in Renville County Area. *St. Paul Pioneer Press*, unknown.

PIoneer Press Staff. (1989, November 19). Family Welcomed Media as Jacob's Best Hope. *St. Paul Pioneer Press*, unknown.

Pioneer Press Staff. (1989, October 27). Mounted Patrols Join Search for Kidnapped Boy. *St. Paul Pioneer Press*, unknown.

Pioneer Press Staff Report. (1990, February 15). Boy's Body Stolen from a Lakewood Crypt. *St. Paul Pioneer Press* .

Pioneer Press Staff Report. (1997, August

15). Police Doubt Car Bombing, Wiess Linked / Explosion Occurs on Street of Accused Child Molester. *St. Paul Pioneer Press*, unknown.

Pioneer Press Staff Report. (1989, October 25). Small Red Car Spotted Near Kidnapping Site. *St. Paul Pioneer Press*, unknown.

Prentice, E. a. (2013, May 8). Trial for Tim Huber Coming to a Close—Jury Begins Deliberations in Murder Case. *Paynesville Press*, 1, 11B.

Prentice, E. (2011, November 23). Hubers Indicted for First-Degree Murder. *Paynesville Press*, 1.

Rassier, D. (2012, July). Formal Complaint Letter to the Jacob Wetterling Investigation. St. Joseph, MN, USA.

Ross, J. a. (2015, October 15). Possible Link in Wetterling Case. *Star Tribune*, 1.

St. Cloud Times Editorial Board. (2010, July 10). Silence in Jacob's Case Raises Questions. 4B.

St. Cloud Times Staff and Wire Report. (1990, May 2). Drifter Cleared in Wetterling Probe—Man Never Reached St. Joseph. 1, 2B.

St. Cloud Times Staff and Wire Report. (1990, February 15). Police Confirm Body in River Not Jacob. 1B.

St. Cloud Times Staff Report. (1990, January 9). FBI Narrows Focus in Jacob Probe. 1B.

St. Cloud Times Staff Report. (1991, October 20). Foundation Seeks Donations. 6A.

St. Cloud Times Staff Report. (1989, December 3). Fridley Abduction Try Not Tied to Jacob. 1, 2B.

St. Cloud Times Staff Report. (1990, October 21). Grafft Tones Down Optimism on Lead. 1B.

St. Cloud Times Staff Report. (1990, April 22). Investigators Checking Tips in Jacob Case. 7A.

St. Cloud Times Staff Report. (1990, Octoberr 12). Jacob Lead Fizzles. 1B.

St. Cloud Times Staff Report. (1989, February 24). Man Wanted for Abducting, Assaulting Boy. 5A.

St. Cloud Times Staff Report. (1991, September 20). Man with BB Gun Causes Scare at Wetterling's Albany Office. 1A.

St. Cloud Times Staff Report. (1989, December 29). New Reward Prompts 100 Tips. 1B.

St. Cloud Times Staff Report. (1989, November 4). No New Clues Found in Jacob's Abduction. 1, 12A.

St. Cloud Times Staff Report. (1990, May 9). Officials Reveal Reverse Pornography Sting. 2B.

St. Cloud Times Staff Report. (2010, September 30). Paraprofessional Pulled from Rassier Classroom. 1B.

St. Cloud Times Staff Report. (1990, February 17). Party Marks Jacob's 12th Birthday. 1A.

St. Cloud Times Staff Report. (1991, July 19). Patty Wetterling Comments on Reports. 8A.

St. Cloud Times Staff Report. (1991, October 24). Pond Search Turns Up No Clues. 1A.

St. Cloud Times Staff Report. (1990, April 18). Search of Quarries Yields No Leads on Jacob. 1A.

St. Cloud Times Staff Report. (1990, November 3). Search Donations Keep Coming. 5A.

St. Cloud Times Staff Report. (1989, November 27). St. Cloud Man Held on Sex Charge. 2B.

St. Cloud Times Staff Report. (1989, December 22). Tips Still Sought—Redwood Falls Boy Reports Abduction Attempt. 1, 2B.

St. Cloud Times Staff Report. (1990, April 30). Wisconsin Man Questioned in Abduction. 1B.

St. Joseph Newsleader Editorial Staff. (1992, September 25). We're Just Doing Our Job. 2.

St. Joseph Newsleader Staff Report. (1990, March 16). Grammer Benefit Concert for Jacob Is March 25. 5,12.

St. Joseph Newsleader Staff Report. (1990, May 11). Jacob Reward Upped to $200,000—Police Seek Caller with Information. 1.

St. Joseph Newsleader Staff Report. (1993, February 5). New Exec Director Named for Wetterling Foundation. 1.

St. Paul Pioneer Press Staff Report. (1989, October 29). Attempted Kidnapping May Uncover New Leads.

St. Paul Pioneer Press Staff Report. (1989, October 24). National Alert Issued for Boy, Kidnapper.

St. Paul Pioneer Press Staff Report. (1989,

December 15). Wetterling, Earlier Case "Similar."

San Jose Mercury News Staff. (1990, January 25). Boy's Kidnapping Mobilizes His Hometown Residents—Sense of Security Stolen Too. *San Jose Mercury News*, unknown.

Savage, D. (1989, November 6). Letters—Reporter Defends TV Coverage of Abduction. *St. Cloud Times*, 7A.

Schugel, J. (2012, June 06). *Authorities Reopen 30 Year Old Case of Kimball Post Office Bombing*. Retrieved November 27, 2014, from Minnesota.cbslocal.com: www.minnesota.cbslocal.com/2012/06/06/authorities-reopen-30-year-old-case-of-kimball-post-office-bombin.

Scott, K. (2004, October 22). 6th-Grader's Abduction Touches Community Members. *St. Cloud Times*, 4A-5A.

Scott, K. (2004, February 2). Answers in Wetterling Case Elude, but Hope Doesn't—Reminders of the Boy Taken 14 Years Ago Remain, Inspire Those Hunting for Closure. *St. Cloud Times*, 1A, 6A.

Scott, K. (2004, February 25). Investigators Explore New Path in Wetterling Case—Kidnapper May Have Been on Foot, Not in Car. *St. Cloud Times*, 1A, 4A.

Scott, K. (2004, February 25). Police Ask People to Help in Wetterling Case. *St. Cloud Times*, 1A.

Scott, K. (2004, May 6). Sheriff Cautious on Abduction Links—Victim Sees Several Similarities to Wetterling Case. *St. Cloud Times*, 1B, 3B.

Scott, K. (2004, February 26). Sheriff's Officials, Wetterlings Discuss New Twist. *St. Cloud Times*, 1A, 4A.

Scott, K. (2004, October 22). Still Searching—Community, Family Take Day to Remember Jacob. *St. Cloud Times*, 1A, 5A.

Scott, K. (2004, May 8). Tips Come in After Reports on Wetterling. *St. Cloud Times*, 1B.

Shortal, J. (2015, October 29). *Jacob Wetterling Abduction Tied to Child Porn Suspect*. Retrieved November 15, 2015, from usatoday.com: www.usatoday.com/story/news/nation-now/2015/10/29/jacob-wetterling-1989-kidnapping/74819588/.

Simons, A. a. (2010, July 4). In the Search for Jacob, Another Shot in the Dark: Two Days of Excavating on Land Near Where the 11-Year-Old Was Taken Comes Six Years After the Property Was Last Targeted. *Minneapolis Star Tribune*, unknown.

Simons, A. (2010, July 3). Items Seized in Search by Wetterling Investigators: Analysis of Items Taken from St. Joseph, Minn., Farm Near Where Jacob Wetterling Was Abducted Could Take Weeks. *Minneapolis Star Tribune*, unknown.

Smith, K. (2015, October 31). FBI Push Revived Wetterling Case. *Star Tribune*, unknown.

Somasundaram, M. (1990, August 9). Reported Sighting of Jacob Has Investigators Scrambling. *St. Cloud Times*, 1A, 10A.

Star Tribune Staff Report. (2004, May 7). Assault Victim Hopes His Story Will Lead to Break in Wetterling Case.

Star Tribune Staff Report. (1989, November 19). FBI Investigates Report on New Kidnap Attempt.

Star Tribune Staff Report. (1989, November 19). FBI Probing Second Kidnapping Attempt of a Boy in 10 Days. *Minneapolis Star Tribune*.

Star Tribune Staff Report. (1989, October 26). FBI Profiles Type Likely to Kidnap Child as Search Grows.

Star Tribune Staff Report. (1990, January 31). FBI Reduces Number on Wetterling Task Force.

Star Tribune Staff Report. (2004, February 29). From the Start, Wetterling Case Drew Range of Tips.

Star Tribune Staff Report. (1989, November 5). Kidnap Attempt Probed.

Star Tribune Staff Report. (1998, October 31). Letter Stirs Up Leads in Wetterling Case.

Star Tribune Staff Report. (1989, November 7). Police Seek Man Seen Lurking at Stores in St. Joseph Area.

Star Tribune Staff Report. (1989, October 24). St. Joseph Boy, 11, Kidnapped at Gunpoint.

Star Tribune Staff Report. (1989, November 19). Where Is Jacob?

State Fire Marshal Division. (2009). *Inves-*

tigation Report. St. Paul: State of Minnesota.

Statement of Kevin H., ICR# 89005407 (Stearns County Sheriff's Department October 21, 2003).

Stearns County, State of Minnesota. (1986, October 1). Criminal Complaint, Case K7–86–2667. *Criminal Complaint.* St. Cloud, Minnesota, USA: Stearns County.

Stearns County, State of Minnesota. (1984, March 16). Criminal Complaint, K34–987. *Criminal Complaint, K34–987.* St. Cloud, Minnesota, USA: Wright County.

Stearns County, State of Minnesota. (1984, November 19). State of Minnesota Vs Danny James Heinrich, Case K8–84–987 and K1–84–988. *State of Minnesota Vs Danny James Heinrich.* St. Cloud, Minnesota, USA: Stearns County.

Stelling, L. (1990, December 11). Wetterling Urges Children to Speak Out. *Paynesville Press*, 1–2.

Suzukamo, L. (1990, January 25). Man Held. *St. Paul Pioneer Press*, unknown.

Thyen, D. (1987, May 26). Local Police Seek Help in Accosting Incidents. *Paynesville Press*, 1–2.

Thyen, D. (1987, June 23). Police Still Working for Arrest. *Paynesville Press*, 1.

United States Attorney Office, Shane Ball. (2015, October 27). Criminal Complaint, Case 15-mj-838JJK. *Criminal Complaint.* St. Paul, Minnesota, USA: United States Attorney Office.

United States of America vs. Danny James Heinrich, File No. 15CR340 (United States District Court of Minnesota September 6, 2016).

Unze, D. (2009, October 22). Cases Have Changed Society. *St. Cloud Times*, 1A, 4A.

Unze, D. (1999, October 22). A Decade of Hoping—Through Education, Legislation and Love, Wetterling Family and Friends Keep Hope's Flame Burning for Jacob. *St. Cloud TImes*, 1A, 8A.

Unze, D. (2014, October 18). Hope Rises with Wetterling Billboard Campaign. *St. Cloud Times*, 1A.

Unze, D. (2001, January 26). Man May Be Linked to Wetterling Case—Child Pornography Allegations, Sketch Similarity Prompt Background Check. *St. Cloud Times*, 1B.

Unze, D. (1999, June 25). Media Still Drawn to Wetterling Case—as 10th Anniversary of Son's Abduction Nears, Mother Holds Hope He'll Be Found. *St. Cloud Times*, 3A.

Unze, D. (2015, November 22). Private Investigator's Notes 1990 Notes Mention Heinrich. *St. Cloud Times*, 1A, 6A.

Unze, D. (1999, September 11). Unsolved Case Investigators Ask About Blom. *St. Cloud Times*, 1A.

Urseth, W. A. (2010). *The Line.* Prior Lake, MN: William Urseth.

Van Pilsum, T. (2013, February 25). *Investigators: Feeney Fascinated with Wetterling Case.* Retrieved September 14, 2014, from myFoxTwinCities.com: myFoxTwinCities.com/story/21348273/investigators-feeney-and-wetterling.

Van Pilsum, T. (2013, February 18). *Investigators: In Feeney's Words.* Retrieved September 14, 2014, from myFoxTwinCities.com: myFoxTwinCities.com/story/21237086/investigators-in-feeney's-words.

Various, L. (1989, November 12). Letters Reflect Hope, Frustration for Jacob. *St. Cloud Times*, 11A.

Vezner, T. (2010, July 2). Retrieved September 26, 2014, from Twincities.com: Twincities.com/ci_15424697.

Vezner, T. (2010, June 30). Law Enforcement Converge on Site Near Wetterling Abduction in St. Joseph. *St. Paul Pioneer Press*, unknown.

Vezner, T. (2010, July 2). Wetterling Investigators at Nearby Farm for 2nd Day. *St. Paul Pioneer Press*, unknown.

Wade, B. (1989, December 16). New Tips Encourage Abduction Investigators. *St. Cloud Times*, 1B.

Wade, B. (1989, November 9). Wolves Tip Off for Jacob's Hope. *St. Cloud Times*, 1A.

Welsh, J. (1994, October 22). Five Years After Abduction, Jacob Leaves Legacy. *St. Cloud Times*, 1A, 7A.

Welsh, J. (1992, October 20). Former Prep Student to File Sex Abuse Suit. *St. Cloud Times*, 3A, 5A.

Welsh, J. (1993, October 20). His Pal Lives Jacob's Football Dream—"I Always Wish That He Will Come Home," Friend Says. *St. Cloud Times*, 1A, 4A.

Welsh, J. (1993, October 22). Jacob's Hope Still Alive—Police, Friends Not Ready to Give Up—Search for Leads Now Focuses Locally. *St. Cloud Times*, 1A.

Welsh, J. (1990, August 10). Leads Dry in Illinois Sighting, FBI Says. *St. Cloud Times*, 1B.

Welsh, J. (1994, February 3). Man Claims Sex Ring Took Jacob—Authorities Unconvinced; Jerry Wetterling Wants More Information. *St. Cloud Times*, 2A.

Welsh, J. (1994, October 19). Remembering Jacob Five Years Later—Wetterlings: Little Has Changed as Sad Anniversary Nears. *St. Cloud Times*, 1A, 5A.

Welsh, J. (1993, June 3). Soul Asylum's New Video to Help Search for Jacob. *St. Cloud Times*, 1A.

Welsh, J. (1996, May 17). Warrants Reveal Early Wetterling Suspects—but New Information Doesn't Center on top Suspects, Police Say. *St. Cloud Times*, 1A, 8A.

Wetterling, C. (1989, December 8). Carmen's Plea. *St. Joseph Newsleader*, 7.

Wetterling, (2007, June 8). "Hello, I'm Jacob 'Edwin' Wetterling." *Sartell Newsleader*, 3, 11–12.

Wetterling, (1989, November 10, 24). Jacob's My Son. *St. Joseph Newsleader*, 2.

Wood, D. (1989, November 24). Jacob's Hope. *St. Joseph Newsleader*, 1.

Wright County, State of Minnesota. (2015, July 24). Application for Search Warrant and Supporting Affadavit. *Application for Search Warrant and Supporting Affadavit*. Wright County, Minnesota, USA: State of Minnesota.

Wright, R. (2009). *Sex Offender Laws: Failed Policies, New Directions*. New York, NY: Springer.

Index